Rachel Weeping

JEWS, CHRISTIANS, AND MUSLIMS AT THE FORTRESS TOMB

Fred Strickert

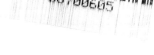

A Michael Glazier Book

LITURGICAL PRESS
OCM 768200669
Collegeville, Minnesota

www.litpress.org

A Michael Glazier Book published by Liturgical Press

Cover design by David Manahan, O.S.B. Cover illustration is a (Photochrom) print © of an early photo of the Tomb of Rachel, Jerusalem, Israel and courtesy of U.S. Historical Archive.

Unless otherwise indicated, photos and illustrations are provided by the author and are in public domain.

1   2   3   4   5   6   7   8   9

Library of Congress Cataloging-in-Publication Data

Strickert, Frederick M.
    Rachel weeping : Jews, Christians, and Muslims at the Fortress Tomb / Fred Strickert.
        p.   cm.
    "A Michael Glazier book."
    Includes bibliographical references and index.
    ISBN-13: 978-0-8146-5987-8
    1. Rachel's Tomb (Bethlehem).   2. Rachel (Biblical matriarch).   I. Title.
DS110.B4S77   2007
203'.50956952—dc22
                                                                2006038090

For my own
Rachel,
Benjamin,
and
Angela:
always on the way

Contents

List of Illustrations

Prologue

On October 17, 2000, in the streets outside Bethlehem's Rachel's Tomb, thirteen-year-old Muayad Jawarish was shot to death. It was one of those AP headlines that caught my attention. Only weeks earlier the second *intifada* had erupted after then-Minister of Housing Ariel Sharon paid a visit to the area in Jerusalem that some call the Noble Sanctuary and others the Temple Mount. Religious sensibilities play a big role in this part of the world. Reports spread to the four corners of the world about scores of people injured and killed, and the world shuddered as yet another peace plan was pronounced dead on arrival. Now the violence had spread from the streets of Jerusalem to the cities of the West Bank.

For a long time the main Jerusalem-Hebron road that ran along Rachel's Tomb had been a flashpoint for violence. It was relatively close to the Bethlehem checkpoint manned by the Israeli border police, and in recent years an Israeli security post had been constructed just north of the tomb. This location was thus natural for Palestinian demonstrations. Youth often gathered, and stone throwing occasionally ensued. On this particular day, the stone throwing was supplemented with Coke-bottle gasoline bombs, and the soldiers retaliated with tear gas and gunfire.

According to the newspaper reports, young Jawarish was not one of the demonstrating youth. At two o'clock in the afternoon, he was on his way home from school when his route took him near the action. Like many youths, he paused to watch, curious about what was going on. He paused, seemingly at a safe distance. Unexpectedly, a high-velocity bullet from the gun of an Israeli sniper stationed atop Rachel's Tomb hit him in the base of the skull. That evening Muayad Jawarish died at al-Hussein Hospital in Beit Jala.

Everyone would agree that something's wrong with this picture. Any time children are killed it is a tragedy. The wartime setting only multiplies the emotional pull. In this particular case there are other factors. The holy city of Bethlehem. The century-long conflict in a land of promise. The setting outside Rachel's Tomb. Youth showing lack of respect for religious space. Soldiers shooting from the roof of a shrine. Add to all these the name of Rachel. It is not just any holy place. It is Rachel's Tomb. Rachel is the age-old symbol of the grieving mother. Her children are dying, Palestinian and Israeli alike. And Rachel continues to weep for them. Rachel cries, and so do Israeli and Palestinian mothers. How appropriate that a reporter recorded the lament of Muayad Jawarish's mother: "My son! My son! They killed my son! God give me strength!"[1]

When I read the newspaper account of Muayad Jawarish's death, it stirred up memories of my own visits to Bethlehem. My first trip in 1974, similar to the experience of most tourists, is a blur of images and seemingly hundreds of historic sites and stories. I vaguely remember the Bethlehem shrine. It was the only time I ever set foot inside. If I had kept a journal, I imagine the entry would have been rather short with words like "quaint," "insignificant," "the same old thing." Little did I know that the shrine would find its way to center stage in later years.

I drove by that same Rachel's Tomb almost every day during my 1995–96 sabbatical when I was a senior fellow at the Albright Archaeological Institute in Jerusalem and lived at the Lutheran Church compound in Bethlehem. How well I recall one such trip in the back seat of a *sherut*, one of the shared taxis that left Damascus Gate in Jerusalem and dropped off passengers at the Beit Jala junction along the Jerusalem-Hebron Road in Bethlehem for two shekels. On that particular day an unfamiliar woman was sitting in the back of the vehicle. I, too, made my way to the back where three passengers usually sat, but she would not allow me to sit beside her. Speaking no English, she motioned that I was to leave a seat vacant between us. The Palestinian driver motioned, but she signaled that no one was to sit in that middle seat. With a shrug of his shoulders he started the engine, seeming to understand. She was a Hasidic Jew with strict rules forbidding men and women touching each other. I watched her closely throughout that twenty-minute taxi ride before she exited at Rachel's Tomb. Most Jewish visitors to the tomb travel there in bulletproof buses or in police-escorted caravans.[2] How different this woman

---

[1] Denis Barnett, "Palestinian boy, policeman die in day of anti-summit rage," *Agence France Press* (October 17, 2000); Jamie Tarabay, "For ninth-grade boys, clashes are a game of cat and mouse," *The Associated Press* (October 18, 2000). Charles Sennott also was moved by this incident to write about it in *The Body and the Blood: The Holy Land at the Turn of a New Millennium* (New York: Public Affairs, 2001) 357–60.

[2] "To Rachel's Tomb in a Bulletproof Bus," *Haaretz* (November 23, 2000); Doron Geller, "Sense of Mission," *The Jerusalem Post* (November 12, 1997).

appeared on this particular day!

This woman in the taxi, totally humble, totally quiet, bobbed her head in prayer while focusing on the Hebrew prayer book inches in front of her face. How different from the other visitors to Rachel's Tomb! What was it that brought her, a Hasidic Jew, to ride in a shared taxi with mainly Palestinian

Engraving of Rachel's Tomb—year 1881

men? Why wasn't she in one of those escorted vehicles? I don't know the answers. Yet the more I've learned about Rachel's Tomb, the more I'm willing to hazard a guess. Likely this young woman was having trouble conceiving. She was different from the many Hasidic wives leading around a large flock of children. Her trip to Rachel's Tomb was motivated by human need. It was likely a case of desperation. With no children her family role was threatened. She lived in shame. Unless something changed quickly, she might end up divorced and shunned. Being barren was not something she would want to discuss openly, especially with her husband. In desperation she, like other women before her, was making a quiet trip in a Palestinian taxi to seek the aid of Rachel, the symbol of motherhood. Who knows what became of that young mother? I, of course, never saw her again. Yet her image stays fixed in my memory, a figure of sincere devotion.

Months later in early 1996, things began to change at Rachel's Tomb. My daily taxi rides were diverted through Bethlehem side streets while construction workers began to change the face of this ancient monument. That historic route taken by several-millennia-worth of travelers was changed permanently four years later so that traffic no longer passes in front of Rachel's Tomb. The renovations took eighteen months and cost well over two million dollars. Part of the reason for the project was to facilitate larger numbers of pilgrims; the prayer area multiplied five-fold. But most of the changes were in the name of security. Thirteen-foot-high security walls now block the view of the well-recognized white dome from all directions but above.

Photo of Fortress Tomb—year 2000

The Israeli government unveiled the new Rachel's Tomb to an estimated thirty-thousand ultra-orthodox Jews at the commemoration of the matriarch's death on November 11, 1997. Associated Press reporter Dina Kraft characterized the scene as one of celebration, with festive music booming from loudspeakers and individuals swaying in prayer as they waited in long lines for their turn inside the tomb. The mood inside had a different tone, "Worshippers crowded shoulder-to-shoulder despite the expansion of praying space. Wails and sobbing were heard from the women's side of the tomb where young women fervently prayed for safe pregnancies and births."[3]

Most of the worshipers and seemingly the reporter were buffered from the commotion in the streets outside. According to Associated Press writer Samar Assad, the crowd of pilgrims had attracted young stone throw-

[3] Steve Rodan and Margot Dudkevitch, "Rachel's Tomb reopens after renovations," *The Jerusalem Post* (November 12, 1997) 2. Dina Kraft, "Thousands worship at fortified tomb," *AP News Service* (November 11, 1997).

ers, most only eleven years old. Into that crowd walked nine-year-old Ali Jawarishe with his bright red backpack on his way to buy pencils to do his homework after school. He was hit in the head with a rubber-coated steel bullet fired at close range by an Israeli soldier trying to disperse the boys. Ali died the following day, and his parents donated his organs to save the lives of other children, both Palestinian and Israeli.[4]

Again, it is obvious that something is not right with this picture. Jews traveling to a holy shrine in armored vehicles. Soldiers guarding a holy place and shooting young children. Inside the tomb, women wailing with tears over pregnancy and childbirth. Outside, mothers sobbing uncontrollably over the deaths of their sons.

It is a scene repeated all too often in recent years in Bethlehem. Rachel's Tomb, a holy place, has been turned into a fortress. The thing about fortresses is that they mark power and exclusivity. In late October 2000, after the second *intifada* had begun and shortly after thirteen-year-old Muayad Jawarish's death, thousands of pilgrims made their way for the annual commemoration of Rachel's death. The words spoken by one worshiper to *Reuters* reporter Christine Hauser are telling: "It's terrible that we are praying in our holy spot, to our God, in a fortress."[5]

In this particular case a fortress is totally out of character. Rachel, as the ideal mother, is the mark of vulnerability and faithfulness. Her appeal over the centuries is to victims, who like her remain vulnerable and faithful at the same time. Her burial is significant because it is located at the side of the road, still on the way to her destination and still vulnerable. That's what makes her so appealing. And her tomb on the way has given access over the centuries to all, no matter their national identity or religion.

The purpose of this book is to take another look at Rachel and her tomb. We will read her biblical story fresh as the vulnerable and faithful woman

[4] Samar Assad, "Palestinian boy fights for life," *AP News Service* (November 12, 1997). Joel Greenberg, "Strife Claims Small Victim As Rachel's Tomb Is Reopened," *The New York Times* (November 12, 1997) A3. Margot Dudkevitch, "Parents of child killed by IDF: 'Organs can go to Jew or Arab,'" *The Jerusalem Post* (November 16, 1997) 2. Although having similar last names the two boys described in this prologue, Muayad Jawarish and Ali Jawarishe, are not related.

[5] Christine Hauser, "In Bethlehem, faithful pray in the shadow of the gun," *Reuters News Service* (October 28, 2000). "MKS Pray at Besieged Tomb," *Haaretz* (November 10, 2000); Margot Dudkevitch, "Activists try to reach Rachel's Tomb despite IDF ban," *The Jerusalem Post* (November 10, 2000) 3A.

always "on the way." We will also survey the later traditions about Rachel, especially how she becomes a model for victims in various situations: the exiles heading to Babylon; the boy babies slaughtered in Bethlehem; and individual women struggling with motherhood and pregnancy. What we will see is that the matriarch Rachel is held in esteem by all three monotheistic religions. We will also analyze carefully the biblical references to Rachel's Tomb, coming to the conclusion that the location of Bethlehem is ironically wrong. The biblical witness points to a location north of Jerusalem. This finding is nothing new. Biblical scholars have recognized the problem of a Bethlehem location for years. Yet this conclusion has often been presented only as short notes in biblical commentaries or encyclopedia articles. The topic has not been the subject of a full treatment. The exception is the fifty-four page article in Italian by G. Lombardi in *Liber Annuus* in 1970.[6] A comprehensive, up-to-date study in English is overdue. Lastly, we will survey the literature about the Bethlehem tomb over the last two thousand years, asking how this tomb came to be associated with Rachel. We will see that Christians, Muslims, and Jews have all had a share in the various stages of building and have been tolerant of one another in their prayers over most of this period. In the final analysis we will see that the idea of Rachel's tomb as a fortress with exclusive access is totally contrary to the character of Rachel, the woman of faith, always on the way.

Finally, the purpose of such a critical analysis has a practical bent. In our ever-smaller world, we need to learn to live together. Perhaps we might even imagine Rachel speaking through her tears, "Children, please share."

—Fred Strickert

---

[6] G. Lombardi, "H. Farah—W. Farah presso Anatot e la questione della Tomba di Rahel (Gen 35,16-20; 1 Sam 10,2-5; Ger 31,15)," *Liber Annuus*, XX (1970) 299–352. The article was later published as a monograph G. Lombardi, *La tomba de Rahel* (Jerusalem, 1971).

Introduction

At the end of the Book of Genesis, the patriarch Jacob reflects on his adventurous life—a story that began in chapter 25 and reaches its culmination in chapters 48–49. The episode that strikes him most is the tragedy of his wife Rachel. With an efficiency of words he recalls: "'For when I came from Paddan, Rachel, alas, died in the land of Canaan on the way, while there was still some distance to go to Ephrath; and I buried her there on the way to Ephrath' (that is, Bethlehem)" (Gen 48:7).[1]

Claus Westermann attributes this section to the Priestly writer in sixth-century Babylon in exile.[2] The story of Rachel is quite fitting for exiles who reflect on their own loss: the failure of the Judaic monarchy; the destruction of the temple; the fall of Jerusalem; the end of the Israelite nation; the separation from land. What does this all mean in relationship to the covenant, to their role as people of God, to their hope for the future?

Rachel's loss is their loss; their loss is Rachel's loss.

There is nothing in the Genesis text that explains the meaning of the tragedy. Joseph does not ask "why," and Jacob only tells him the what, the when, and the where of his mother's death. Rachel died. That's a fact of life.

As far as the future, Genesis 48:7 provides few clues. Nevertheless, it is significant that Jacob's reminiscence about Rachel was elicited by the death-bed visit of Joseph, Rachel's firstborn. It is followed by Jacob's blessing of their grandsons Ephraim and Manasseh who now will stand on the same level as his twelve sons—tribal patriarchs in their own right. How sad that Rachel was not still alive to see this moment for herself.

The fact is that Rachel died years before and now Jacob himself is dim of sight so that he has no clear vision of the future. This is the stuff of the

---

[1] All Bible citations are from the NRSV unless otherwise noted for the sake of pointing out variations from the Hebrew and Greek.

[2] Claus Westermann, *Genesis 37–50: A Commentary*, trans. by John J. Scullion (Minneapolis: Augsburg, 1986) 182. Contrast Martin Noth, *A History of Pentateuchal Traditions* (Chico, CA: Scholars Press, 1981) 36, who attributes verse 7 as well as 8-22 to the Elohist. Noth, like Westermann, agrees that verses 3-6 belong to the Priestly writer.

great faith chapter of Hebrews. "Now faith is the assurance of things hoped for, the conviction of things not seen" (Heb 11:1). Jacob is, of course, mentioned in that long list of ancestors for his faith in blessing the two sons of Joseph (v. 21). Of all the events in his long life, this typifies the stance of faith. Hope is a glimpse of the future that even the dim of sight might grasp, not seeing but believing all the same.

So Jacob is counted in Hebrews 11 among the faithful. But what about Rachel? Is it possible for someone with such a sudden and unexpected death—for someone youthful and dying before her time—to die with such faith and hope? Certainly from the perspective of the Priestly writer, history has given meaning to her tragic death. Generations have come forth from her. Stories innumerable have been written about her offspring—their successes as well as failures, acts of piety and charity as well as acts of selfishness, lives of faith as well as lives of sin. Stories of Rachel's offspring weave together a tapestry that influenced a significant part of the world over a period of several centuries. Figures such as Saul, Samuel, Jeremiah, Esther, and the Apostle Paul himself are a tribute to her beginning. Though not seen, these were surely the things Rachel hoped for. The words of Jacob in that final reminiscence underscore the characterization of Rachel as a woman who was on the move—someone with a past and with a goal.

Rachel's death occurred when she and Jacob "came from Paddan" and yet had "still some distance to go to Ephrath." These words are rather significant for the reader who has followed her story with interest, for she has for all practical purposes cut herself off from her past in Paddan, having left the house of Laban in much the same way that her husband's grandfather Abram left "his father's house" for the land that God would show him. Like the patriarchs and matriarchs before her, Rachel had staked her claim with Jacob on the promise expressed repeatedly in Genesis in terms of numerous offspring and land. Her death in childbirth points to the fragility and vulnerability of the former. The author's reference "in the land of Canaan" points to the "not yet" character of the latter.

This brings to mind Walter Brueggemann's study of land. "The Bible itself is primarily concerned with the issue of being displaced and yearning for a place," he says in the opening chapter.[3] The patriarchs and matriarchs were living out the twofold promise of Genesis 12:1-3 for land and progeny,

---

[3] Walter Brueggemann, *The Land: Place as Gift, Promise, and Challenges in Biblical Faith*, 2nd ed. (Fortress: Minneapolis, 2002) 2.

with land functioning as a symbol of all they were seeking. So Jacob and Rachel are the perfect example of homeless people who were constantly on the way to landedness. Still, land always became a problem. "The very land that contained the sources of life drove kings to become agents of death. Society became the frantic effort of the landed to hold on to turf, no matter what the cost."[4] Thus the story is in constant movement from landlessness to landedness and back to landlessness. Appropriately, at the moment Rachel moves into the land and bears her child Benjamin, she loses her stake in it.

The expression that best captures the Genesis characterization is perhaps found in the three words "on the way." In fact, the expression occurs twice in this lengthy sentence: "'For when I came from Paddan, Rachel, alas, died in the land of Canaan *on the way*, while there was still some distance to go to Ephrath; and I buried her there *on the way* to Ephrath' (that is, Bethlehem)" (Gen 48:7). Rachel was a woman on the way. This expression captures the tragedy of her life, yet it also reveals her faith and hope.

The Genesis story of Rachel can be divided into five basic parts—a prologue, three acts, and an epilogue—each typified by her on-the-way character.

> **Prologue:** Rachel, the young shepherdess, on the way to water her flocks, encounters the traveler Jacob at the well.
>
> **Act 1:** Rachel, on the way to marriage, patiently and faithfully endures seven years waiting and then is delayed by Laban's deception.
>
> **Act 2:** Rachel, now married, is on the way to motherhood—barren and struggling to conceive, giving birth yet crying out "give me yet another!"
>
> **Act 3:** Rachel is on the way with Jacob to the land of his birth, struggling as he struggles, though not victorious as he, when she succumbs to the pain of childbirth, naming her second born Ben-oni, son of my sorrow.
>
> **Epilogue:** The on-the-way character of Rachel's offspring, Joseph, is sent on his way far from the land of promise to Egypt. He in turn awaits reunion with father and brothers only when the risk is taken of sending the youngest son Benjamin, the epitome of vulnerability.

Unlike the other matriarchs whose stories do not extend beyond the pages of Genesis, Rachel's story continues through people, like Joseph and Benjamin, who themselves are on the way. Following the sixth-century destruction of the Jerusalem temple, when the exiles are amassed for

---

[4] Ibid., 11.

deportation, Jeremiah describes faithful Rachel still by the roadside, weeping for her children, offering her lament, but also a word of hope (Jer 31:15).

Later Matthew quotes these same words of Rachel weeping at the death of boy babies at the birth of Jesus as the holy family, forced from Bethlehem, finds itself also on the way.

For nearly two millennia Jews and Christians have reminded themselves of the on-the-way character of the life of faith, reading these words of Rachel weeping at the transition point of human life, the New Year. For Christians this takes place at the commemoration of the Slaughter of Innocents on December 28 at the end of the calendar year. For Jews the reading occurs at the beginning, on Rosh Hashanah II. People of all faiths can resonate with Rachel because they, too, are people of faith.

In a later midrash, Lamentations Rabbah, Rachel weeping mercifully for her children is a reflection of the divine attribute of mercy and faithfulness. This midrash describes the situation of the beginning of exile in Jeremiah's day. Jeremiah explains exile as punishment for the people's unfaithfulness to God, their idolatry while living in the land. First, Moses is called from his grave beyond the Jordan to appeal on the people's behalf. Then all the patriarchs from their common grave at Machpelah make their appeal. Yet it is to no avail. The people have broken the covenant. They have not been faithful while God remained faithful. Finally, Rachel appears from her road-side grave where she had been buried alone. Her tears of mercy are justified because her faithfulness exceeds all others. She speaks:

> "Lord of the world! It is perfectly self-evident to you that your servant, Jacob, loved me with a mighty love, and worked for me for father for seven years, but when those seven years were fulfilled, and the time came for my wedding to my husband, father planned to substitute my sister for me in the marriage to my husband. Now that matter was very hard for me, for I knew the deceit, and I told my husband and gave him a sign by which he would know the difference between me and my sister, so that my father would not be able to trade me off. But then I regretted it and I bore my passion, and I had mercy for my sister, that she should not be shamed. So in the evening for my husband they substituted my sister for me, and I gave my sister all the signs that I had given to my husband, so that he would think that she was Rachel. And not only so, but I crawled under the bed on which he was lying with my sister, while she remained silent, and I made all the replies so that he would not discern the voice of my sister."[5]

---

[5] *Lamentations Rabbah* 24, ed. and trans. by Jacob Neusner, *Scripture and Midrash in Judaism*, vol. 3 (Frankfurt: Peter Lang, 1995) 57.

While this midrash clearly elaborates and takes liberties with the details of Leah's marriage in Rachel's stead, it eloquently expresses the depth of torment that Rachel suffered in her obedience and faithfulness to Jacob while he was less than faithful to her. So who better to understand what it means to be faithful in the midst of unfaithfulness?

Like Abraham and Job, Rachel has solid ground to appeal for God to be true to the attributes of mercy and faithfulness. So she continues:

> "I paid my sister only kindness, and I was not jealous of her, and I did not allow her to be shamed, and I am a mere mortal, dust and ashes. Now I had no envy of my rival, and I did not place her at risk for shame and humiliation. But you are the King, loving and enduring and merciful. How come then you are jealous of idolatry, which is nothing, and so have sent my children into exile, allowed them to be killed by the sword, permitted the enemy to do whatever they wanted to them?"[6]

These words appeal to all people of faith. Rachel's relationship with her sister Leah is a model of faithfulness. Rachel is not a matriarch who can be tied down to one time and place but is available to all on the way. This is the prevailing theme of this book.

While chapter 1 treats the biblical story of Rachel, chapters 2–4 look at the ways in which this story is interpreted by Jews, Muslims, and Christians. Chapter 5 turns to the part of the Genesis story yet to be mentioned, Rachel's Tomb. It is altogether fitting that Genesis describes her burial place on the way, and not in the established tomb of the patriarchs and matriarchs at Machpelah near Hebron. However, like Rachel, the tomb itself is more a matter of faith than sight. Debates about the actual location continue even today. A more detailed discussion about the exact location of Ephrath as Rachel's burial place is given in an appendix. As far as Rachel's Tomb outside Bethlehem, the location of this shrine has led to centuries of cooperation; Muslims, Christians, and Jews have all made pilgrimage and said their prayers at this tomb. Chapters 6–8 explore the relationship of Jews, Muslims, and Christians to the tomb, as pilgrims and caretakers, throughout history. In recent times Rachel's Tomb has changed in character. No longer an easily accessible shrine to the memory of Rachel, it has become a fortress tomb representing permanence and exclusiveness. This is the subject of chapter 9, "The Politicization of Rachel's Tomb." Sadly, Rachel's Tomb has once again become a place of violence.

---

[6] Ibid., 57–58.

PART ONE

Mother Rachel

CHAPTER 1

The Biblical Rachel

Prologue: At the Well (Gen 29:1-12)

It is appropriate that the story of Rachel begins at a well.[1] Wells are places for people along the way. Strangers meet. Strangers converse. Often they go again on their own separate ways. Wells are meeting places. At a well, a tired and weary Jesus paused for rest and engaged in a memorable conversation with a woman from Samaria (John 4). Jews and Samaritans did not normally interact. Yet this encounter was possible at the well, among people on the way. At a well, Moses met his future wife.[2] He, a Hebrew; she, a Midianite. They were strangers, yet he came to the aid of the young women harassed by the local shepherds (Exod 2:15-22). The reward was hospitality, a place of refuge.

Rachel is introduced to the reader of Genesis as a young woman on the way. Jacob had previously arrived at the well and was inquiring about Laban[3] with men from Haran when they announced her arrival. "And here is his daughter Rachel, coming with the sheep" (Gen 29:6). Her arrival is a surprise to Jacob. It is not the appropriate time for the sheep to be gathered together and watered. Yet here she is coming to the well.

---

[1] A most helpful source for this entire section is Samuel H. Dresner, *Rachel* (Minneapolis: Fortress, 1994).

[2] Susan Niditch notes that the four Genesis scenes at wells (Gen 16:7-14; 21:8-21; 24:10-27; and 29:1-12) have an underlying theme in the ancient world associating fertility and water, "Genesis," in Carol A. Newsome and Sharon H. Ringe, eds., *The Women's Bible Commentary* (Louisville: Westminster John Knox Press, 1992) 16.

[3] Sharon Pace Jeansonne suggests that the narrator withholds introduction of Laban to prolong the drama. *The Women of Genesis: From Sarah to Potiphar's Wife* (Minneapolis: Fortress, 1990) 70–86, especially 71. However, this is a story of Jacob and Rachel, not Jacob and Laban.

Perhaps it is surprising also that she is a woman shepherdess. Such a profession points to a measure of vulnerability in the world of men. That element is certainly part of the story of Moses' future wife encountering ruffians at the well. It also comes across in the name Rachel, because *RHL* in Hebrew means "lamb." Innocent as a lamb, they often say, yet as a shepherdess she would also have attributes of resourcefulness and strength. However, the implication of vulnerability is always present just below the surface. She is vulnerable and dependent. Her trips to the well must coincide with those of the male shepherds. The stone covering the well was too large for her to lift by herself. Only the cooperation and coordination of all the shepherds would result in access to the well's cool and refreshing water. Rachel was resourceful, but that meant working together to complete this daily task.

In some ways, Jacob and Rachel are a lot alike. He, too, is on the way, having traveled from Beersheba in the south to Haran north of the Euphrates, carrying with him the burden of his estrangement from his brother Esau, of guilt over deceiving his father, of loneliness from saying good-bye to mother and home, and of separation from land and covenantal promise. He is a stranger at the well and to some degree also vulnerable. Yet he is a man of strength, self-reliance, and resourcefulness. He proved that already in his dealings with his own father Isaac in obtaining his brother's birthright. At the well he is not dependent upon his hosts from Haran to offer him a drink of water. Rather, in a demonstration of machismo, he shows off to young Rachel, rolling away the stone from the mouth of the well and watering the flock.[4] Finally, in a show of impulsiveness completely unexpected and foreign to social norms, Jacob publicly shows his emotions, kissing the young Rachel and weeping aloud.

This initial scene ends with Rachel running to tell her father that she has met Jacob. The reader is left wondering about the meaning of Rachel's response. Is she afraid or excited, shocked or pleased? Will she keep her distance or seek to learn more about this stranger from the south? Is she merely a messenger that prepares the way for greater things for Jacob, or will she, a stranger from a far-off land, emerge to play a major role in this developing story of God's covenant relationship with the children of Abraham? What is the meaning of such an encounter at the well? Rachel offers no answer; she is silent.[5] Yet as the encounter comes to a close, she is on her way once again, back home to her father.

---

[4] E. A. Speiser, *Genesis: The Anchor Bible* (Garden City, NY: Doubleday, 1964) 223.

[5] Her lack of description and voice leads the reader to await further character development. Jeansonne, 71.

Act One: On the Way to Marriage (Gen 29:13-30)

Marriage in the world of Rachel was determined by men. Previously, the reader was told that Jacob's journey to Paddan-aram was for the purpose of finding a wife. The covenant had passed from Abraham and Sarah to Isaac and Rebecca and then to Jacob, who must find the appropriate mate with whom to share the promises of God and to pass them on to future generations. For the biblical reader, the journey is not merely an aside in order to buy time, nor a detour that diverts from the main story line. The quest of Jacob to find a wife is of highest import. Now, after a month of hospitality at the home of Laban, it is Rachel's father who raises the question of marriage. "Because you are my kinsman, should you therefore serve me for nothing? Tell me, what shall your wages be?" (v. 15).

To the modern reader, this carries all the marks of a business transaction.[6] Rachel still has no speaking part. Her opinion does not seem to matter. The men arrange the marriage, not for the immediate future, but after Jacob has served Laban for seven years.

Rachel is presented, therefore, on the way to marriage, patiently waiting seven years. Then her own father goes back on his word and deceptively and secretly substitutes Rachel's older sister whose hand he gives to Jacob in marriage. Leah, not Rachel, becomes the patriarch's bride. It is clearly a matter of deception since Jacob does not discover the truth until the following morning. He rushes angrily to the tent of Laban, both girls' father, where he protests.

The story is told from the perspective of Jacob, and the reader's sympathies align with the husband who has been outsmarted. Jacob, however, has in fact achieved his goal in traveling to Haran. He has found a wife from among his kinsmen. True, it wasn't his first choice, but he is now married. It is a fitting reward for seven years' labor, since Jacob out-tricked his own brother Esau in obtaining the birthright and deceived his own father in receiving the blessing of the first-born.[7] Laban and Jacob deserve each other, and the rewards of their dealings are most fitting. So Jacob married Leah. Another seven years' labor would be the price for Rachel's hand in marriage.

Only on a subsequent reading of the text focusing on the woman's perspective does it become clear that Rachel is the real victim. She is a victim

---

[6] Gerhard von Rad, *Genesis: A Commentary*, trans. by John Marks (Philadelphia: Westminster, 1961) 285.

[7] In his excuse for substituting Leah, Laban uses the term "first-born," rather than "elder," drawing a connection with the Esau story. Jeansonne, 73.

thrice over. A victim because her own father has bargained away her future, not giving her a say in the matter. A victim because Jacob has played along with Laban's game, making her wait seven years without asking how it affected her. A victim because the men went back on their agreement, relegating her to a lifetime playing second fiddle to Leah. The insightful reader might add yet a fourth reason. Rachel was also victimized by the storyteller who totally ignored her voice, simply passing over the ways that this agreement and the subsequent breaking of the agreement would affect her life. The poor woman waits seven years for marriage and the storyteller gives the story a twist so that our sympathies rest with her fiancé.

Rachel was likely but a child when she first met Jacob at the well, perhaps just thirteen or fourteen years of age. She would spend one-third of her life on the way to marriage, the seven years agreed upon, then the week of Leah's matrimonial limelight, and even then the debt is not paid. Jacob must still work an additional seven years' labor before the marriage transaction is completed. Hers is a story of patient and faithful waiting, suffering in silence. One can only imagine the silent tears while older sister Leah took her place as the honored bride, the mistress of the house, the sharer of Jacob's bed. One can only imagine how one formerly known for her chosen status would always be known only as the second wife.

In the prologue, it is Rachel and Jacob who stand side by side for comparison and contrast. In Act One, the comparison shifts to Rachel and Leah. Rachel is the youngest, Leah the oldest. Rachel is graceful and beautiful, Leah distinguished by her eyes. Yet the reader doesn't know whether Leah's eyes are a positive or negative attribute. The Hebrew *rak* is uncertain. Modern translations range from "lovely" (NRSV; NAB; NJB) to "pretty" (New Living Bible) to "tender"[8] (KJV) to "delicate" (NKJV) to "gentle"[9] to "clouded" (Bible in Basic English) to "weak"[10] (NIV; NAS; RSV).

The element of love pervades the story, mentioned explicitly with respect to Rachel no less than three times. Rachel is loved; Leah is not. Even earlier in the episode at the well, there seems to be the connotation of love at first sight. Jacob's public display of affection, his impulsive kissing and weeping (v. 11), were the cause of embarrassment for later interpreters. This simply isn't done

---

[8] Speiser, 225.

[9] B. Jacob, *Genesis* (New York: KTAV, 1974) 196.

[10] von Rad, 286; Jeansonne, 72; John Skinner, *Genesis: The International Critical Commentary* (Edinburgh: T & T Clark, 1956) 283.

among persons not yet married, for in that age people married and fell in love, not the other way around. Shortly afterward (a few verses for the reader; a month's visit for Jacob) when Jacob begins negotiations with Laban, the storyteller makes clear what has been assumed, "Jacob loved Rachel" (v. 18). With the agreement settled, the reader is immediately told that Jacob's seven years of service "seemed to him but a few days because of the love he had for her" (v. 20). Then followed the first marriage and the agreement for another seven years of service because Jacob "loved Rachel more than Leah" (v. 30).

Act One shows Rachel as beloved, yet on the way to marriage. In contrast, Leah, though married, is presumably on the way to love. In fact, the situation is worse for Leah than the comparatives "more" and "less" in verse 30 would suggest. Once Rachel's marriage was finally realized, Leah is described by the label "unloved" (v. 31).[11]

Act Two: On the Way to Motherhood (Gen 29:31–30:24)

Just as Rachel spent seven plus years on the way to marriage, so, when finally married, she must journey to motherhood. In Genesis 29:31, the narrator reports that "Rachel was barren." It will take twenty-nine verses and seven additional years before she reaches her goal of motherhood.

The situation is dramatized by Rachel's first speaking part: "Give me children, or I shall die!" (Gen 30:1).[12] Motherhood for her is life. Ironically, motherhood will be the death of her. Nevertheless, at the birth of her firstborn, she has only partially reached her goal. "God has taken away my reproach," she says (Gen 30:23). Yet she names her child Joseph or Yusuf, which literally means "he adds." Her understanding of that name is linked directly to her understanding of her own essence. "May the Lord add to me another son!" she says (Gen 30:24). Her motherhood is incomplete.

In Act Two the comparison between Rachel and Leah reaches a new level. They now become rivals. Just as the women's father arranged that Leah be married first, so it is that the Lord opens Leah's womb first. The narrator underscores the contrast by mentioning in the very same verse that

---

[11] von Rad understands "hated" as legal terminology (Deut 21:15), 289. Jeansonne suggests that "hated" can mean "sexual revulsion," 74.

[12] Robert Alter notes that the term for "give" is often used for "peremptory and crudely material requests," emphasizing the brusqueness of the request, *The Art of Biblical Narrative* (New York: Basic Books, 1981) 187.

the Lord opened Leah's womb but "Rachel was barren" (29:31). Leah will bear six sons to Jacob before Rachel bears her first.

Perhaps it is the understanding of the word "barren" that is the most difficult leap for the modern reader. Today, women in the West have more choices. They are not defined only by their ability to bear children, especially male children. This was not the case in Rachel's world, where motherhood, and motherhood alone, provided identity.[13] Not to bear children was a one-way ticket to a perpetual journey without purpose or meaning. Not to bear children meant nothing less than to be always "on the way." The barren state was sufficient reason for divorce, rejection, and banishment. It was fully within Jacob's right to send Rachel packing.

So Rachel's plea to her very own husband betrays her utter desperation, her feeling of worthlessness, her own constant reproach. "Give me children, or I shall die!" she pleads, yet it seems that she is all but dead. Only divine intervention can save her. Rachel's plea also signals that Jacob's patience has been exhausted, his love tested, his devotion to her trumped by the bad hand dealt to her. "Til death do us part" had been the common adage. Yet Rachel's on-the-way status has brought her to the brink of death.

Under such circumstances, Jacob's love for Rachel soon turns to anger. "Am I in the place of God, who has withheld from you the fruit of the womb?" (30:2). It is God who kills and makes alive. The gift to Jacob of her maidservant Bilhah,[14] the acquisition of the mandrake aphrodisiac,[15] the sending of her own rival Leah to her lover's bed, all show love as the most powerful motivation and faith that with God all things are possible. All the vital signs suggest that a child is not possible. Yet Rachel's faith in God and love of Jacob say otherwise. She continues on the way.

In the end, God hears her reproach, and Jacob perseveres, while Rachel holds onto the thinnest of threads. God opens her womb. Jacob begets her child. And Rachel finds motherhood, joining the ranks of the Genesis matriarchs. And it comes to pass that Rachel bears Joseph. This twelfth of Jacob's offspring—eleven sons and the single daughter Dinah—completes God's plan. The baby cries; Jacob smiles; the midwife sighs in relief; and Rachel seemingly reaches her destination. Against all odds, motherhood found her.

---

[13] Jeansonne, 75. See Mary Callaway, *Sing O Barren One: A Study in Comparative Midrash*, Society of Biblical Literature Dissertation Series (Atlanta: Scholars Press, 1986).

[14] For the practice of "giving birth on a woman's knees" see von Rad, 186, 289–90; Speiser, 230.

[15] Jeansonne, 77–79; Jacob, 200–01.

Yet, even then, it was not enough. There must be another, a number thirteen, lucky or unlucky. "May the Lord add to me another son!" was her prayer. And so, the name Joseph—Hebrew for "The Lord adds."

Not satisfied, Rachel—now mother Rachel—continued.

Act Three: On the Way to the Land (Gen 30:25–35:20)

Rachel's status as wife and mother meant that she must be on the way again. As matriarch in the family of the covenant, she must return with Jacob to the land of Canaan and to Isaac's home in Hebron. "And it came to pass that when Rachel had born Joseph, then Jacob said to Laban: 'Send me away that I may go to my own place and to my own country'" (30:25). The culmination of one stage in Rachel's life initiates the next: "When Rachel," "then Jacob." The Genesis writer underscores the cause and effect. "Send . . . that I may go." Jacob had come to Haran for a wife. With the attainment of marriage and motherhood for Rachel, they must again be on the way. The return to Canaan and Hebron is a given.

By now the reader has been conditioned to expect that nothing happens according to plan in the Genesis story. Timetables, schedules, and well-laid plans are all out the window. The decision to return and the departure date are separated by another six years. Six more years are added to the fourteen for Rachel and Leah. Twenty years in all. Once again Laban intervenes to complicate Jacob's plans.

Yet once again God provides the only intervention that ultimately matters. "Return to the land of your ancestors and to your kindred," the Lord said to Jacob, "and I will be with you" (Gen 31:3). Jacob provides the only strategy capable of disrupting the counter plans of Laban. Taking his wives out to the fields—where not even Laban could spy on them—he informs both Rachel and Leah of the plan. Now the mother and fulfilled wife of Jacob, Rachel's name has attained precedence. No longer is it "Leah and Rachel," the older then the younger. The younger precedes the older. The second wife precedes the first wife. The mother of a single child precedes the mother of a half a dozen. So it is Rachel,[16] especially, who confirms Jacob's desire to be on the way. Leah is relegated to the silent spouse, while Rachel revels center stage in her speaking part.

---

[16] The Hebrew word "replied" is singular.

"We are regarded as 'outsiders'"[17] is how she sizes up the situation (31:14). So there is indeed no place in her father's house, no status, no wealth, no security.[18] They are in Haran, but in reality they are already on the way. So the only solution is to do as God has told them. They depart without informing Laban.

There is the mysterious detail that Rachel takes along the house-gods of her father (31:19-35) while obeying without question the God of Jacob who calls for their departure and who promises to be with them. The presence of the *terafim* diminishes neither Jacob nor his God. However, their absence provokes Laban to action. Rachel finally shows that she has got the best of him.[19]

Being on the way implies vulnerability and risk. The journey is hard and long. Jacob's enemies are many. From behind, Laban chases them down, while Esau's forces lie in wait before them. Strangers surround them on all sides, and even God wrestles with Rachel's husband and protector while camped at the River Jabbok.

Conscious of the risks and threats of the journey and the potential confrontation with Esau, Jacob positions the traveling party strategically. Jacob goes ahead to meet his estranged brother. Bilhah, Zilpah, and their children follow, with Leah and her offspring behind. In the rear are the most vulnerable of them all, the now-pregnant Rachel and young Joseph (33:1-3).[20] The encounter is risky, but it achieves its goals: peace and reconciliation. It is Jacob's willingness to bring humiliation upon himself, to bow seven times to the ground before his estranged brother, and to offer extravagant gifts, that make it possible to enter Canaan in peace. Reconciled to his brother, he can return to the altar at Bethel where God appeared twenty years earlier at the beginning of the journey (Gen 28:10-22), and where God appears to him once again, forgiving, reconciling, and confirming the promise first spoken to Abraham ages ago (Gen 35:1-15).

Peace. Reconciliation. A return to the land. They come with promise. Yet life's realities continue to hit them square in the face. The pangs of death give

---

[17] This term for "foreigner" is the translation of Jeansonne. The NRSV has "are we not regarded by him as foreigners?" carrying with the term "foreigner" a negative connotation. Jeansonne, 81.

[18] The language of verse 15 is very strong, the only time in the Bible that the word "to buy" is used for acquiring wives. Niditch, 20.

[19] Rachel establishes herself as a trickster equal to Laban. Niditch, 21. Jeansonne, 81.

[20] Jeansonne, 85.

a somber tone to their celebration. The narrator first reports the death of the nurse Deborah outside Bethel (Gen 35:8) and later that of aged Isaac in Hebron (Gen 35:29). Both are reported merely in passing. But sandwiched in between in the course of five full verses, Rachel's death is recounted in elaborate detail (Gen 35:16-20). It was the worst thing that could happen at the worst possible time. Having just returned to Canaan to begin a new era in peace, she was ready to bear a second son. It is the worst of all imaginable worlds—death for Jacob's most beloved, death while giving life, death along the way. Twice the Genesis writer notes that Rachel's death occurred on the way—four times if one counts both the narration in chapter 35 and the summary statement in chapter 48.[21] It was so unexpected, and it happened on the way. So many questions remain. On the way to where? The best the writer could say was a place named Ephrath, a place otherwise unnamed in the rest of the Pentateuch.[22] How far along the road? At what point? The Hebrew is vague: a *kbrt* from Ephrath, a term only used elsewhere in Genesis 48:7 and 2 Kings 5:19.[23] At best the translators guess "a long ways off."

Rachel's labor increased in the midst of their journey, the pains became great, and childbirth ensued. It was a particularly difficult birth with the pangs described as "hard labor." Only divine intervention could save her. Why not? God had seemingly rescued her every time before. Perhaps that was the expectation of the midwife whose "Do not be afraid" echoes divine pronouncements. Had Jacob expected this development surely he would have planned otherwise—prolonging their stay at Bethel or hastening their arrival in Hebron. Such was the love of Jacob for Rachel, he would not have placed her in such jeopardy. But he didn't know better and he had no resource to change her fate. She had lived on the way and she would die on the way.

There was nothing Jacob could do but mourn and grieve with all the emotion of a man for the woman he loved dearly. He had wept openly upon meeting Rachel at the well some twenty years before and he would weep openly upon hearing the news that his son Joseph supposedly fell victim to

[21] In addition, the paragraph about Rachel's death is sandwiched between two similar statements: "Then they journey . . ." (v. 16) and "Israel journeyed on . . ." (v. 21).

[22] The reference to Bethlehem is clearly a later insertion attempting to clarify. Claus Westermann, *Genesis 12–36: A Commentary*, trans. by John J. Scullion (Minneapolis: Augsburg, 1985) vol. 2, 555.

[23] "An unknown measure of distance" according to Westermann, vol. 2, 554. "As far as a horse can run" implied by the Greek Septuagint translation. "About a mile," according to Ernst Vogt, "Benjamin geboren 'eine Meile' von Ephrata," *Biblica* 56 (1975) 30–36.

wild animals. Yet the writer does not include such details at Rachel's death. His description suggests more the elements of shock. Jacob matter-of-factly digs her grave and reaches into the recesses of his strength to lift a large pillar to mark the spot. Dying on the way meant that Rachel would not share the family tomb at Machpelah and find a resting place alongside the matriarchs Sarah and Rebecca, as even her rival Leah would. She would not have a resting place at Jacob's side in the Machpelah tomb. Just as he had lifted that heavy stone from the well when he had first laid eyes on her, so now at this farewell, Jacob lifted the stone in its place.

The harshness of this moment could not escape Jacob's ears. Rachel's final words still echoed as a reminder of her tragic life: "Son of my sorrow." As a final act, she named him Benoni,[24] yet Jacob would not have it. Rachel deserved more, so he did the one thing possible. "Son of my sorrow" must not become the final word. Her newborn must be transformed as a tribute to Rachel. Benoni would be called Benjamin, "Son of my right hand."

Epilogue: Children on the Way—Joseph and Benjamin

Jacob lost Rachel whom he loved dearly. His only hope was to remain close to her through their two sons. As for Joseph, Rachel's firstborn, his handsome appearance was a constant reminder of Rachel (Gen 27:17; 39:6).[25] He soon rose to be the father's favorite. As for Benjamin, the last born, if he was to be truly the son of Jacob's right hand, he would have to keep him close, protected and secure. So Jacob finally found himself in the settled life, no longer on the way. His ten eldest to be sure were often out and about, pasturing their flocks and competing with the inhabitants of the land. As for Joseph and Benjamin, they remained home with Jacob.

However, this was not to be. Like their mother Rachel, they were destined to be always on the way. Joining his brothers in the field, the teenage Joseph became the brunt of sibling rivalry. The gifted dreamer, the wearer of a colorful coat, the sheltered favorite soon found himself the possession of a trade caravan making its way to Egypt. As for Jacob, he was told Joseph had met his death. With such an end, the memory of Rachel was bound to cease,[26] so Jacob wept as if he were weeping for Rachel.

---

[24] Westermann, vol. 2, 555.

[25] Their appearance is described with the same terms. von Rad, 359.

[26] Dresner, 109–10.

Like mother, like son. Joseph is marked by his beautiful appearance, by the love of Jacob, and a life on the way. Like his mother, he too would die on the way in far-off Egypt. Like his mother, he too would find a burial place other than the Machpelah tomb of patriarchs and matriarchs.

Before the story of Joseph's death, of course, is the surprising story of Joseph's life in Egypt, a story that encompasses a significant portion of the book of Genesis. With an unexpected reversal, Joseph, now the successful government administrator, draws father and brothers away from the comfort and security of the famine-oppressed home in Canaan to this southern breadbasket. The story is told in high drama with ten brothers first making the trek (42:4), then also Benjamin (43:7), and finally also Jacob. The meeting comes not without tears, but also tricks and deception with Joseph first hiding his identity and planting the silver goblet in Benjamin's sack. Rachel's firstborn had been placed at risk. Yet life on the way meant a life of abundance in a time of famine. In the end there is reconciliation. For seventeen years Jacob and sons would join Joseph, living in Egypt, but because of Joseph they would live with full stomachs.

Instead of Reuben, Jacob's firstborn, it was Joseph who rose to the status of patriarch. Rachel's firstborn became the preeminent leader both materially and spiritually—a prince among his brothers (49:26). As his final act, Jacob called forth all his sons for a blessing. When Joseph's turn came, there was a double blessing. Placing his hands upon the heads of Ephraim and Manasseh, the two sons of Joseph, Jacob claimed them as his own two children and established them as leaders of the tribes of Israel (48:21). The irony was that Rachel's two grandsons became equals of Leah's sons. So it was that Rachel was remembered through her children.

Postscript: Jeremiah—On the Way to Exile

For more than a millennium following Rachel's death, she was remembered through her offspring. First, it was through her children Joseph and Benjamin, even as they found themselves in Egypt. Then grandsons Ephraim and Manasseh found themselves elevated as equals of Leah's sons. Later, generations of descendants found themselves still on the way during hard times in Egypt, and later still, others found themselves in the settled life with the tribes of Benjamin, Ephraim, and Manasseh calling forth her memory. Rachel's children produced leaders like Joshua, the successor of Moses; the prophet Samuel; and the first king Saul. With the division into

Northern and Southern Kingdoms, Ephraim soon became synonymous for the north while smaller Benjamin latched onto Judah in the south. It seemed that Rachel's offspring had found an end to life on the way. They were settled and secure at last. Rachel could rest in peace.

Yet Bible stories don't always end happily ever after. Rachel's offspring eventually found themselves again on the way, first with the Assyrians, then the Babylonians disrupting their lives. In the late eighth century, Ephraim and the other northerners found themselves in exile. By the sixth century, Benjamin and Judah followed. After a siege of three years, Jerusalem fell and its inhabitants were processed for deportation to Babylon at the town of Ramah. They were experiencing the spiritual death of exile from the land, and the only response was tears of grief. These were the same tears shed by mother Jerusalem for her children in Lamentations. Yet the most poignant expression of grief was that which Jeremiah imagined would be expressed by his own ancestress Rachel.

In the context of the deportation to Babylon, Rachel's descendant, the Benjaminite Jeremiah from the village of Anathoth, responded with a vision that marked Rachel with immortality.[27] Dead for over a millennium, she was still alive with her children, suffering through their misfortunes, pleading to God on their behalf:

> Thus says the Lord:
> A voice is heard in Ramah,
>   lamentation and bitter weeping.
> Rachel is weeping for her children;
>   she refuses to be comforted for her children,
>   because they are no more. (Jer 31:15)

This single verse, remembered through the ages, is part of a larger section in Jeremiah known as the Book of Consolation (chs. 30–33).[28] After decades of proclaiming doom and gloom of impending destruction, Jeremiah

---

[27] As background E. Burrows points to a Semitic belief that mothers who died in childbirth became weeping ghosts in "Cuneiform and Old Testament: Three Notes," *Journal of Theological Studies* (JTS) 28 (1927) 185. Terence E. Fretheim states, "the image presented in v. 15 is not that of a dead Rachel weeping in her grave, but Rachel as the personification of all Israel's mothers," *Jeremiah: Smyth & Helwys Bible Commentary* (Macon, GA: Smyth & Helwys, 2002) 434.

[28] The contrast between Rachel's Lament and the hopeful tone of the whole chapter and section provides a startling impact. Frederick A. Niedner, "Rachel's Lament," *Word & World* 22 (Fall 2002) 409.

offers a word of comfort. With Jerusalem captured and the exiles gathered for deportation at the town of Ramah[29]—including the prophet himself (40:1)—Jeremiah provides a word of hope. Following exile in Babylon, God will intervene and bring about a return to the land.

Yet the return will not come through any merit of the exiles, rather only because of the emotion-filled plea of their all-deserving mother Rachel. The lament begins, "A voice is heard." It is not a meaningless babbling or an endless repetition of empty words. The meaning is clear. God has heard.

> Thus says the Lord:
> Keep your voice from weeping,
>   and your eyes from tears . . .
> There is hope for your future,
>   says the Lord:
> your children shall come back to their own country. (31:16-17)

God has heard, and only because it is Rachel pleading. As Terence Fretheim has noted, "Recognizing her weeping and her tears, God seeks to comfort her with a word of unconditional promise, completely without motivation or rationale."[30] There is a strange aspect to this section because among the specific names, Ephraim is mentioned no less than six times with most endearing language:

> Is Ephraim my dear son?
> Is he the child I delight in? (31:20)

Although the northern kingdom had been exiled years earlier, the prophet now sees Ephraim as symbolic of all Israel.[31] They are Rachel's children. Yet more than that, Yahweh now identifies with Rachel as parent.[32] Strangest of all is the fact that the typical ways of the world no longer provide the answers. The ways of power and strength, of exclusivity and manipulation, have all failed. Instead, Rachel's faithfulness and patient waiting have become a model for all.

---

[29] The issues around understanding Ramah as an ambiguous "height" rather than a specific place name are discussed in detail by William L. Holladay, *Jeremiah: Hermeneia Commentary Series* (Minneapolis: Fortress, 1989) 186–87. See also Robert P. Carroll, *Jeremiah: Old Testament Library* (Philadelphia: Westminster, 1986) 598.

[30] Fretheim, 434.

[31] Kathleen M. O'Connor, "Jeremiah," *The Women's Bible Commentary*, 176.

[32] Phyllis Trible, *God and the Rhetoric of Sexuality* (Philadelphia: Fortress, 1978) 45.

> For the Lord has created a new thing on the earth;
> A woman encompasses a man. (31:22)[33]

In the male-dominated society of Jeremiah's day, God has turned the world inside out. It is not surprising that Rabbi Shimon ben Yohai later said, "Everything depended upon Rachel."[34]

Rachel has emerged as the preeminent matriarch. How odd that Sarah, Rebecca, and Leah are hardly mentioned outside the Pentateuch, but Rachel found a lasting role as the mother figure who weeps for all those on the way. Certainly, her own character prepared her for that. Yet her earlier suffering and tears make it possible to suffer for others. Finally, one cannot discount the significance of her own death and burial. Unlike the other three matriarchs buried in the Machpelah tomb, Rachel was given a simple burial on the way. Her place there by the roadside remained accessible to all no matter their status, their family, their ethnicity. So it was that Rachel's tears extended also to her own rival Leah's children.

It is significant that Jeremiah placed the lament of Rachel in Ramah, a city within the borders of Benjamin north of Jerusalem. It is along this same road that Rachel once accompanied Jacob from Mesopotamia. Now the exiles were gathered to make that march in reverse. They were experiencing their own spiritual death and annihilation, just like Rachel years before. In mentioning Ramah, Jeremiah was clearly alluding to the memorial pillar erected by Jacob that the Genesis writer noted was standing "to this day." For some, this would be a sign of providence that her death and burial had taken place, not in Hebron, but there on the way where the exiles would one day be passing. For others, it was a mere coincidence. Whatever the case, it provided a powerful symbol in Jeremiah's day for those on the way. In future generations, the image of Rachel weeping for her children provided meaning for other passersby who saw Rachel's Tomb and remembered her story.

---

[33] The second part of this couplet literally means "a female surrounds a warrior." O'Connor, 176.

[34] *Genesis Rabbah* 71.2 according to the translation of Dresner, 163. See also Neusner, 116.

CHAPTER 2

Rachel in Judaism

The story of Rachel was told and retold in later generations. Sometimes it was repeated verbatim; sometimes just a brief allusion to Rachel was made. Sometimes it was retold with a surprising twist, an elaborate detail, or an expanded insertion. Sometimes it was used to teach a moral lesson. It was told a myriad times over by people in numerous places, in multiple languages, and in a variety of faiths. Rachel's on-the-way character made it fitting that Rachel could not be contained by a single group of people or faith. She was accessible to all, a model of faith. To understand Rachel's character, it is important to survey the retelling of her story in Judaism, Christianity, and Islam—three children sharing a common spiritual mother. Chapters 3 and 4 will look at Rachel's story in Christianity and Islam. This chapter will explore Rachel in Judaism.

Josephus

The first-century Jewish historian Flavius Josephus tells the story of Rachel in substantial detail in his *Jewish Antiquities*.[1] Although the story fills sixty paragraphs, it is generally shorter than the Genesis account. Yet it is clearly not an abbreviation of the well-known narrative. Rather, Rachel's story is told with creativity that suggests the use of independent traditions that likely existed already in the biblical era.[2] Therefore, it is fitting to begin with Josephus.

[1] Josephus, *Jewish Antiquities* 1.285–344 in *Josephus*, vol. IV, trans. by H. St. J. Thackeray and Ralph Marcus. *The Loeb Classical Library* (Cambridge, MA: Harvard University Press, 1977) 139–65.

[2] Thomas W. Franxman, *Genesis and the "Jewish Antiquities" of Flavius Josephus* (Rome: Biblica et Orientalia 35, 1979).

The one episode that is told at much greater length is the initial meeting at the well in Haran. In this account, Rachel is not present at the well at Jacob's arrival but is significantly depicted as on her way to the well. When the encounter takes place, she immediately offers "the stranger" hospitality. There is no show of Jacob's unusual strength or physical attributes. He merely reveals that he is her cousin. Rachel is characterized with youthful excitement, acting out of "childish delight." As for Jacob, he is moved by the physical appearance of the young woman, "amazed at the sight of beauty such as few women of those days could show." Already at this point in the story, Jacob is moved by "love for the maid." Yet as is characteristic of Josephus, the Greek word here is *eros*, the physical erotic love.[3] However, unlike the biblical account, Jacob does not act on his feelings. He does not offer the young woman a kiss. Rather, Rachel has the more active role. She bursts into tears, flings her arms around the stranger, and leads him to her father.[4]

Jacob, of course, begins working for his uncle Laban, but it is some time before he raises the question of marriage. Eventually, Laban agrees to the marriage of Rachel in exchange for Jacob's labor over seven years. The narrator again notes that she deserved his esteem, especially for her services of hospitality. Again Jacob's love (*eros*) is noted.

Only at the time of the wedding is Leah introduced. She is older and "devoid of beauty." However, a totally new element is introduced to the story. Jacob is "all-unconscious" completely "deluded by wine and the dark." To the reader, Jacob deserves what he gets. There is less sympathy for him and, in turn, more for Rachel. This leads to the "morning-after" confrontation with Laban. His new father-in-law asks if he still has *eros* for Rachel, and Jacob responds that indeed because of his *eros* for her, he will work an additional seven years for her. In this case, the marriage itself will not take place for another seven years. The plight of Rachel is doubled, waiting fourteen years altogether.

The rivalry between the two sisters is abbreviated and also told in a way that emphasizes the positive qualities of Rachel. Josephus notes that the two handmaids, Zilpah and Bilhah, were not really slaves, but merely

---

[3] Harold W. Attridge, *The Interpretation of Biblical History in the Antiquitates Judaicae of Flavius Josephus* (Missoula, MT: SBL, 1976) 126–40.

[4] James L. Bailey, "Josephus' Portrayal of the Matriarchs," in Louis H. Feldman and Gohei Hata, ed., *Josephus, Judaism, and Christianity* (Detroit: Wayne State University Press, 1987) 154–79.

subordinates. Leah's desire to bear children was the only way she might gain the favor of Jacob because his passion (*eros*) for Rachel was so great. Totally omitted is the confrontation between Rachel and Jacob in which she blames God for her barren state. She silently submits, faithful all the while. When it comes to the mandrake episode, Rachel merely desires to eat the apple of the mandrake as food. Leah responds in anger. So Rachel offers her bed that night to Leah to appease her. Jacob then sleeps with Leah "to please Rachel." Finally, Josephus mentions in passing that Rachel gave birth to Joseph.

When Jacob and family depart from Haran after twenty years, Rachel takes with her the images of the gods, not because they were important to her—Jacob had taught her to despise them—but in order that she might have some recourse over Laban. Jacob defends her as following him freely because of her "affection" for her husband. Later he approaches his encounter with Esau with caution, but also with confidence because he had "committed to God his hopes of salvation." Jacob is reconciled with his brother and then settles for a time near Bethel. Josephus presents the final episode with brevity: "Thence he [Jacob] proceeded on his way, and when he was come over against Ephratene Rachel died in childbirth and there he buried her, being the only one of his family who had not the honor of burial at Hebron. Deeply he mourned her and called the child whom she bore Benjamin because of the suffering which he had caused his mother."[5] The final statement suggests some knowledge of the longer story with the name Benoni. Although the grief of Jacob is emphasized, there is no reference to the pillar or the continued significance of her tomb. The location of Bethlehem is not mentioned. Rachel is merely buried on the way to Ephrathene.

Early Translations

Unlike Josephus who highlights the erotic love of Jacob for Rachel, the Septuagint Greek translation consistently employs the verb *agapan*—the Greek word used for an unconditional and unmerited form of love—to express the deeper relationship between the two (Gen 29:18, 20, 30). The contrast between Rachel and Leah is emphasized so that Jacob comes to "hate" (*misein*) Leah (Gen 29:31). Earlier when the two sisters were introduced, the Hebrew text clearly described Rachel in favorable terms ("graceful and beautiful" in the NRSV translation), but the description of Leah is

---

[5] Josephus, *Jewish Antiquities* 1.343, in *Josephus*, vol. IV, 165.

unclear: "her eyes were _____," with the final Hebrew term uncertain (Gen 29:17). Many commentators believe that the original intention was positive. However, the Septuagint has translated the uncertain term as *astheneis*—her eyes were weak.

In the episode of Rachel's death, several geographical terms are changed. While the Greek text continues to emphasize that Rachel died and was buried on the way (*en tē hodē*), the Greek translator sought to clarify details that seemed uncertain. Unlike Josephus, the translator includes the parenthetical explanation "that is, Bethlehem" that is found also in the Hebrew. The translator, however, recognized the problematical nature of this reading so that even the order of the verses has been rearranged. The final verse, "Israel journeyed on, and pitched his tent beyond the tower of Eder" (Gen 35:20 in Hebrew and NRSV), has been moved in the Greek to the beginning of the episode in verse 16. This change, as we will see in more detail later, is certainly because the tower of Eder was often associated with Jerusalem, a location north of Bethlehem.

The translator apparently does not understand the unusual Hebrew term *kbrt* that designates the distance from Ephrath. Rather, the assumption is that it must be the name of a place along the road and thus the place name *Chabratha* was created and used in the Septuagint passage in Genesis 35. This term also occurs in Genesis 48:7. However, in that latter summary statement, the confusion of the translator produces yet another unusual reading: Jacob and his traveling party were drawing near to the hippodrome of Chabratha (*ton hippodromon chabratha*). Here the translator has taken a cue from 2 Kings 5:19—the only other occasion that *kbrt* is used in the Hebrew Scriptures—where it refers to the distance a horse can run at a full gallop,[6] while the modern reader is likely to understand hippodrome in terms of the many stadium-like horse tracks throughout the Roman Empire. There is evidence for such a hippodrome in Hasmonean Jerusalem and later in Caesarea Maritima, but not in Bethlehem. Yet there's another possible connotation, as 2 Kings 5:19 suggests. The term "hippodrome" literally means "the running of a horse." In other words, the intended meaning was that Rachel died "about as far as a horse can run" from Ephratha, although the Septuagint gives it as a location by an actual hippodrome. The fact that the Septuagint text includes both *hippodromon* and *Chabratha* sug-

---

[6] Westermann, *Genesis 12–36: A Commentary*, vol. 2, 554. Ernst Vogt, "Benjamin geboren 'eine Meile' von Ephrata," *Biblica* 56 (1975) 30–36.

gests a tradition of interpretation already in existence. Then to underscore this interpretation the term is repeated at the end of the verse: "And I buried her on the way *of the hippodrome*"—a reading that led to further confusion among early Christian writers as we will see below.

Targums

In Targum Jonathan, an Aramaic translation and interpretation from perhaps the first or second century, Rachel has disappeared as the figure weeping for her children in Jeremiah 31. She has been replaced by Jerusalem herself, reminiscent of the mother figure and weeping goddess motif in Lamentations. The text reads:

> Thus the Lord has said:
> A voice in the height of the world has been heard,
>> the house of Israel is lamenting and moaning after the prophet Jeremiah,
>>> when Nebuzaradan, the chief of the murderers, sent him from Ramah:
> Lamentations and weeping out of bitterness;
> Jerusalem weeps for her children, refusing to be comforted
> for her children, since they have gone into exile. (TJer 31:15)[7]

No longer does Rachel play a special role as the figure suffering on behalf of the people as she did in other manuscripts. Instead, Jeremiah the prophet is now mentioned within the text, becoming the model servant, representing the imprisonment and suffering of the exiles. As a conflation with chapters 39–40 of Jeremiah, his imprisonment is located at the city of Ramah. However, the familiar "voice heard in Ramah" is missing. In Hebrew the word *Ramah* means *height*, thus the opening words of the Targum: "A voice in the height of the world has been heard." The voice is no longer connected with a site near the biblical Ramah, north of Jerusalem.

Historical Works of the Late Biblical Period

The third-century B.C.E. chronographer Demetrius repeats the basic details of the Genesis story of Rachel.[8] There is no recalling the meeting

---

[7] Translation by Ida Zatelli, "Rachel's Lament in the Targum and Other Ancient Jewish Interpretations," *Revista Biblica*, 39 (1991) 477–90.

[8] Demetrius is known in six fragments preserved in Eusebius, *Praeparatio Evangelica* 9. See James Charlesworth, *The Old Testament Pseudepigrapha*, vol. 2, Anchor Bible (Garden

at the well and the deception of Laban related to Jacob's marriages, but Rachel's barren state is mentioned. The concern of Demetrius is to designate the specific dates of the biblical events. Thus Joseph was born in the eighth month of the fourteenth year of Jacob's sojourn in Haran. He was six years and four months old at the time of their departure. In order to fit the biblical events together, Demetrius has to add an even ten years to the chronology so that Dinah was a young woman of sixteen when the events of Genesis 34 took place. As a result there is a difference in age of sixteen years and four months between the births of Joseph and Benjamin. Demetrius concludes that Jacob lived with Rachel a total of twenty-three years at her death (thirteen in Haran and an additional ten years after the return to Canaan). The death of Rachel is recounted only in passing. Dependent upon the Septuagint translation, Demetrius notes that Jacob traveled from Bethel to Chaphratha, and from there to Ephrath, which is Bethlehem. There she died giving birth to Benjamin.

The book of Jubilees[9] is also concerned in providing a chronological framework for biblical events, describing various seven-year periods as weeks. Thus in the first year of the third week, Jacob made his agreement with Laban to work for a wife, and in the sixth year of the fourth week Joseph was born. The story of Rachel is told in some detail, although again the encounter at the well is omitted. The deception by Laban is told in short order, noting that Jacob "did not know it because Jacob assumed she [Leah] was Rachel." Like the biblical text, the author of Jubilees notes that Jacob loved Rachel more than Leah. The reason is simple: "Rachel had good eyes and good appearance and she was very beautiful." Interestingly, the report about Leah is mixed. Like the Septuagint, the writer notes that Leah's eyes were weak, but perhaps more like the Hebrew text, "her appearance was very beautiful." Jacob agrees to a second "week" in exchange for Rachel. As in other traditions, Rachel was barren. Here her barren state is explained "because Leah was hated, but Rachel was loved." Rachel's plight is noted in her exchange with Jacob, but in a much less dramatic way. "Give me sons," she says (not "Give me children, or I shall die!"). Jacob replies, "Have I withheld from you the fruit of your womb? Have I forsaken you?" (not "Am I in the place of God who has withheld from you the fruit of the womb?"). The

City, NY: Doubleday, 1985) 843–50. The story of Rachel occurs in Fragment 2 = Eusebius, *PrEv* 9.21.1–19.

    [9] Charlesworth, *Pseudepigrapha*, vol. 2, 109–18.

birth of sons is reported matter-of-factly without the intrigue of the rivalry, the episode of the mandrakes, or Rachel's sending Leah to her husband's bed. In Jubilees, the final two children, Zebulun and Dinah, are twins. Finally, the Lord had mercy upon Rachel and opened her womb so that Joseph was born, as with Demetrius, "on the first of the fourth month in the sixth year, of that fourth week." The author omits the cry of Rachel, linked to the naming of Joseph, "Lord, add to me another!"

The Jubilees account continues with Jacob agreeing to work further for Laban for an unspecified period of time. Eventually, Jacob calls Leah and Rachel (not "Rachel and Leah" as in the Genesis text) to inform them of his intention to return to Canaan. "We will go with you anywhere you go," they responded in unison. They left in the seventh year of the fourth week, in the first month on the twenty-first day, eventually being overtaken by Laban, but without any mention of Rachel taking the house-gods. By the first year of the fifth week in that jubilee, they crossed over the Jordan and entered Canaan. The interval before Rachel's death includes, in addition to the Genesis material, an encounter between Jacob and his parents, the designation of Levi for priesthood, and a vision which restrained him from building a sanctuary at Bethel (in deference to the later importance of the Jerusalem temple). Following the death of Rebecca's nurse Deborah at a place called "Deborah's River" near an oak tree south of Bethel, Jacob traveled on to dwell in the land of Kabratan. This detail is completely absent from the Genesis account and is apparently dependent upon the Septuagint mistranslation of the unusual term *kbrt* of distance.

The death of Rachel is then recounted, not while they are traveling but while they are living "in the land of Ephrata, i.e., Bethlehem." So it is "in the night" that Rachel bore a son on the eleventh day of the eighth month in the first year of the sixth week of that jubilee. The author of Jubilees notes that Rachel first named her new child "son of my sorrow" while Jacob called him Benjamin. Following her death Jacob built a pillar on her tomb "on the road." In Genesis, Rachel's death and tomb are revisited in Jacob's final words. However, Jubilees adds one further tradition. Following the announcement of Joseph's death by wild animals, Rachel's servant Bilhah died while grieving for him as did also Dinah. At the time they were dwelling in a place called Qafrateh, a name apparently alluding to Ephrath. The two women were then taken, not to Hebron for burial, but were buried "opposite the tomb of Rachel" (Jubilees 34:15-17). Leah's death is passed over in Genesis. However, Jubilees 36:21-24 notes that she died in the fourth year of the second week of the 45th Jubilee. In describing her burial at the Machpelah cave with all the sons present, the writer notes that Jacob "loved her exceedingly after Rachel her sister died; for she was perfect and upright in all her ways . . . and he lamented her exceedingly; for he loved her with all his heart and with all his soul." Here begins a branch of tradition, continuing with Philo and the Hasidic mystics, that elevated the role of Leah.

Another pseudepigraphic work that draws from Genesis is the Testaments of the Twelve Patriarchs.[10] Twelve separate sections relate the perspectives of the twelve sons of Jacob. Naphtali thus announced that Rachel had a special love for him because he, a son of Bilhah, was born on the knees of Rachel. So she would kiss him and say, "May I see a brother of yours, like you, from my own womb!" So Joseph was in every way like Naphtali.

Issachar recounted the episode when he was conceived after Reuben brought the mandrakes from the field and Rachel then "hired" a woman for Jacob for the night, Issachar's own mother, Leah. Issachar then goes on to relate a vision of Jacob in which he was informed by God that Rachel would bear him two sons. The reason was that Rachel despised intercourse with her husband, choosing rather continence. It was true, according to Issachar, that Rachel wanted to sleep with Jacob. However, it was because she wanted to bear children, not for sexual gratification.

Benjamin notes an unusual explanation for his name, meaning "Son of days." He received this name because he was conceived in his father's old age, noting that Jacob prayed that he might have two sons from Rachel, whom he loved exceedingly. Between the birth of Joseph and that of Benjamin, twelve years elapsed. It was only through prayer and fasting that she finally became pregnant. He adds no further information concerning his birth or his mother's death, though he notes that he was nursed by Bilhah. The remainder of the Testament of Benjamin is devoted to the story of his family's journey to Egypt to be restored to Joseph his brother.

The Testament of Joseph recounts exclusively his Egypt experience. The one significant detail noted is the instruction that Joseph gives to have his wife, Asenath, transported to Canaan after her death to be buried near Rachel. Following the Septuagint reading, the writer notes the location of her burial place "by the hippodrome." A separate manuscript mentions the name Zilpah rather than Asenath, perhaps a reflection of a separation tradition. Thus, along with the notation in Jubilees concerning Bilhah and

---

[10] Charlesworth, *Pseudepigrapha*, vol. 1 (1983) 782–828.

Dinah, the tradition is preserved that other women of Genesis were buried along with Rachel.

Philo: Allegorical Interpretation

The first-century Alexandrian Philo approaches the story of Rachel in a totally different way because he attempts to read Genesis through the perspective of dualistic Platonic philosophy. Thus the figures of Rachel and Leah are perfect grist for contrast. Since Rachel is noted in Genesis for her physical beauty, she does not fare well with Philo. In *Sob.* 12, Philo writes: "Thus Rachel, who is comeliness of the body, is described as younger than Leah, that is beauty of soul. For the former is mortal, the latter immortal, and indeed all the things that are precious to the senses are inferior in perfection to beauty of soul."[11] Rachel is the model of sense perception common to women, and she shows weakness throughout her life, including her plea to Jacob, "Give me children, or I shall die!"[12] Rachel thus finds herself in a barren state. In contrast, Leah receives children by God's own gift,[13] a sign that God brings forth "worthy practices and excellent deeds."[14] Leah, not Rachel, should be the model for women because it is said "Leah was hated." This means that Leah "was above the passions" and "cannot tolerate those who are attracted by the spells of the pleasures that accord with Rachel, who is sense-perception."[15] Thus, following Leah's example, one should turn away from mortal things.

In *Congr.* 24-30, Philo interprets the meaning of the names.[16] Jacob as the practitioner of virtue seeks out Leah because she is smooth movement which leads to the noble life. In contrast, Rachel is like a whetstone to sharpen the mind. Rachel's name means "vision of profanation," not because she is profane, but because she judges the world of senses to be profane. However, even the name of Rachel's handmaid, Bilhah, betrays her character, which he interprets as "swallowing," denoting attraction to eating and drinking. Leah, however, has a handmaid named Zilpah, interpreted

[11] Philo, *On Sobriety* 12, in *Philo*, vol. III, trans. by F. H. Colson and G. H. Whitaker, *The Loeb Classical Library* (Cambridge, MA: Harvard University Press, 1968) 449.

[12] Philo, *Allegorical Interpretation* 2.46, in *Philo*, vol. I (1981) 253.

[13] Philo, *Allegorical Interpretation* 3.180, in *Philo*, vol. I (1981) 423.

[14] Philo, *Who Is the Heir?* 50, in *Philo*, vol. IV (1968) 309.

[15] Philo, *On the Posterity and Exile of Cain* 135, in *Philo*, vol. II (1979) 406.

[16] Philo, *The Preliminary Studies* 24–30, in *Philo*, vol. IV (1968) 471–73.

by Philo as "walking mouth," signifying the vocal organs by which humans make arguments and offer persuasive speech.[17]

While the death of Rachel calls for sympathy in other writers, in Philo it is a final sign of weakness. Her suffering leads her to name her newborn "son of sorrow," because she has been swept along by "the current of empty opinion" faced with "envy, jealousies, continuous quarreling, rancorous enmities unreconciled till death, feuds handed down successively to children's children, an inheritance which cannot be possessed."[18] Jacob's name for his offspring is Benjamin, interpreted as "son of days." However, Philo's understanding is not the same as in the Testament of Benjamin in which the name denotes Jacob's old age. Rather, Benjamin is a child of the daylight where our senses perceive outward beauty but miss inner virtue, thus a sign of vainglory. So Philo concludes: "And so God's interpreter could not but represent the mother of vainglory as dying in the very pangs of childbirth. Rachel died, we read, in hard labor, for the conception and birth of vainglory, the creature of sense, is in reality the death of the soul."[19] Thus it is significant that Rachel is not buried in the Machpelah cave. For Philo, the wives of the patriarchs are generally symbolic of virtue and the double cave near Hebron is thus the appropriate resting place: "But the soul wedded to goodness obtained inhabitants excelling in the virtues, whom the double cave received in pairs, Abraham and Sarah, Isaac and Rebecca, Leah and Jacob, these being virtues and their possessors."[20] As for Rachel's offspring, Joseph fairs no better than Benjamin.

Philo is not unique in seeing the positive qualities of Leah. However, in his treatment of Rachel, he must be understood as an aberration in the long Jewish tradition of praise and admiration for the character of Rachel.

Rabbinic Literature

"Everything depended upon Rachel," said Rabbi Shimon ben Yohai. There is no question about the high esteem for Rachel in rabbinic literature. This statement quoted earlier is from the fifth-century c.e. Rabbinical work *Genesis Rabbah* where the entire book of Genesis is treated through Rabbinic interpretation, providing new eyes for the story of Rachel. A full treat-

[17] Philo, *Allegorical Interpretation* 2.96, in *Philo*, vol. I (1981) 285.

[18] Philo, *On the Change of Names* 92–96, in *Philo*, vol. V (1968) 189–91.

[19] Ibid., 191.

[20] Philo, *On the Posterity and Exile of Cain* 62, in *Philo*, vol. II (1979) 361.

ment of rabbinic texts on Rachel could fill whole books.[21] So as an example, we will merely highlight the presentation of Rachel in *Genesis Rabbah*.[22]

When considering the episode at the well, the rabbis are concerned about the morality of two strangers meeting. That Rachel is a shepherdess is puzzling, since this profession would place such a beautiful young woman at risk. Some explain it as a necessity, assuming that Laban had no sons or that the flocks had been depleted by disease. Whatever the reason, they concluded that God's protection looked out for her virtue in view of her chosen role as matriarch.[23] Nevertheless even Jacob responded to her with kisses, the only example in Scripture besides the Song of Solomon of an unmarried man and woman kissing. *Genesis Rabbah* 70.12 states the common position, "Every form of kissing is obscene except for three purposes, the kiss upon accepting high office, the kiss upon seeing someone at an interval after an absence, and the kiss of departure." Still, Jacob's actions do not fit these reasons. So Rabbi Tanhuma, noting the Genesis verse that Rachel was Jacob's kinswoman, adds a fourth permissible kiss: "the kiss exchanged among kin." Any ideas of immorality or the potential of immorality are therefore unfounded.

Jacob's willingness to deal with a deceitful character like Laban, even in order to obtain a wife like Rachel, might appear suspect, yet Jacob was a stronger bargainer than even the biblical record implied. He made an agreement that left no room for misunderstanding. "For Rachel, not for Leah. For your daughter, and you cannot bring someone from the market place whose name is Rachel. The younger one, so you may not change their names for another."[24] Yet when it came to the wedding night, Jacob's judgment was dulled from drinking and the darkness of night blurred his vision so that it was only in the morning that he realized it was Leah.[25] Although this detail is not recorded in *Genesis Rabbah*, other rabbinic sources report that Rachel complied with her father's wishes to such a degree that she spent the night under the bridal bed answering for Leah whenever Jacob spoke to her.[26]

---

[21] See Dresner for extensive rabbinic commentary on Rachel.

[22] *Genesis Rabbah*, ed. and trans. by James Neusner, *Scripture and Midrash in Judaism*, vol. 2 (Frankfurt: Peter Lang, 1995) 19–170.

[23] Ibid., 70.11.

[24] Ibid., 70.17.

[25] Ibid., 70.19.

[26] See introduction above. *Lamentations Rabbah, petikhta*, 24 and *TB Megillah* 13b. Louis Ginzberg, *The Legends of the Jews*, vol. 2, trans. by Henrietta Szold (Philadelphia: The Jewish Publication Society of America, 1910).

Leviticus 18:18 forbids a man to marry two sisters lest they become rivals. The midrash above is thus an example of the attempt to present both Leah and Rachel on most favorable terms. From the women's perspective it was a marriage of necessity. As the eldest, Leah had been marked for marriage to Esau. So the description of Leah as having "weak" eyes is understood in terms of her constant crying over that arrangement.[27] The agreement that both be married to Jacob is thus a positive solution, and the cooperation of both women is held up as virtuous. When Genesis 30:1 says that Rachel envied Leah, it is only envy of her piety and many good deeds.[28] Though Rachel endures the arrangement in silence, it is still a struggle, thus she names the son born to her maidservant Naphtali, meaning "wrestling." Rachel reflects on her situation: "With mighty wrestlings I have wrestled with my sister and have prevailed. . . . I perfumed [my bed], I was persuaded [to give place to my sister], I placed my sister above me. . . . Had I sent word to him and told him, 'Pay attention for they are going to deceive you,' would he not have separated from her? But I thought, 'If I am not worthy of having the world built up from me, let it at least be built up from my sister.'"[29] Rachel's silent wrestling is thus explained. She is a model of the patient, long-suffering wife.

Rachel's barren state is cause for concern. Like a number of other situations in life, the barren state is no less than a walking death. Yet like Sarah and Rebecca before her, Rachel is loved by her husband. Here the Hebrew wordplay explains the irony. The word *akarah* means barren, and the word *ikarah* means the principal one. Rachel is Jacob's first love, not in spite of, but because she is barren.[30] Eventually, of course, God intervenes to open Rachel's womb. In later tradition, the details are presented in an even more miraculous way. Rachel at first was pregnant with Dinah, not Joseph, and God switched the embryos at the last minute so that Rachel could bear a son. Here the rabbis noticed that Genesis 30:21 reads, "Afterwards she [Leah] gave birth to a daughter." In her other pregnancies, there is a standard formula, "she conceived and bore." They conclude that Leah did not originally conceive Dinah, but rather another son. However, because of the

[27] *Genesis Rabbah* 70.16.

[28] Ibid., 73.4.

[29] Ibid., 71.8.

[30] Ibid., 71.2-6.

prayer of Rachel, the child was turned into a girl.[31] In later rabbinic tradition, the reason is attributed to Leah, who in her good-heartedness remembers how she had been exchanged with Rachel on her wedding night and prays for God to exchange the embryos of Dinah and Joseph.[32] Thus it was that Leah bore a daughter, Dinah, and Rachel bore a son.

As the twelfth child of Jacob (counting Dinah), the birth of Joseph marks a transition. It is now time to consider leaving Haran and returning to Canaan. This is made clear by the Genesis writer: "*When* Rachel had born Joseph, *then* Jacob said to Laban: Send me away" (Gen 30:25). This sets in motion the chain of events that leads to the death of Rachel while traveling from Bethel to Hebron. There is no question that her death is tragic. The Hebrew first notes that she was dying and then that she died, emphasizing both the prolonged and painful nature of her death. In *Leviticus Rabbah* 30.10, the rabbis compare the four matriarchs to the traditional plants used in the celebration of the annual festival of Succoth: the lulav, etrog, myrtle, and willow.[33] When they looked at Jacob's first wife, Leah, she seemed much like the myrtle with its many leaves because of her numerous children. Rachel, however, resembled the willow, the first to wither and fade.

A major debate took place among rabbis concerning Jacob's decision to bury her along the way, while he left careful instructions that his own body be carried back from Egypt for burial in the Machpelah cave. Samuel Dresner provides a long list of possible reasons, including the condition of the road, the weather, absence of a physician, Jacob's own burden of family and flocks, and Jacob's own grief at the situation.[34] However, ultimately there was one sufficient reason. To Jacob it was revealed that his children one day would be carried off to exile in Babylon and that they would pass by this same grave where she would rise up to comfort them.[35] This is elaborated in *Lamentations Rabbah* 24 (quoted in the introduction to this book) where Rachel alone is found worthy of interceding on behalf of Israel.

With Genesis 37, the focus turns to Joseph. The rabbis noted that the summary in Genesis 37:1, "This is the history of the family of Jacob," is

---

[31] Ibid., 72.6.

[32] "Torah Shlemah," *Encyclopedia of Biblical Interpretation*, ed. by M. M. Kasher (New York: KTAV, 1979); Dresner, 59–60.

[33] *Leviticus Rabbah* 30.10, ed. and trans. by James Neusner, *Scripture and Midrash in Judaism*, vol. 3 (Frankfurt: Peter Lang, 1995).

[34] Dresner, 177–78. See also Ginzberg, vol. 2, 132–36.

[35] *Genesis Rabbah* 82.10.

followed immediately by reference to Joseph. "Joseph was feeding the flock" (Genesis 37:2). This was not an accidental juxtaposition. Rather, the intention was that biblical history focused on both Jacob and Joseph: "This is the history of the family of Jacob-Joseph." In other words, the whole history of Genesis and Exodus must be understood for the sake of the family of Joseph, Rachel's offspring.[36]

The special treatment offered by his father and the jealousy of his brothers play an important role in the early part of the story. Then Joseph is tricked, sold to caravaners, and reported as dead. Just as Rachel plays a key role for the exiles leaving the land of promise, so she is there for her own firstborn as he is forced on the way. Later Jewish legends tell how the journey took them to Ephrath, the place of Rachel's sepulcher. The young man threw himself on the grave, crying, "O mother, mother, that didst bear me, arise, come forth and see how thy son hath been sold into slavery, with none to take pity upon him. . . ." He remained immovable until a voice with heavy tears spoke to him from the grave, "My son Joseph, my son, I heard thy complaints and thy groans, I saw thy tears, and I knew thy misery, my son. I am grieved for thy sake, and thy affliction is added to the burden of my affliction. . . . Fear not, for the Lord is with thee, and He will deliver thee from all evil."[37]

The text continues to focus in detail on Joseph's travels to Egypt, noting the description of Joseph's beauty is the same as that of Rachel in Genesis 29:17. The story of Potiphar is developed further so that his motive for purchasing Joseph was for his own sexual pleasure.[38] Later, however, Joseph's greatest temptation came from Potiphar's wife. Joseph was able to resist only through reliance on his strong moral upbringing. Most important, when he looked at the window in this moment of crisis, he saw the image of his mother Rachel, the model of patient waiting, and his passions were cooled.[39] As a result of Joseph's strong virtuous character, he eventually brought his brothers and father to Egypt where they were rescued during the time of famine. Thus Joseph was rewarded as a prince among his own brothers.

---

[36] Ibid., 84.5.
[37] Ginzberg, 20–21.
[38] *Genesis Rabbah* 86.3
[39] Ibid., 98.20

The Mystical Tradition

The mystical tradition in Judaism flourished during the Middle Ages and is expressed in the book *Zohar* and later in the writings of Hasidic rabbis. The most important contribution to Jewish thought about Rachel is the identification of Rachel with the indwelling of God, known as the *Shechinah*. This Hebrew term as a feminine is perfect for the model of the patient and long-suffering mother. *Zohar* 3.187 reads: "To Abraham [the *Shechinah*] appeared as 'Lord' as it is written, *And the Lord appeared to him in the plains of Mamre* (18.1). . . . She is called 'Lord' when she rests upon the two cherubim. . . . When she first appeared to Moses, she was called 'angel'. . . . For she is called 'angel' when she is a messenger from on high. . . . But to Jacob she appeared only under the figure of Rachel, as it is written, *And Rachel came with the sheep.*"

The idea of linking Rachel with the divine had already surfaced in the interpretation of Jeremiah 31:15. As noted earlier, the Targum had identified weeping Rachel with "the house of Israel" and "Jerusalem" praying on the heights. *Tana deBe Eliyahu* later understood the reference to Rachel in terms of God's own spirit: "Read not Rachel weeping for her children, but *RuaH EL*— the spirit of God—weeping for her children."[40] This interpretation is derived from the three consonants of Rachel's name *RHL* and the Hebrew term for Spirit, *RuaH*, or more precisely the spirit of God, *RuaH EL[ohim]*. The *Zohar* continues by identifying Rachel with the collective soul of the nation. She is the spiritual community or the *Keneset Israel*.[41] Taking a cue from Psalm 91:15 ("I shall be with you in time of trouble"), the Talmud had already understood the *Shechinah* as exiled with Israel. This concept is developed in the *Zohar* so that Rachel, as *Shechinah*, weeps as Israel marches past her grave into exile and then follows, suffering with them and continuing alongside as long as exile lasts.[42]

The eighteenth-century Hasidic Rabbi Nahman of Bratslav incorporated this understanding of the *Zohar* in his prayers: "Master of the world, take pity on the tears and the wailing of our mother Rachel, who is the *Shechinah* and who moaned over our great anguish. For Rachel wept for her children who were dismissed from their father's table and exiled from their land, 'weeping sorely at night, her tears upon her cheeks, and among all her

---

[40] Dresner, 183–84.

[41] *The Zohar* 3.29, ed. and trans. by Maurice Simon, five vols. (Brooklyn: Soncino Press, 1984).

[42] Ibid., 3.187.

friends none to comfort her' (Lam 1.2). . . . So take pity on us, O merciful one. . . ."[43] At the same time, the location of Rachel's Tomb plays an important role for mystics, along with Jerusalem's Western Wall and Hebron's Machpelah cave, as one of the three holiest sites of Jewish pilgrimage.[44] Here the on-the-way character of Rachel's life and death is best understood, she "achieved more than any of the patriarchs, for she stationed herself at the crossroads whensoever the world was in need."[45]

Eventually, according to the *Zohar*, exile comes to an end when the Messiah appears and leads the people home along the road by Rachel's grave.[46] In this time of rejoicing, Rachel's tears will finally cease:

> Where shall this be?
> On the way to Ephrat
> At the crossroads,
> Which is Rachel's grave.
> To mother Rachel he will bring glad tidings.
> And he will comfort her.
> And now she will let herself be comforted.
> And she will rise up
> And kiss him. (2.7–9)

There is another important aspect of the mystical writings. Leah is interpreted as a model of faith equal to Rachel or even superior. Noting that her "weak" eyes may have restricted her natural vision, Leah was influenced by the Holy Spirit—as with Rachel the *Shechinah* also was with her—to see deeply into the mysteries of the world. Thus she represented the invisible or the spiritual realm while Rachel represented the visible or worldly aspect of Israel's task. To some degree, Jacob's life can be divided into two, with his early concern for the physical (Rachel) and his later concern with the spiritual (Leah).[47] Jacob naturally was willing to settle for a lower level of spirituality and thus was not attracted to Leah. However, when Laban substituted the older sister in marriage, Jacob protested, "What is this you have done to me? Did I not serve with you for Rachel? Why then have you deceived me?" (Gen 29:25). However, the similarity between the Hebrew

---

[43] Dresner, 248–49, fn. 23.

[44] Dresner, 63.

[45] *Zohar* 3.29.

[46] Ibid., 1.175.

[47] Dresner, 60.

words *rimitani* (deceived) and *romamtani* (raised) suggests that Laban's goal was to raise him to a higher level of spirituality.[48]

Though the Genesis text suggests that Jacob loved Rachel for her physical beauty, there was more to it. The Hasidic Rabbi Levi Yitzhak presents a rather interesting interpretation of Genesis 29:30, "He loved Rachel more than Leah." Because the Hebrew term *gam* ("more than") in this verse can be translated "also," Yitzhak says: "It is clear that, while Jacob's purpose in working for Laban was to marry Rachel, Jacob, in fact, wed Leah. And it was Rachel who was responsible for this. Now Jacob's love for Rachel was twofold: he loved her for herself, but he loved her also, i.e., even more, because she brought him so pious a wife as Leah. This then is what the verse is telling us: *Jacob loved Rachel 'also because of' Leah.*"[49] Hasidic Rabbi Shlomo of Radomsk argues that the statement in Genesis 29:31 that "Leah was unloved" misunderstands the Hebrew term *sanuah* (unloved) when it should be *shinui* (changed). When her womb was opened she was changed to become a compassionate person, as might be suggested by the similarity in the Hebrew words womb (*rehem*) and compassion (*rahmanut*).[50] While the Genesis text is generally read to highlight the rivalry between Leah and Rachel, the mystical interpretation suggests that it isn't really so. The culmination of that rivalry would seem to come in the episode of the mandrakes when Rachel sends Leah to her husband's bed in exchange for the mandrakes. Genesis 30:16 reports, "Leah went out to meet him, and said, "You must come in to me." The *Zohar* interprets this verse in a way that makes Leah the model wife:

> On the surface this language appears to be immodest, but in truth it is a proof of Leah's modesty. For she said nothing in the presence of her sister, but *went out* to meet Jacob, and there told him in a hushed tone that, though he properly was Rachel's, she had obtained permission from Rachel. She spoke to him outside and not in the house, that he not become upset before Rachel. Should Jacob once enter Rachel's tent, Leah felt it would not be right for her to ask him to leave it, and so she intercepted him outside. . . . Leah went to all this trouble because the Holy Spirit stirred within her, and she knew that all those holy tribes would issue from her; and so she hastened the hour of union in her loving devotion to God.[51]

[48] *Zohar* 2.316; Dresner, 225, fn. 12.

[49] R. Levi Yitzhak, *Kedushat Levi* (Jerusalem, 1958) 53, quoted in Dresner, 72.

[50] Shlomo of Radomsk, *Tiferet Shlomo* (Tel Aviv, 1962) 58, quoted in Dresner, 231, fn. 39.

[51] *Zohar* 2.157.

In the end, Leah's spiritual contributions were rewarded with a resting place alongside Sarah and Rebecca in the Machpelah cave, while Rachel was buried on the way.[52]

In the rituals of Judaism, the role of Rachel found a place at an early date. Rachel's lament in Jeremiah 31:15 became the reading for the second day of the New Year (*Rosh HaShanah*). Her death was commemorated on the fourteenth day of the month Heshvan (in late October or early November). Another occasion was the remembrance of the destruction of the temple, when the custom was established to rise at midnight for prayer that centered on the lament of Rachel. However, the sixteenth-century mystic from Safed, Isaac Luria, established a two-part liturgy that placed equal stress on Rachel and Leah. For Luria, both Rachel and Leah were aspects of *Shechinah*. The *Tikkun Rachel* focuses on the suffering and exile of the *Shechinah*, reading Psalm 137 and the last chapter of Lamentations. The *Tikkun Leah* focuses on redemption and the reading of the messianic Psalms. Sometimes the latter is known as the Rite of Jacob and Leah because it refers to the fruitfulness of their union and symbolizes her spiritual union with God.[53] Beginning with the seventeenth-century messianic movement of Shabbetai Tzevi and a movement back to the land, some have argued that the Rite of Rachel is no longer appropriate and that only the Rite of Leah should be celebrated. For others, however, the two rites continue to be said.

---

[52] *Zohar* 2.316; 1.158, 168, 223.

[53] Gershom Scholem, *On the Kabbalah and Its Symbolism* (New York, 1965) 149–50.

CHAPTER 3

Rachel in Christianity

Matthew's Infancy Account

For most Christians, Rachel is a favorite character from their childhood Christian education, especially the dramatic Genesis love story, the rivalry of sisters, the birth of twelve sons, and yes, her tragic death. There's also an awareness that Rachel is somehow connected to the Christmas story. Again, this is a case of striking contrast. Every child's favorite is the celebrative Christmas story of a manger, of shepherds, of angelic messengers. Yet the story is measured with pathos at the death of the boy babies of Bethlehem.[1] Yes, that same Rachel from Genesis weeps at the birth of the Christ-child. The commemoration of the Holy Innocents is given its own special day three days after Christmas on December 28.[2] There one recognizes that the world into which Jesus was born was neither idyllic nor peaceful. Jesus was born into a world of political intrigue, self-centered fits of paranoia and rage, and flagrant displays of power and violence. When the magi fail to report back to King Herod about their findings concerning the one born king of the Jews, he took matters into his own hands, making sure there would be no messianic pretenders in Bethlehem. All the male children, not just of the small village but those in and around Bethlehem, faced the wrath of the raging tyrant. Not just the newborns, but all under the age of two, met their death at the time when one called God's Messiah was breathing his first breaths. It was not an ideal time to be a mother in Bethlehem. The tears flowed, and the cries of grief must have filled the sky with mourning and

---

[1] Raymond E. Brown, *The Birth of the Messiah* (Garden City, NY: Doubleday, 1977) 204–23.

[2] In later Christian tradition there was a tendency to exaggerate the number of deaths, numbering them in the thousands. Brown, 205.

lamentation. In contrast, one couple fled for their lives. Joseph and Mary, warned in a dream, were sent fleeing for safety with the baby Jesus. The holy family found no refuge in Bethlehem but soon became refugees themselves on the way. In this context, one could imagine no other voice more appropriate, no other tears more fitting, than Rachel weeping for her children.

So it is that mother Rachel finds herself alongside mother Mary at the Christ-child's bed. It is often said that the infancy accounts provide the gospel in a nutshell. Mary and Rachel thus form a perfect pair. The tears of mother Rachel foreshadow the tears of Mary, walking the Via Dolorosa, standing by the cross, embracing her son's dead corpse before burial. Rachel's son Benoni prefigures Mary's child, the man of sorrows. Renamed *Son of my Right Hand*, Benjamin also prefigures the victorious offspring of Mary. In other ways, they are a perfect contrast. Rachel dies giving life, while Mary lives giving birth to one destined for death. So it is that Matthew needed to record this somber note about a joyful birth. So it is that the mothers weeping for their Bethlehem children would one day join those weeping along the streets of Jerusalem as this newborn made his way to the cross. How could this story be told without the presence of Rachel, the weeping mother?

Matthew is recognized for the literary artistry in these two chapters, shaping the infancy account by the older biblical story. Through a series of dreams, God intervenes to guide Joseph just as his namesake was guided in the Genesis story. The allusions, however, are not always distinct and precise, but rather they become interwoven to form a tapestry of images, including those of Moses saved from the biblical tyrant (as Herod).[3] Like Joseph the dreamer, the father of Jesus must find himself on the way to Egypt so that out of Egypt God will call his son.

These two chapters are designed around a series of five Old Testament quotations, including Rachel's lament from Jeremiah 31:15. For some, this is evidence that the Rachel traditions had already been fixed to Bethlehem. However, Matthew's creative and free use of Scripture suggests otherwise. The quotation, "He will be called a Nazorean," in Matthew 2:23 helps to locate Jesus in Nazareth but derives from a prophetic context (Isa 11:1) that knows neither a town named Nazareth nor a name resembling the later sect. Likewise, Matthew 2:15 uses only the first part of Hosea 11:1, "Out of Egypt I have called my son," leaving off the more negative assessment of

---

[3] Matthew thus combines images from the two greatest trials of the Hebrew Bible, the Exodus and the Exile, to set the stage for the life of Jesus. Brown, 216.

Hosea that follows in 11:2: "The more I called them, the more they went from me." So, while the allusions are significant, it is best not to make too much of the geographic connections.

This is especially clear with the Micah 5:2 passage:

> But you, O Bethlehem of Ephrathah,
>> who are one of the little clans of Judah,
> from you shall come forth for me
>> one who is to rule in Israel,
> whose origin is from of old,
>> from ancient days.

Here the intent is clear. There is an extreme contrast between the insignificance of the little town of Bethlehem and the greatness of the coming ruler. In Matthew's quotation, the idea of contrast has been lost. The focus is on the greatness of Bethlehem:

> "And you, Bethlehem, in the land of Judah,
>> are by no means least among the rulers of Judah;
> for from you shall come a ruler,
>> who is to shepherd my people Israel." (Matt 2:6)

Had Matthew wished to play up the connections with Rachel, he missed the perfect opportunity, for the Genesis account had located her death and burial on the way to Ephrath, that is, Bethlehem. However, Matthew omitted Micah's reference to Ephrathah and included in its stead a second reference to Judah. For Matthew, there was no significance in Rachel's offspring Benjamin, rather in the lineage of the Christ child through Leah's son Judah (Matt 1:2).

However, when it came to Rachel's Lament, Matthew included the reference to the city of Ramah, north of Jerusalem:

> "A voice was heard in Ramah,
>> wailing and loud lamentation,
> Rachel weeping for her children;
>> she refused to be consoled,
>>> because they are no more." (Matt 2:18)

Scholars have wondered which of the several possible sources Matthew had at his disposal for the Jeremiah 31:15 quotation. It was certainly not the

Aramaic Targum that had omitted reference to Ramah, as we saw earlier.[4] The NRSV of Jeremiah 31:15 is as follows:

> A voice is heard in Ramah,
>   lamentation and bitter weeping,
> Rachel is weeping for her children,
>   she refuses to be comforted for her children,
>   because they are no more.

For Matthew, the importance of this text is in the continuing significance of the figure of Rachel. Just as she wept for the exiles who had made their way from Ramah centuries before, so she wept for the victims of a violent King Herod at the birth of Jesus. Like the exiles sent on their way to Babylon, so the holy family now found themselves on their way to Egypt. They were not alone. Rachel was weeping for her children.

The Church Fathers: Allegorical Interpretation

As the church adopted allegorical interpretation of Scripture, the contrasting sisters became a favorite for the church fathers. The second-century Justin Martyr argued that one should not take the Genesis stories literally and marry more than one wife. Rather, they should be understood as a typological prophesy leading to Christ because "Jacob was called Israel; and Israel has been demonstrated to be the Christ, who is, and is called, Jesus." It was necessary for Jacob to have two wives as a foreshadowing of the work of Christ: "The marriages of Jacob were types of that which Christ was about to accomplish. For it was not lawful for Jacob to marry two sisters at once. And he serves Laban for [one of] the daughters; and being deceived in [the obtaining of] the younger, he again served seven years. Now Leah is your people and synagogue; but Rachel is our Church." So here, in the earliest centuries of Christianity, the two sisters are types of faith, one modeling the synagogue and the other the church. Other details of the story find their

---

[4] Neither does Matthew's Greek correspond with either of the two Septuagint traditions. Brown concludes that Matthew has relied on a Hebrew text that was older than the Masoretic text of Jeremiah 31:15. Brown, 221–23. Menken, on the other hand, argues that Matthew's source was a revised version of the Septuagint. Martinus J. J. Menken, "The Quotation from Jeremiah 31 (38).15 in Matthew 2.18: A Study of Matthew's Scriptural Text," in Steve Moyise, ed., *Old Testament in the New Testament* (Sheffield: Sheffield Academic Press, 2000) 106–25.

fulfillment in Justin's world: "Jacob served Laban for speckled and many-spotted sheep; and Christ served, even to the slavery of the cross, for the various and many-formed races of mankind, acquiring them by the blood and mystery of the cross. Leah was weak-eyed; for the eyes of your souls are excessively weak. Rachel stole the gods of Laban, and has hid them to this day."[5]

In the early fifth century, Cyril of Alexander developed further the typology of Leah and Rachel to contrast synagogue and church:

> Leah, the eldest, surely stands for the Synagogue of the Jews. . . . For the synagogue came first and begot for God the multitudes of the Jews . . . as it is written, "Israel is my first-born" (Exod 4:22). The barrenness of Rachel, who stands for the church of the nations, refers to the period preceding the coming of our Savior. But Isaiah told of the time to come when she would bear and nurture many children: "Sing, O barren. Thou that didn't not bear, break forth into song. . . . For more are the children of the desolate than the children of the married wife" (Isa 54:1; Gal 4:27). . . . The church, having accepted the mystery of Christ . . . became mother to the peoples which so increases that it cannot be counted. . . . So the church of the nations joins the flocks from Israel.[6]

As the conflict between church and synagogue developed further, other characteristics of Leah, such as her poor eyesight, are used to establish a deficiency.[7] Earlier, Philo of Alexandria had taken the detail about Leah's eyes to argue for her superior spiritual insight in contrast to the emphasis on the physical senses in Rachel. Yet Rachel is always treated as superior in Christian writings. The two Genesis sisters are thus frequently compared with the sisters Mary and Martha of Luke 10:38-42. It is Rachel who, like Mary, sits listening at the feet of Jesus while Leah, like Martha, busies herself in the kitchen.

Augustine of Hippo sets forth this typology: "Two lives are held out to us . . . the one temporal, in which we labor; the other eternal, in which we shall contemplate the delights of God. The names of Jacob's wives teach us

---

[5] Justin, *Dialogue with Trypho*, 134; Alexander Roberts and James Donaldson, eds., *The Anti-Nicene Fathers*, vol. 1 (Grand Rapids, MI: Wm. B. Eerdmans, 1981) 267.

[6] Cyril 4.213-24. E. Giannarelli, "Rachele e il pianto della madre nella tradizione cristiana antica," *Annali de storia dell'esegise* 3 (1986) 215–26. L. Zatelli, "Lea e Rachele," in *Atti del seminario "Giacobbe, o l'avventure del figlio ruinore,"* Biblia (Florence, 1990) 51–74.

[7] Dresner, 66.

to understand this. For it is said that Leah is interpreted as 'laboring' and Rachel 'the beginning seen' or 'the word by which is seen the beginning.' Therefore the action of human and mortal life, in which we live by faith, doing many laborious works, is Leah. But the hope of the eternal contemplation of God, which has a sure and delightful understanding of the truth, is Rachel."[8] Similarly, Gregory of Nyssa interprets the name Rachel as "vision of principle" that "signifies the contemplative life."[9] In his *Homily on Ezekiel*, Gregory states that the goal of "the contemplative life is to keep with one's soul the love of God and neighbor."[10] Because of the focus in Genesis on the beauty of Rachel, this is to be understood as the beauty of the contemplative life in the soul.

As others before him, Thomas Aquinas, in the section on "Active and Contemplative Life" in his *Summa Theologiae*, sees the natural parallel between the two sisters of Genesis and Mary and Martha of Luke 10:38-42. "These two modes of life are exemplified by the two wives of Jacob—the active life by Leah and the contemplative by Rachel—and by the two women who received Christ as a guest—the contemplative life by Mary and the active life by Martha."[11] While Augustine understood all of life as active and the contemplative life as only a promise to be realized in the eternal, Aquinas understands both as aspects of the present life. Still, beautiful Rachel is held as supreme.

This tradition of theological interpretation became dominant in the culture of the Middle Ages, as can be seen from Dante's *Divine Comedy*. Dante portrays Leah observing the reflective Rachel, sitting before her mirror:

> Whoso would ask my name, I'd have him know
> That I am Leah, who for my array
> Twine garlands, weaving white hands to and fro.

---

[8] Augustine, *Contra Faustum*, 22.52, trans. by Richard Stothert, *A Select Library of the Nicene and Post-Nicene Fathers of the Christian Church*, vol. IV, ed. by Philip Schaff (New York: Charles Scribner's Sons, 1909) 292.

[9] Gregory of Nyssa, *Moralia* VI, 37. *Patrologia Latina*, vol. 75, ed. by Jacques-Paul Migne (Paris, 1844–1864) 764.

[10] Gregory, *Homil. In Ezech*, II, hom. 2.2.10. *Patrologia Latina*, vol. 76, ed. by Jacques-Paul Migne (Paris, 1844–1864) 952.

[11] St. Thomas Aquinas, "Active and Contemplative Life," *Summa Theologiae*, vol. 46, trans. by Jordan Aumann (New York: McGraw-Hill, 1964) 7.

To please me at the glass I deck me gay;
The while my sister Rachel never stirs
But sits before her mirror all the day,

For on her own bright eyes she still prefers
To gaze, as I to deck me with my hands;
Action is my delight, reflection hers.[12]

The contrast between the two sisters is then reflected in the visual arts by Michelangelo in his design of the tomb of Pope Julius II in 1545. There Rachel is portrayed in a nun's habit postured in contemplative prayer with hands and eyes raised to heaven while Leah is depicted in simple peasants' garb, poised to carry out her daily tasks.[13]

The mystics also were fascinated with the contrasts between Rachel and Leah. In his meditation on *Benjamin*, Richard of St. Victor develops the allegory in even greater detail: "For as we read, Jacob is known to have had two wives. One was called Leah; the other Rachel. Leah was more fruitful; Rachel, more beautiful. Leah was fruitful but with poor eyesight. Rachel was nearly sterile but of singular beauty. Now let us see what these two wives of Jacob are so that we may more easily understand what their sons are. Rachel is teaching of truth; Leah, discipline of virtue. Rachel is pursuit of wisdom; Leah longing for Justice."[14] It is natural for Richard to identify Rachel with wisdom since the apocryphal book Wisdom 7:29 describes wisdom as "more beautiful than the sun." Jacob thus burns with love for her since that same work says, "I loved [wisdom] more than health and beauty" (Wis 7:10). It is also understandable that men would shun Leah, because justice demands so much from them. This is the meaning of the name Leah, laborious. Yet Leah, with her poor eyesight, errs in judgment.

Richard goes on to refer to Scripture as "the bedchamber of Rachel" because "wisdom is hidden beneath the veil of attractive allegories."[15] There one finds what is needed to cleanse one's soul of the sordidness of life and to prepare oneself for the contemplation of heavenly things. No wonder then that many who take the easy way find themselves losing out on Rachel. There are

[12] Dante Alighieri, *The Divine Comedy*, Purgatorio 27.100-108, trans. by Dorothy Sayers (New York: Penguin Classics, 1962).

[13] H. Hibbard, *Michelangelo* (New York, 1978) 174. See Dresner, 67.

[14] Richard of St. Victor, *The Twelve Patriarchs: Benjamin*, trans. by Grover A. Zinn (New York: Paulist Press, 1979) 53.

[15] Ibid., 56.

also roles in the allegory for the two handmaids. Since Rachel is understood as "reason," her handmaid Bilhah is "imagination." Since Leah represents "affection," her handmaid Zilpah is "sensuality."[16] Rachel pleads, "Give me children," because reason tells us that wisdom is desirable. However, the pursuit of wisdom often falls short. Affection is successful in producing offspring. This is understood as a necessary step. Rachel, seeing Judah, only burned with desire for children, the pursuit of knowing. Still, she must first have children through her handmaid. Imagination is a first step to achieving one's goal through reason.[17] In Richard's allegory, the mandrakes, because they are known to scatter widely their sweet odor, represent the fame of good opinion.[18] Rachel only begs for part of the mandrakes because reason knows that the appetite for human favor must be moderated in order to turn back to the glory of God. In contrast, Leah does not speak to Jacob of only a part, but of "the mandrakes," showing that affection leads to praise of oneself.

In the end, the birth of Benjamin is the sign that Rachel has achieved her goal; she has heard the voice of God and perfectly achieves the contemplation of the divine. She is much like the disciples on the mount of transfiguration. They fall because they do not truly hear. Human reason fails. But when Rachel dies, Benjamin is born.[19] The birth of Joseph had not achieved this goal. Her arrival at motherhood was rather like the ascent of the mountain that prepared her for this ultimate gift, the true knowledge of God. This is how Richard understands Psalm 68:27, "There is Benjamin, the least of them, in the lead." In his allegory, Benjamin is "ecstasy of mind."[20] Richard thus concludes: "There are those two kinds of contemplation, one of which pertains to the death of Rachel, the other to the ecstasy of Benjamin. In the first, Benjamin kills his mother when he goes above all reason. However, in the second he goes beyond even himself when he transcends the mode of human understanding in that which he comes to know from divine showing.[21] In the death of Rachel, contemplation ascends above reason.

---

[16] Richard of St. Victor, 57. Contrast Philo, *The Preliminary Studies* 24–30, in *Philo*, vol. IV (1968) 471–73.

[17] Richard of St. Victor, 65–66.

[18] Ibid., 82–83.

[19] Ibid., 138.

[20] Ibid., 142.

[21] Ibid., 145.

The Reformation: The Plain Message of Scripture

For Martin Luther and other reformers, it was important to emphasize the simple message of the biblical text. In his *Lectures on Genesis*, Luther gives a verse-by-verse explication of the biblical text. This is a classical case of "love at first sight," as Luther describes the meeting at the well that inflames Jacob with "the impulse of both faith and love" and leads to unusual strength as he moves the stone to capture the maiden's heart.[22] Luther is especially concerned about Jacob's "disgraceful" behavior in kissing Rachel publicly, though it must be understood in response to the announcement that she was the daughter of his kinsmen. Cultural awareness may be helpful, as Luther says, "This is a custom today in Belgium and also in other lands. Our people only hold out the hand, and they embrace maidens or matrons modestly and shyly. There are as many customs as there are lands."[23] Luther chides Jacob for his childish behavior since, taking the text literally, he assumes that Jacob is now an old man of eighty years.[24] In his crude way, Luther at times refers to Leah simply as "ugly." Elsewhere he describes Leah as being "weak of sight" and goes on to link this to the reason she did not find favor with Jacob, "for she had eyes less sharp and charming." Rachel on the other hand was beautiful. Using Aristotelian categories for beauty, Luther notes that her "eyes had the right shape, and her forehead, her cheeks, and her whole body had the proper arrangement and symmetry of its members."[25] It is thus understandable that a man even of Jacob's age would fall in love with Rachel.

As far as the substitution of Leah for Rachel, Luther has nothing but contempt for Laban. But what about the guests, the "fickle and worthless fellows, good-for-nothing rascals" who did not speak out when Leah was brought forward?[26] At the same time, Luther wonders how Jacob could not have been aware that it was Leah, not Rachel. The only possible excuse is that he was so much in love that he lost awareness of his senses, "that powerful ardor of love blinded him."[27] As for Rachel, Luther shows nothing but

---

[22] Martin Luther, "Lectures on Genesis: Chapters 26–30," in Jaroslav Pelikan, ed., *Luther's Works*, vol. 5, American Edition (St. Louis: Concordia, 1968) 281.

[23] Ibid., 283.

[24] Ibid., 288.

[25] Ibid., 294.

[26] Ibid., 297.

[27] Ibid., 301.

sympathy: "One can see here how great paternal power was among those people."[28] It was a patriarchal society. To some degree he also blames the writer: "How Rachel herself felt is not told,"[29] so he imagines the indignation and tears that must have followed. Yet he credits the writer for not referring to Leah as wife.[30] Some "ask whether there was a true marriage that night between Leah and Jacob. I reply that there was not."[31] At the same time, Luther refrains from calling it adultery. The blame rested on Laban.

Laban, of course, offered Jacob a second deal, another seven years for Rachel. "What should the saintly man do?" asks Luther. "He lets it pass. He bears this wrong with equanimity in order that he may obtain Rachel."[32] At the same time he reasons that he must not repudiate Leah because she has become an unwanted woman. "This is an outstanding example of the special mercy and virtue because of which he keeps with him the woman who, as he knows, has been substituted for his bride."[33] Then there is the question about the law's prohibition against marrying two sisters. For Luther, Jacob is a kind of "heroic man" chosen by God who must break the law, yet without leaving a precedent for others. Similarly, Jacob will bear children also with two handmaids. Yet "Jacob lived most continently with so many wives, and far more chastely than anyone else with one wife."[34] Luther emphasizes that later generations should emulate "the faith, patience, and hope" of the patriarchs and matriarchs, but not imitate their "heroic examples."[35]

As for Rachel, Luther describes her as a "very saintly woman, who called upon God in true faith."[36] It is true, Luther notes, that Genesis speaks of her envy when Leah bore children, but properly speaking this is not envy because she sought the noble cause of bearing offspring according to divine promise so much that she was willing to die.[37] Although Rachel pleads with Jacob, and he replies in tones of anger, "in these sordid matters the greatest virtues shine forth, namely, outstanding faith, completely certain hope, and

[28] Ibid.
[29] Ibid., 297.
[30] Ibid., 297.
[31] Ibid., 302.
[32] Ibid., 307.
[33] Ibid.
[34] Ibid., 324.
[35] Ibid., 326.
[36] Ibid.
[37] Ibid., 328.

unconquerable patience toward God and toward men."[38] Luther is a bit perplexed by the episode of the mandrakes; he spends most of his effort trying to understand them from a botanical point of view. Yet the apparent quarrel between the women is simply evidence of their desire to bear children.[39]

Luther demonstrates the modern critical mind when trying to understand the order of the birth of Jacob's children.[40] He reasons that Jacob begat twelve children in twelve years.[41] Since Joseph was clearly born in the seventh year of marriage, he should not be considered the twelfth born, but rather the seventh.[42] Thus it is necessary at times to employ reason over the plain text of Scripture. At the birth of Joseph, the Genesis text states that God remembered Rachel. Again, Luther attempts to understand the situation from Rachel's perspective:

> It is as though Moses were saying: "The only feeling Rachel has was that all her prayers and tears had been in vain and useless, and that she had been utterly obliterated and deleted from the heart and memory of God." But you should not come to this conclusion, my dear Rachel; for you would be making a big mistake. . . . God has not forgotten you, but from the beginning, when you began to ask for offspring, He immediately heard and marked all the words of your sobbing. But your prayer was not yet ardent and strong enough. Therefore it had to grow and become strong. . . . But your sobbing did not yet find rest. God still seemed turned away. Therefore God remembered, although He had never forgotten you for one moment. But this was finally the time for him to hear your sighs, when you thought that they had been completely buried, covered, and forgotten.[43]

Here in a nutshell is the Genesis foundation for the lament of Jeremiah 31:15—Rachel weeping for her children. And with Joseph's birth she prays, "Lord add to me another."

Luther gives brief attention to Rachel's death, consistent with the Genesis report. He does spend a little time discussing the rare Hebrew word *kbrt*, criticizing Jerome for his long-winded, yet bad interpretation. The Septuagint

---

[38] Ibid., 332.
[39] Ibid., 354.
[40] von Rad, 306.
[41] Ibid., 338–40.
[42] Ibid., 357–58.
[43] Ibid., 360.

translation hippodrome simply does not make sense. Rather, in his folksy way, Luther concludes that "the distance to Bethlehem was as far as one has to go to breakfast, a short distance, so that one might gain an appetite for the breakfast morsel."[44] Yet the main issues of concern were Rachel's vocational role in bearing yet another child, Jacob's grief, and the contrast of names Benoni and Benjamin. Most of all, Luther holds up Rachel as a model of faith. He says: "It was certainly better for Rachel to die in this way while praying to God and believing in Him than if she had been permitted to enjoy all the joys of this life. . . . There she died and was buried in a neighboring field or on a road just as if the wife of a shepherd died in the fields in the midst of the flocks. There was no house nor any lodging house except Jacob's tent. This is the way of the saints to heaven."[45]

Allusions in Popular Literature

The character of Rachel becomes so well known in Western culture that allusions are common in art and literature. Perhaps the most significant is in Herman Melville's *Moby Dick*, first published in 1851—five years before his own trip to the Holy Land. Chapter 128 begins, "Next day, a large ship, the *Rachel*, was descried, bearing directly down upon the *Pequod*." Captain Ahab describes his conversation with the captain who informed him about his lost crew. Rejected, the *Rachel* sailed off, "so wept with spray" and remaining "without comfort." In case the allusion has not been sufficient, Melville turns more specific, "She was Rachel, weeping for her children, because they were not."[46] Later in the Epilogue, Ishmael, the narrator of the tale, describes his rescue at sea, "*Rachel . . .* in her retracing search after her missing children, only found another orphan."[47]

From Chaucer's *Prioress' Tale* to Charles Lamb's "In Praise of Chimney Sweepers" to T. S. Eliot's *The Waste Land*, Western literature is filled with allusions to Rachel weeping for her children. Elsewhere, authors have introduced their own Rachels in novels, such as Charles Dickens' *Hard Times* and Thackeray's *Henry Esmond* (as well as allusions in *The Virginians*). In

[44] Martin Luther, "Lectures on Genesis: Chapters 31–37," in Jaroslav Pelikan, ed., *Luther's Works*, vol. 6, American Edition (St. Louis: Concordia, 1970) 266–67.

[45] Ibid., 272–73.

[46] Herman Melville, *Moby Dick* (New York: Quality Paperback, 1996) 466–69.

[47] Melville, 507.

Hardy's *Tess of the D'Urbervilles*, the character Angel Clare has "three Leahs to get one Rachel."[48]

Through two thousand years of Christianity the figure of Rachel has been held up as a model for patient suffering and faithfulness. Unlike Judaism, where Rachel has sometimes been criticized for her sensuality and where Leah has been lifted up as the model of spirituality, Christianity has been consistent in its view of the biblical matriarch. Rachel is a model of faith.

[48] Linda Beamer lists various references to Rachel in literature in "Rachel," in David Lyle Jeffrey, ed., *A Dictionary of Biblical Tradition in English Literature* (Grand Rapids, MI: Wm. B. Eerdmans, 1992) 652.

CHAPTER 4

Rachel in Islam

The matriarch Rachel is revered in Islam. This may seem surprising to non-Muslims who think of Islam as a religion born in Arabia only fourteen centuries ago. What is the connection between Muhammed and Rachel? What is the relationship between Mecca and Haran or Bethlehem? Yes, Muslims do revere Abraham as the common ancestor, but don't they trace his descendants through Ishmael rather than Isaac? So, as the daughter-in-law of Isaac, where does Rachel fit in?

In treating this topic, it is important to begin with the *Qur'an*, the sacred revelations to Muhammed beginning in 610 C.E. Then we will turn to a body of literature less known in the Western world, the commentaries titled *Qisas al-anbiyā'*. The term *Qisas* has variously been translated as *The Tales of the Prophets* or *The Lives of the Prophets*. This body of literature includes a variety of stories that help to illustrate the revelation of the *Qur'an*, often including contrasting traditions side by side. Some of the traditions come from Middle Eastern folklore. Others come from the Bible and are introduced with the expression "Some of the people of the Torah have said." Three particular collections have been cited. *The History of Prophets and Kings* by Abū Ja'far Muhammad b. Jarīr al-Tabarī contains thirty-eight volumes of about two hundred pages each in Arabic. Al-Tabari lived in Tabaristan in Northern Iran from 839–923 and recorded traditions, some as early as the time of Muhammed, up to 915.[1] *Lives of the Prophets* by Abū Ishāq Ahmad b. Muhammad b. Ibrāhīm al-Tha'labī al-Nīsābūrī al-Shāfi'ī is considered the longest and most diverse collection. Al-Tha'labī was born in Nishapur, Iran, but spent most of his life in Baghdad and died about

---

[1] al-Tabari, *The History of al-Tabari: Volume II: Prophets and Patriarchs*, trans. and annotated by William M. Brinner (New York: State University of New York Press, 1987).

1036.[2] *Tales of the Prophets* by Muhammad b. ʿAbdallāh al-Kisāʾī contain fifty-six brief tales from creation through the prophets. Little is known about al-Kisāʾī except that his work cites sources from the late tenth century through the twelfth century.[3]

Rachel in the *Qurʾan*

A significant portion of the *Qurʾan* deals with the age of the patriarchs and matriarchs, the material described in Genesis 12–50. Especially prominent is the story of Abraham, his call by God, his dealings with his nephew Lot, the difficulty in having children, then the birth of both Ishmael and Isaac, and the test of faith in taking his son to the mountain of sacrifice. Of the 114 *suras* (or chapters) of the *Qurʾan*, Abraham is mentioned in twenty-five of them. Like Genesis, there are also references to the next three generations after Abraham.

The patriarchs are treated with highest respect because they are viewed in the long line of prophets. A typical passage reads:

> That was the reasoning
> About Us, which
> We gave to Abraham
> (To use) against his people:
> We raise whom We will,
> Degree after degree:
> For the Lord is full
> Of Wisdom and Knowledge.

> We gave him Isaac
> And Jacob: all (three)
> We guided:
> And before him,
> We guided Noah,
> And among his progeny,
> David, Solomon, Job,
> Joseph, Moses, and Aaron:

---

[2] Abū Isḥāq Aḥmad b. Muḥammad b. Ibrāhīm al-Thaʿlabī al-Nīsābūrī al-Shāfiʿī, *Lives of the Prophets*, trans. and annotated by William M. Brinner (Leiden: E. J. Brill, 2002).

[3] Muḥammad b. ʿAbdallāh al-Kisāʾī, *Tales of the Prophets*, trans. by Wheeler M. Thackston, Jr. (Chicago: Great Books of the Islamic World, Inc., 1997).

> Thus do We reward
> Those who do good. (*Qur'an* 6:83-84)

Unlike Genesis, where the focus falls on Isaac to the exclusion of Ishmael (e.g., "the God of Abraham, Isaac, and Jacob"), the *Qur'an* recognizes both Ishmael and Isaac as prophets:

> Say ye: "We believe
> In Allah, and the revelation
> Given to us, and to Abraham,
> Ismā'īl, Isaac, Jacob,
> And the Tribes, and that given
> To Moses and Jesus, and that given
> To (all) Prophets from their Lord:
> We make no difference
> Between one and another of them:
> And we bow to Allah (in Islam). (*Qur'an* 2:136)[4]

One quickly notices in reading the *Qur'an* a totally different character from that of Genesis. In contrast to the narrative of the latter, the poetry of the former is more of the nature of the Psalms. Thus numerous details are omitted. Since the prophets are to present examples of faith, there is less emphasis on the human frailties and personal side of the story than comes across in Genesis, including the romance and the struggles of daily life. Thus it is not surprising that the stories revolving around Rachel are simply absent from the *Qur'an*. In fact, the names of the other matriarchs of Genesis are lacking as well. Among women, only the name of Mary, mother of Jesus, is mentioned specifically in the *Qur'an*.[5]

Nevertheless, one must say that Rachel's role is still important. She is wife of the prophet Jacob and mother of the prophet Joseph. The *Qur'an* itself recognizes the role of wife and mother of a Prophet:

> We did send messengers
> Before thee, and appointed
> For them wives and children. (*Qur'an* 13:38)

Sura 12 presents the story of Joseph, the longest continuous narrative in the *Qur'an*. Here his role is highlighted among the twelve sons of Jacob. He

---

[4] Also *Qur'an* 3:84; 4:163–164.

[5] Barbara Freyer Stowasser, *Women in the Qur'an, Traditions, and Interpretation* (Oxford: Oxford University Press, 1994).

alone is given the title prophet and his exemplary model in Egypt is held up for later generations to follow.[6]

Muslim Commentaries

The love story of Jacob and Rachel, known from Genesis, is paralleled in *The Tales* and *Lives of the Prophets*. Following his conflict with Esau, Jacob has been sent to Haran to find a wife lest he marry among the Canaanites. While working with his maternal uncle Laban he agrees to provide seven years' labor in place of a dowry for his daughter Rachel's hand in marriage.

How Jacob had come to fall in love with Rachel is not explained. In most versions of the story the elements of their meeting at the well have been totally omitted. In Kisa'I, however, Laban's daughter reported to him how she had observed a stranger at the well on a particular day. He had filled his bucket like everyone else, but then he had performed the prayer ritual the same as Laban, first completing the ablutions and then reciting two *rak'as*. At Laban's insistence she returned to fetch the young man.

In all the commentaries the bargaining is described in detail and Jacob's objective is quite clear: he desires Rachel. Al-Tabari cites al-Husayn b. Muhammad b. 'Amar al-'Abqāri who received the tradition from his own father who received it from Asbāt who received it from al-Suddī who said, "Jacob fell in love with the younger daughter." He specifically told Laban, "I want only Rachel."[7] Likewise al-Thalabi records Jacob's words, "For Rachel alone shall I serve you."[8] In Kisa'I it is noted that Leah was in fact very beautiful, though she was "bleary-eyed."[9] "I want the girl who wears the veil," Jacob said about the one who veiled herself lest she tempt anyone with her beauty.[10] Later in the story he goes on to mention that Rachel was the most beautiful of all Laban's daughters. She was thus given the name Shamsun-nahâr. Her beauty comes up in other commentaries as well, in relation to the beauty of Joseph. According to al-Tabari, "Joseph had, like his mother, more beauty than any

---

[6] Muhammad Abdel Haleem, "The Story of Joseph in the *Qur'an* and the Bible," in *Understanding the Qur'an: Themes and Style* (New York: St. Martin's Press, 1999) 138–57; John Kaltner, *Inquiring of Joseph: Getting to Know a Biblical Character through the Qur'an* (Collegeville, MN: Liturgical Press, 2003).

[7] al-Tabari, 138.

[8] al-Thalabi, 171.

[9] al-Kisa'I, 165.

[10] Ibid.

other human being." He quotes the Prophet Muhammed himself that "Joseph and his mother were given half of all the beauty in the world."[11]

One element that is repeated frequently in the Muslim traditions is an apologetic that Jacob married both Leah and Rachel, two sisters. *Qur'an* 4.23 forbids such a practice: "And [it is forbidden to you] that you should have two sisters together, except for what has already happened in the past." Al-Tabari thus includes one tradition that Leah had already died before Jacob married Rachel.[12] This of course conflicts with the rest of the story about the competition between the two sisters in producing offspring for Jacob. So, most other commentaries face up to the reality of this unusual marriage. "In those days people used to marry two sisters to the same husband, until Moses came and the Torah was revealed."[13] Here the recognition is that *Qur'anic* law is consistent with Torah.

As a prophet, Jacob's actions are treated as exemplary. There is no hint that he might have been complicit in sleeping with Leah. Several commentaries emphasize that Laban brought her to Jacob *at night* when he would have been unable to recognize her. Only in the morning did he realize what had happened. Then he placed total blame upon Laban, referring to his actions as unlawful and fraudulent. He says, "You have deceived and cheated me."[14]

The role of Rachel as mother to Joseph and Benjamin is central to all the commentaries. In some of the commentaries there is no hint of competition between the sisters, nor is there any reference to the barrenness of Rachel. In listing the children of Jacob, there is sometimes confusion about which sons were Leah's. Likewise the role of the handmaids is not always clear. In Kisa'I they are yet other daughters of Laban. Yet all accounts agree that Rachel bore two children, Joseph and Benjamin. Al-Tabari, however, accurately reports the complete tradition preserved in Genesis listing twelve sons in all, six from Leah, two each from Zilfah and Bilhah, and two from Rachel. "After he had given up hope of having any children by Rachel, she bore him Joseph and Benjamin."[15]

---

[11] al-Tabari received this tradition from ʿAbdallāh b. Muhammad and Ahmad b. Thābit al-Rāzayyān who received it from ʿAffān b. Mulim who received it from Hammād b. Salamah who received it from Thābit who received it from Anas who received it from the Prophet. al-Tabari, 148.

[12] Ibid., 134–35.

[13] Ibid., 136; al-Talabi, 172.

[14] Ibid., 135.

[15] Ibid., 136.

The tragedy of Rachel's death is remembered, though the details are fuzzy. "It is said that Rachel died in childbirth while delivering Benjamin," writes al-Tabari.[16] According to al-Thalabi her son was called Shaddād in Arabic, but he was also called Benjamin as a reminder of the sorrow of this moment. The commentator notes that although the name means son of my right hand in Hebrew, *yāmīn* means "complication" in Arabic.[17] Thus, the name Benjamin is appropriate.

The location of Rachel's death is not clear. The description of Kisa'I is most consistent with the Genesis tradition. Her death occurred when Joseph was two years old and it took some time for the news to reach her father Laban.[18] In other traditions it is less clear whether the death occurred while Jacob was still in Haran or after he had parted from Laban. In al-Tabari, the former seems to be the case. In recounting the episode of the stealing of Laban's idols, it was not Rachel that took them, but her sons. She instructed Joseph, "Take one of my father's idols; perhaps we may seek money from him."[19] The significance of Joseph's role is linked to the *sura* on Joseph in the *Qur'an* where a statement is made about Benjamin, "If he steals, a brother of his stole before" (*Qur'an* 12:77). Yet the commentator notes that the stealing took place while Joseph and Benjamin were together in the tent, although Benjamin would not yet have been born. At the same time, al-Tabari does note that the departure from Haran occurred when Jacob announced his plans to return to his father's house in Palestine. In another place, he specifically mentions as his destination Bayt al-Maqdis, an Arabic name for Jerusalem.[20]

The commentaries then describe Jacob's reconciliation with Esau and his settling down in Palestine. They all agree that Jacob's love centered upon Joseph and Benjamin, Rachel's two sons. Kisa'I recounts a tradition from Kaab al-Ahbar that Laban sent Jacob yet a younger daughter as his wife to raise the two boys. Others, however, report that Jacob's own sister (a daughter of Isaac and Rebekah), named Tumel, helped to raise the boys. This came about when she secretly obtained the belt of Isaac and tied it around the waist of Joseph. According to custom, this was to give her authority over

---

[16] Ibid., 139.

[17] Ibid., 172.

[18] al-Kisa'I, 167.

[19] al-Tabari, 139.

[20] Ibid., 136, 139.

the boy. This episode was also used to explain the origins of the *Qur'anic* statement mentioned above that this boy had stolen before.

Because of the importance of *Sura* 12 in the *Qur'an*, the commentaries treat in great detail the story of Joseph in Egypt. Although this is not pertinent to the story of Rachel, it does underscore once again her role as wife of Jacob and mother of Joseph and Benjamin. In this last generation of the patriarchal age, it is significant that Rachel's son Joseph is considered in the line of prophets.

Thus it is that the matriarch Rachel is highly esteemed in Islam, just as she is in Judaism and Christianity.

Implications for the Reverence of Rachel's Tomb

Rachel is one of those larger-than-life figures whose importance continues to grow with the passage of time. Because her portrayal in Genesis is so human, her appeal is to be expected. Every generation looks to its mothers in gratitude, especially when hardship and sacrifice have been part of their story. Every son or daughter also learns from his or her mother the message of hope, for in the act of childbirth mothers say yes to the future. No one models faithfulness and hope better than biblical Rachel. So it is only to be expected that later generations—offspring both natural and adopted—would continue to honor her. Already in the biblical era, the descendants of Leah, Zilpah, and Bilhah in the north proudly took the name Ephraim. At the time of the exile, all Judah found comfort in her lament and, in later years, her memorial tomb became recognized in Judah. For Christians, it was mother Rachel who wept over the tragedy of the murder of innocents after Jesus' birth—that is, Jesus, son of David, offspring of Judah; and it was Rachel, like Mary, whose faithfulness showed attentiveness to the life-giving word. For Muslims, her example was no less revered. Like a beloved mother figure whose kitchen acts as a magnet for all the children of the neighbor, so mother Rachel has attracted to her circle every child of the monotheistic faith. When such a popular mother finally succumbs to death, all join in mourning. All weep as if she were their very own. All gather at her gravesite to offer final respects, to remember, and to appropriate her lessons as they continue on their ways. This brings us to Rachel's Tomb. It is only natural that Christians, Muslims, and Jews alike—who gather around the written word to hear her story—should also desire a place at her lasting memorial, the shrine in Bethlehem.

PART TWO

Rachel's Tomb

CHAPTER 5

Rachel's Tomb in Biblical Texts

The portrait of Rachel as a woman on the way seems to come to an end with her death and Jacob's decision to build a tomb to remember her. The Genesis writer suggests this new idea of permanence and stability with the concluding words, "which is there to this day" (Gen 35:20c). The stone pillar upon her grave transformed the biblical matriarch into a permanent fixture that was visible to the biblical writer and, so it would seem, to people of the modern era. A Google search in this technological age identifies "Rachel's Tomb" with 113,000 sites, many complete with photos and descriptions of the memorial by this name in Bethlehem.

As is often the case with biblical memorials, the façade may mask reality. Even the stones recede into the surrounding, ever-changing, political landscape, and the tradition eludes the modern quest for historical certainty. It is not just the modern quest that brings uncertainty. The biblical record itself confounds the search for Rachel's Tomb.

Long ago, biblical scholars recognized that there are two traditions for the location of Rachel's tomb: a northern tradition and a southern tradition. The northern tradition locates Rachel's death and burial north of Jerusalem near the town of er-Ram. The southern tradition places the tomb on the west side of the Jerusalem-Hebron road just at the entrance to Bethlehem. Perhaps it is Matthew's Christmas story that makes the connection of Rachel and Bethlehem so appealing. Likewise, the popular Genesis narrative so clearly names Bethlehem when recounting Rachel's death that an alternate proposal would seem unlikely. Yet our approach to the biblical record must be open to the unexpected.

The Northern Tradition

We will begin with the northern tradition for Rachel's Tomb for the simple reason that it is all but forgotten. There are two primary witnesses, the

Lament of Rachel from the time of the sixth-century B.C.E. Babylonian exile (Jer 31:15), discussed in chapter one, and 1 Samuel 10:1-5, set at the beginning of the monarchy in the eleventh century B.C.E. The Samuel text reads:

> ¹Samuel took a vial of oil and poured it on his [Saul's] head, and kissed him; he said, "The Lord has anointed you ruler over his people Israel. You shall reign over the people of the Lord and you will save them from the hand of their enemies all around. Now this shall be the sign to you that the Lord has anointed you ruler over his heritage: ²When you depart from me today you will meet two men by Rachel's tomb in the territory of Benjamin at Zelzah; they will say to you, "The donkeys that you went to seek are found, and now your father has stopped worrying about them and is worrying about you, saying: What shall I do about my son?" ³Then you shall go on from there further and come to the oak of Tabor; three men going up to God at Bethel will meet you there, one carrying three kids, another carrying three loaves of bread, and another carrying a skin of wine. ⁴They will greet you and give you two loaves of bread, which you shall accept from them. ⁵After that you shall come to Gibeath-elohim, at the place where the Philistine garrison is; there, as you come to the town, you will meet a band of prophets coming down from the shrine with harp, tambourine, flute, and lyre playing in front of them; they will be in a prophetic frenzy.

In the Samuel text, Rachel's tomb is located in the territory of Benjamin. This makes perfect sense because Rachel was giving birth to this twelfth son of Jacob at the time of her death. The tomb would serve as a permanent reminder to all of Benjamin's descendants of his tragic beginning. Likewise the tribe's small size would help to recall the Genesis narratives about the youngest and most vulnerable child in the shadow of larger and stronger Judah to the south and Ephraim and Mannasseh (sons of Joseph) to the north. Most Bibles include illustrative maps that show the distribution of land to the twelve tribal groups. There one can see clearly the boundaries described in Joshua 18:11-18. The southern border of the tribe of Benjamin begins near Kiriath-jearim, and heads east through the Hinnom Valley, south of the slope of the Jebusite city, an early reference to the city of Jerusalem. The Hinnom Valley descends to the west and south of the current old city and joins the Kidron Valley just south of the Pool of Siloam. Jebus was designated within the boundaries of Benjamin, although the city was not yet conquered during the time of the judges.[1] According to 1 Samuel 5:1-10, it was David who captured Jebus and turned it into his capital in

---

[1] For competing traditions see Judges 1:8 and 19:10-12.

an effort to unite all Israel behind him. Thus Jerusalem eventually came to be identified with Judah. The northern boundary of Benjamin began at the Jordan River on the east and followed the slopes of Jericho westward to the "wilderness of Beth-aven" just to the south of Luz or Bethel. Later, during the period of the divided kingdoms, the sanctuary of Bethel was known for its location at the far southern end of the northern kingdom, within the tribal territory of Ephraim. The distance from Bethel to Jerusalem is only ten miles, so the location of Rachel's tomb in the northern tradition within the territory of Benjamin would seem to be not that difficult to determine.

The reference to Rachel's tomb occurs appropriately within the story of one of Benjamin's most famous descendants, the first king of Israel, Saul the son of Kish. In 1 Samuel 9, Saul is introduced while engaged in searching for his father's straying donkeys. The small size of the territory of Benjamin is made clear in the report that he has already searched through the land of Benjamin (as well as the hill country of Ephraim) without finding the donkeys (1 Sam 9:3-4). At that point, a young boy suggests that they consult a prophet who resides in a nearby town and ask if he might help them in their quest. That prophet is Samuel, who proceeds to help them find the donkeys (1 Sam 9:20), but who also surprises them by anointing Saul as king (1 Sam 10:1). The town is not explicitly identified in 1 Samuel 9:6, but it is likely Ramah, where Samuel resided and from where he administered justice to Israel (1 Sam 7:17). Today this is commemorated by the shrine of Nabi Samuel, several miles directly south of Bethel near the modern Palestinian city of Ramallah.[2]

From Ramah, Saul is instructed to go to Rachel's tomb, where he is to learn about the fate of the lost donkeys (1 Sam 10:2). Rachel's tomb, within the territory of Benjamin, is identified as located at Zelzah. From there his itinerary will take him to the "oak of Tabor" (v. 3), Gibeath-elohim (v. 5), and Gilgal, the shrine near Jericho (v. 8). Ultimately he is heading in an eastward direction. Along the way, he meets three men on their way to Bethel to the north (v. 3) and also a band of prophets (vv. 5, 10). Unfortunately, some of the names given here are not well known. Zelzah is not mentioned elsewhere and does not occur on biblical maps. One suggestion is that the meaning is not spatial but temporal. Perhaps it means something like "at the shade of the noonday sun."[3] In Hebrew *slsh: sl* would mean shadows from the rays of the sun as in Isaiah

---

[2] Specifically at er-Ram.
[3] Lombardi, 319.

38:8; Judges 9:36; and Psalms 80:11; and *sh* would mean "brilliance." This might explain why the next stop is at the oak of Tabor.[4] While it is quite possible that this is one of those landmarks known only to those of a particular generation, one should not discount similar references to other trees. In Judges 4–5, the story is told of the judge Deborah who used to render judgments to those who came to her in the hill country of Ephraim. More precisely, she is located near the northern border of Benjamin between Bethel and Ramah, where she used to sit "under the palm of Deborah" (Judg 4:5).[5] While this predated the time of Samuel by several hundred years, it is significant that the first judgment rendered was to engage the enemy Sisera at Mount Tabor in the north (Judg 4:6). So there may or may not be a connection between these two sites. The point is that it is a place where Saul will meet three men on their way to Bethel. Gibeath-elohim may be another name for Gibeah, Saul's home (1 Sam 10:26), south of Ramah but five miles north of Jerusalem (modern-day Tell el Ful). The word literally means hill (in contrast to mountain), so Gibeath-elohim means hill of god. It is identified as the location of a Philistine garrison (1 Sam 10:5). More important, Saul is instructed to go there to meet a band of prophets before heading to the sanctuary at Gilgal where Samuel will meet him and stay with him for seven days. The point of these directions, therefore, is not necessarily to move Saul in a straight line to the east, but to have him encounter several groups of people before he ends up at the sanctuary of Gilgal. The locations generally fit the vicinity of Ramah. While 1 Samuel 10 cannot give more precise details for location, one must conclude that Rachel's tomb was located near Ramah.

This is exactly the sense in which the lamentation recorded by Jeremiah four and a half centuries later is to be understood, "A voice is heard in Ramah . . . Rachel is weeping for her children" (Jer 31:15). This memorable poetic line was written at this significant moment because the prophet undoubtedly assumed a connection with the tomb of Rachel and Ramah. The moment of history was, of course, the beginning of the Babylonian exile. After a siege of three years, Jerusalem had fallen and its inhabitants were being processed for deportation to Babylon. It is especially significant that Jeremiah himself was a Benjamite and very familiar with this area, his hometown Anathoth (Jer 1:1) located only several miles to the southeast. The town is mentioned

---

[4] Not to be confused with Mount Tabor in the Plain of Esdraelon farther north.

[5] Tony W. Cartledge, *1 & 2 Samuel: Smyth & Helwys Commentary* (Macon, GA: Smyth & Helwys, 2001) 131.

several times in his prophesies (Jer 11:21-23; 29:27; 32:7-9), most significantly at the end when he buys a field in Anathoth while Jerusalem is surrounded and the situation is hopeless. Later Jeremiah, too, was captured and held among the captives at Ramah (Jer 40:1). For some reason, Jeremiah was released and allowed to make his own exile in Egypt, but his heart went out to the captives. Yet the most poignant expression of grief was that which he imagined would be expressed by his own ancestress Rachel. The irony is that Jacob and Rachel had arrived in the land of promise by the same route that the deportees would make on their way to Babylon. Now they would take the reverse route: Ramah → Geba → Michmash → Bethel → Shechem → Damascus → Mesopotamia. The location of Rachel's tomb near Ramah is thus central to his prophetic utterance in Jeremiah 31:15.

The witness of 1 Samuel 10:2 and Jeremiah 31:15 is strong. During the time of the monarchy, from the anointing of Saul to the beginning of exile (1040–596 B.C.E.), Rachel's tomb was understood to be located in the north near Ramah.

The Southern Tradition

The primary witness for the southern tradition for Rachel's tomb is the book of Genesis. What adds to the impact of the witness is the fact that the report occurs twice, first in the narrative form describing the events of Jacob and Rachel's arrival in the land (Gen 35) and then as a summary statement (Gen 48:7). The Genesis writer sets the context for this tragic event in some detail. The chapter begins with Jacob at Bethel in the north (35:1) and ends with his arrival at Hebron in the south (35:27), a journey of forty miles likely consuming a full week with a large caravan. Verses 16-21 compose a complete unit which seems to comprise a single day, departing from Bethel in verse 16 and arriving at "the tower of Eder" where Jacob pitches his tent in verse 21. The Hebrew expression in verse 21 is *Migdal Eder* that literally means "tower of the flock." The question is whether this is a specific place name or a general notation of a watchtower where the flocks could be easily watched. The NRSV seems to take a middle ground, rendering the expression as the tower of Eder. With the assumption that there must be many such watchtowers, this notation is often ignored.

More important is the designation of Rachel's death in relation to a place called Ephrath. Rachel's tomb is described as "on the way to Ephrath" (v. 19). Earlier the writer introduced the episode saying that "they were still some distance from Ephrath" (v. 16). Presumably because Ephrath is not a well-known name, the writer adds, in verse 19, "that is, Bethlehem." The matter is handled in a similar fashion in the summary statement of Genesis 48:7. Ephrath is mentioned twice. The final time, the clarification is added, "that is, Bethlehem."

For many, it is the familiarity with the Bethlehem of the Christmas story that makes the location meaningful. Yet, other than being the hometown of King David (1 Sam 17), Bethlehem was a small, insignificant village. Yet one other text helps to solidify the connection of Bethlehem and Ephrath. Micah, the contemporary of Isaiah (about 700 B.C.E.) writes about the coming messiah:

> "But you, O Bethlehem of Ephrathah,
> who are one of the little clans of Judah,
> from you shall come forth for me
> one who is to rule in Israel,
> whose origin is from of old, from ancient days." (Mic 5:2)

At this later date, Ephrathah seems to be understood as a clan name for the area where the village of Bethlehem is located. Bethlehem was but a small village, and Ephrathah, one of the little clans of Judah; yet greatness will come from such meager beginnings in the person of the Messiah, the ruler of Israel whose origin is of old. Thus, in such an important text the connection is made clear between Bethlehem and Ephrathah, paralleling the Genesis account of Rachel's death.

The importance of this text in the Christian era is evident from Matthew's citation in his infancy account of Jesus, one of five prophetic quotations in Matthew 1–2. Yet there is an irony. In Matthew's selective and creative use of quotations, he omits the reference to Ephrathah.

> "And you, Bethlehem, in the land of Judah,
> are by no means least among the rulers of Judah;
> for from you shall come a ruler
> who is to shepherd my people Israel." (Matt 2:6)

It would seem that for Matthew the importance is on connecting the birth to "Judah" so that the name occurs twice. Ephrathah is all but forgotten.[6]

---

[6] Only twelve verses later Matthew quotes Jeremiah concerning Rachel (Matt 2:18).

Making Sense of Multiple Traditions for Biblical Events

For many, multiple traditions for holy sites are simply a fact of life. A dozen different sites are suggested for Mount Sinai, two or three for Jesus' miracle of loaves and fishes, and also several for biblical Cana where Jesus first turned water to wine. The Church of the Holy Sepulchre and the Garden Tomb compete for modern pilgrims' hearts as the place of Jesus' death and resurrection. Medieval pilgrim maps show that convenience was often a more important criterion in commemorations than historical accuracy. In the case of Rachel's tomb, there are other considerations. Rabbinic tradition saw no problem with both a northern and a southern tradition for Rachel's tomb, using two different Hebrew terms to designate them. One site (Bethlehem) can be understood as the actual burial place of Rachel, the other (Ramah) as a memorial. With Rachel dying in the territory of Judah, the Benjaminites would have established their own site. John Wilkinson suggests the opposite: that a location within the tribal territory of Benjamin was original, but as Rachel grew in importance to all Israel, a local site was established in Bethlehem as well.[7] More recently, Zecharia Kallai draws the same conclusion.[8]

In some ways, it seems fitting that two separate traditions of Rachel's tomb occur in the Bible. For an individual characterized as always on the way, it is appropriate that no single place could confine her in death. In a sense Rachel has become like Moses, whose burial place was hidden from people who might make his place of death more important than the accomplishments of his life. In truth, the existence of Rachel's tomb has elevated her memory so that she transcends death and intercedes for her offspring and others in need.

The role of politics complicates the matter further. Anthropologist Susan Sered has noted that the revitalization of the cult of Rachel corresponds to the establishment of the modern state of Israel.[9] Individuals finding themselves perpetually vulnerable to the extreme have found solidarity at one particular physical monument: the tomb of Rachel in Bethlehem. As the fledgling state grew in importance for Jews, so did the Bethlehem

---

[7] John Wilkinson, *Egeria's Travels to the Holy Land* (Jerusalem: Ariel, 1981); also von Rad, 335.

[8] Zecharia Kallai, "Rachel's Tomb: A Historiographical Review," in *Vielseitigkeit des Altes Testaments* (Frankfurt: Peter Lang, 1999) 215–23.

[9] Susan Starr Sered, "Rachel's Tomb: Societal Liminality and the Revitalization of a Shrine," *Religion* 19 (1989) 27–40. See also Gershom Gorenberg, "The Tomb Cult: Outside the Fence," *The Jerusalem Report* (September 23, 2002) 31.

tomb. The result is that any discussion of authenticity may be blurred by the emotional attachment to the site at Bethlehem.

Still, as long as there are two competing sites, absolute claims can be countered. There are arguments available on both sides to counter any conclusion. This is not to say that one should not investigate the matter with every critical tool and to seek the historic truth. Quite clearly one tradition reflects more accurately the original location of Rachel's tomb. With careful critical analysis it may be possible to discover which tradition is original and the reasons that a second tradition developed.

What might the Bible itself suggest? When approached from a canonical point of view, the Genesis account of a Bethlehem tomb would appear original. Then during the monarchy (1 Sam 10), the tradition would seem to shift to Ramah in the north. Then again it would seem to shift back to Bethlehem in the south at the end of the Old Testament era and especially among Christians, perhaps with the help of Matthew's Christmas story.

The difficulty, of course, is that the biblical books were not written in the order that they appear in the Bible. While many books include traditions that go back very early, their final form as we know them does not come about until the fifth and fourth centuries B.C.E., after the Babylonian Exile and return. This is the general view concerning Genesis. So while the stories of Jacob and Rachel reflect a period of time perhaps two millennia before the Common Era, the actual wording of the texts was not finalized until much later. In other words, the accounts of 1 Samuel 10 and Jeremiah 31 predate the actual wording of Genesis 35 and 48. So it may well be that the northern tradition concerning the tomb of Rachel was original and that only later did it shift to Bethlehem. This question requires a more critical reading of the texts.

Genesis 35 and the Northern Tradition

How necessary is the Bethlehem reference to the biblical story of Rachel's death? As we saw earlier, it does not occur in Josephus' version of the narrative, probably reflecting older independent traditions. Josephus simply refers to Rachel going into labor while still some distance from Ephrath. When read from a critical perspective, it has long been suggested that the reference to Bethlehem in Genesis 35:19 is a gloss.[10] In fact, it is presented in modern

---

[10] Claus Westermann, *Genesis: A Commentary*, vol. 2, 555; von Rad, 335. Skinner, 426; Cartledge, 132.

translations as a parenthetical comment. The Hebrew *hî Bethlehem* ("that is, Bethlehem") could easily have been added as the story went through various stages of editing prior to the written composition, or also in the early days of textual transmission by copiers of the text. Whether it was a scribe, an editor, or the biblical writer himself, the addition of the expression "that is, Bethlehem" helps to clarify the meaning of Ephrath. Yet it is surprising that the name Bethlehem occurs only at the end of the story. The name Ephrath occurs twice, yet in the introduction, where one would most expect a clarification, Ephrath stands by itself.[11] In other words, the story was told originally in a setting that understood the location of Ephrath. That was no longer the case when the text reached its current form, likely between the fifth to second century B.C.E.

The real test comes in reading the text without the questionable phrase. Might we read the Genesis account with different eyes were "that is Bethlehem" omitted? Are there difficulties in the text without that phrase? Are there difficulties when it is added? Are there reasons that might account for the change? Without that gloss, might Genesis 35 be compatible with the northern tradition for Rachel's tomb?

As a whole, Genesis 35 is a chapter that centers on the region around Bethel in the north, not, as it might seem, the Bethlehem area. This is significant since God had appeared to Jacob at Bethel upon his departure for Paddan-Aram (Gen 28). So Jacob returns from Paddan-Aram to settle near Bethel at the instruction of God. As a repetition of the Genesis 28 episode, he renames the site Bethel when he establishes an altar, and God appears to him a second time (v. 7). The writer describes Jacob both as journeying (vv. 16 and 21) and as living in that land (v. 22). The chapter also includes a number of life's transitional moments, first the death of Rebekah's nurse who was buried below Bethel (v. 8) and then the death of Rachel on the way to a place called Ephrath (v. 19). Following a summary statement that closes off the Paddan-Aram period (vv. 22-26), Jacob reaches Hebron for the death of his father Isaac (vv. 27-29).

The episode of Rachel's death brings to mind the difficulty of a woman traveling while nine months pregnant. Whether one day or more distant from Bethel, the writer is not specific. The seemingly unnecessary reference to Jacob pitching his tent beyond Midgal Eder (v. 21) may well imply a single day. If that in fact is the case, one can imagine an event-filled day: the departure

[11] Westermann, vol. 2, 555.

from Bethel at daybreak; the slow trek of the large traveling party; the delay during the intense labor of Rachel; the childbirth; the nursing of the child; the mother's death; the mourning of Jacob over his beloved wife; the burial; the raising of a pillar; the reorganizing of the caravan; the journey farther to the place for pitching their tents at Migdal Eder. That's quite a bit for a single day. One can hardly imagine a journey of more than ten miles under such conditions. Ten miles, of course, would not reach past Jerusalem.

This takes us back to Migdal Eder as the destination on that fateful day. The rendering has usually been quite vague, reflecting the translation "tower of the flock." Thus Jerome, for example, suggested a location of prime pasture land east of Bethlehem, traditionally where the Christmas shepherds pastured their sheep. Elsewhere in the Bible, Migdal identifies a particular city such as Magdala on the Sea of Galilee or Migdal-Gad (Josh 15:37) and Migdal-El (Josh 19:38). The NRSV translates the Hebrew in Genesis 35:21 as *tower* of Eder. Yet the exact same name, Migdal Eder, occurs in Micah 4:8 (translated as "tower of the flock" in NRSV) as another name for Jerusalem.[12] More specifically, *Seqal* 7.4 identifies the place as the Ophel near Mount Zion. The tradition linking Migdal Eder and Jerusalem was so firm that the Septuagint translator actually rearranged the text so that Genesis 35:21 immediately follows Genesis 35:16a. Jacob and company depart Bethel and arrive at Migdal Eder, and only then does Rachel begin her labor before her death near Bethlehem in Genesis 35:19. The alternative is to read the text more critically. Jerusalem is located only ten miles from Bethel. Without the Bethlehem gloss to explain the name Ephrath, one could easily conclude that the death of Rachel occurred at a location north of Jerusalem, before arriving at Migdal Eder (Jerusalem).[13]

"Which is there to this day"

In describing the pillar set up by Jacob over Rachel's grave, Genesis 35:20 notes that the pillar was still present "to this day." Such notations often occur in the book of Genesis. Yet the meaning is not always so clear: which day? Was it the time of the original hearer of this story when the words were passed on during the oral tradition stage? Was it the time of

---

[12] Lamonette Luker, "Rachel's Tomb," *Anchor Bible Dictionary*, vol. 5, 608. See also the fortress language in Psalm 46 written about Jerusalem.

[13] For a more in-depth discussion on the relationship between the term Ephrath and Bethlehem, see the Appendix in this book.

the first writer whom we call the Elohist,[14] likely composing the text in the north shortly after the divided monarchy (ninth century B.C.E.)? Here we have confirmation in the report of Samuel and Saul in 1 Samuel 10. Was it the time of the editor who brought the various Pentateuch documents together in fifth-century Babylon? Here we have the evidence of Jeremiah's lament in chapter 31. Yet the prophet's allusion to the tomb is more subtle, and the editor of the Pentateuch, writing in far-off Babylon, was hardly an eyewitness to the monuments of Eretz Israel. Was it the time of a later scribe who added the gloss "that is, Bethlehem?" Was that change undertaken on the basis of reading other biblical texts such as Micah and 1 Chronicles? Was it based on actual knowledge of a still-existing monument? Was it eyewitness testimony or historical memory?

The announcement that the pillar was still "there to this day" is intriguing, but not wholly helpful since we don't really know the time of "this day." For the modern reader of the Bible, there is a Rachel's Tomb today on the outskirts of Bethlehem. There is, in fact, a tomb that one can see and touch, labeled in large print for all to see: "Rachel's Tomb." Yet, the key issue is whether one can draw a line of continuation from the current tomb all the way back to the one mentioned in Genesis. The more recent part of that issue will be dealt with in the next chapter. The more ancient part can be handled here and in short order. There is simply no direct evidence for a Rachel's Tomb in Bethlehem from the time of the Genesis text until the fourth century of the Common Era when eyewitnesses began reporting on the monument outside of Bethlehem. There is a major gap in the line of evidence. The only possible allusion to a Bethlehem tomb is found in Matthew's infancy story where he quotes Jeremiah 31 in reference to the slaughter of innocents. Yet interestingly, Matthew still locates the voice of Rachel at Ramah and in quoting Micah 5:2 he omits any reference to Ephrathah. When one adds to this Matthew's creative use of prophetic quotations in the infancy story, even he must be excluded as a witness to the Bethlehem tradition for the tomb.

What is the evidence for such a monument in the north "to this day"? Three different sites have been proposed, Ophrah, Kiriath-jearim, and Parah, locations where burial tombs are prominent. In the case of Orphah, Albright made a case that an abundance of tombs are found at Ain-Samieh

---

[14] Anthony F. Campbell and Mark O'Brien, *Sources of the Pentateuch: Texts, Introductions, Annotations* (Minneapolis: Fortress, 1998) 175.

a short distance away. In addition, he found evidence for an early sanctuary to the Ewe Goddess and suggested that the origin of the story of Rachel found its roots in this very early cultic center, especially since the name Rachel means ewe.[15] More recently, Matitiahu Tseuat argues for a location eight miles west of Jerusalem at Kiriath-jearim.[16]

The case for Parah, or Farah, two miles east of er-Ram, seems most impressive.[17] Lombardi noted the existence at Hizma in the *wadi ras al-Fara* of five extremely large stone structures that were researched by Vincent a century ago.[18] These range in length from 53 meters to 10 meters and in height from 6.62 meters to 2.8 meters. Each has a funerary room in the center. Vincent concluded from the style that they belonged to nomadic groups and originated in the Bronze Age prior to the conquest of Israel. Likely such wandering shepherds would bring their dead back to this central location for burial. Vincent ascertained from the residents of this area that the monuments as a whole were known as *Qubbur Bene Israin*, or the Tombs of the Sons of Israel. In particular the largest and most prominent tomb went by the name *Qaber Um Bene Israin*, or Tomb of the Mothers of the Sons of Israel. From the title it would seem that this could easily be the Rachel's tomb referred to in 1 Samuel 10. It is also possible that there may be some connection with the story of the nurse Deborah's death and burial "below Bethel" in Genesis 35:8 and the reference to the oak of Tabor near Rachel's Tomb in 1 Samuel 10. Again, it is important to trace the line of continuation from an ancient monument to the present day. In this case, there has been less attention to these monuments over the last two millennia, likely because Farah simply cannot compete with Bethlehem in its importance to Christian history.

---

[15] Albright, 124–37.

[16] Matitiahu Tseuat, "Rachel's Tomb," IDB Supplement (Nashville: Abingdon, 1976) 724–25.

[17] A recent survey of the Israel Antiquities Authority identifies the site as Hizma, site number 480 in Benjamin, located at coordinates 17580 and 13880. Archaeological evidence points to occupation in the Middle Bronze Era. Israel Finkelstein and Yitzhak Magen, eds., *Archaeological Survey of the Hill Country of Benjamin* (Jerusalem: Israel Antiquities Authority Publications, 1993) 63.

[18] H. Vincent, "Cronique," RB (1901) 287–89. This suggestion had already been made by Charles Clermont Ganneau on the basis of his 1873–74 research north of Jerusalem in *Archaeological Researches in Palestine in the Years 1873–74* (London: Palestine Exploration Fund, 1899). This view was also followed by R. A. S. Macalister, "The Topography of Rachel's Tomb," *Palestine Exploration Fund Quarterly* (1912) 74–82, and Lombardi, 323–32.

Yet there may well be late biblical references to these tombs. The book of Jubilees retells the Genesis story. Jubilees 32:34 merely repeats the Genesis account of Rachel's death at Ephrath, that is, Bethlehem. Interestingly, the account also relates independent traditions, including the detail that Rachel's labor and Benjamin's death took place during the night. Jubilees 34:15-17, however, presents entirely new traditions, including descriptions of the deaths of Bilhah, Rachel's handmaid, and Dinah. With regard to Bilhah, the text notes that she died mourning the report of the death of Joseph and then she was buried "opposite the tomb of Rachel." Dinah, too, then died and also was buried in Rachel's tomb. Interestingly, the text gives a place name where Bilhah had been living, *Qafrateh*. This is indeed a strange terminology. It seems to refer to Farah/Parah or Ephrathah. Yet the presence of "Q" is uncertain but perhaps refers to *Qaber* or tomb. The present form could thus be a contraction of *Qaber* and Farah or Ephratha. In the Testament of Joseph there are also references to the burial of Asenath, Joseph's wife, and Zilpah, Leah's handmaid, at Rachel's Tomb.[19] From the structure of the tombs at Farah and from the popular name, one would expect multiple burials. Lombardi also suggests a connection between the five separate monuments and the fact that names of five women are given (Rachel, Bilhah, Dinah, Zilpah, and Asenath).[20] Thus the title, the Tomb of the Mothers of Israel.

In sum, evidence of the northern tradition for Rachel's tomb in the biblical tradition is rather substantial. 1 Samuel 10 and Jeremiah 31 remain primary sources. However, as we saw above, a critical reading of Genesis 35 also fits the northern tradition. Perhaps the most ambiguous evidence concerns the name Ephrath, which can point both to the north and also to the Bethlehem region (see Appendix). The presence of the Tomb of the Mothers of Israel at Farah, north of Jerusalem, provides an alternative to the current tomb of Rachel in Bethlehem. In contrast to the strong evidence for a northern site for Rachel's tomb, biblical evidence for Rachel's tomb in Bethlehem is slim and problematical. However, the situation changes in the Common Era. The northern tradition is all but forgotten. Attention shifts completely to a structure in Bethlehem known as Rachel's Tomb.

---

[19] Actually, the deaths of Asenath and Zilpah are reported in two separate manuscript traditions, so they may be variations of the same report. Yet they could reflect two separate traditions.

[20] Lombardi, "H. Farah–W. Farah," 331.

CHAPTER 6

In the Age of Pilgrims

The history of the current Rachel's Tomb in Bethlehem is preserved through the notations of pilgrims and visitors to the Holy Land over the last two millennia. The notations contain the location, helpful descriptions of the development of architectural style through various stages, and information about the various groups who held the monument sacred: Christians, Muslims, and Jews alike. The early reports also provide helpful clues to understanding the origins of this particular tomb near Bethlehem.

In modern religious literature, it is not unusual to find descriptions of Rachel's Tomb with citations of half a dozen or so ancient witnesses to the existence of the tomb. Often they include the Bordeaux Pilgrim, Eusebius, Jerome, Arcuflo, and one or two from the Middle Ages. The conclusion: There is a continuous line of testimony for the authenticity of Rachel's Tomb going back nearly two thousand years. The problem is that these very texts have not been scrutinized with a critical eye. Most of these texts come from visitors to the Holy Land, pilgrims who, like modern tourists, are herded around to dozens of sites in ten days to two weeks. Listen to any travelogue by a first-time visitor to Jerusalem, and one often hears a line of confusion or uncertainty: "This building marks the burial of some important person. I think it was one of the prophets. Yes, that's right. A prophet. Jeremiah. No, maybe it was Zecharaiah. Was it his tomb? Or maybe his home. Maybe that was the shrine we saw the day before. We saw so much. I can't remember. But it was an important site connected with the Old Testament." We've all heard those reports and, when we do, our minds automatically work to filter out information that is not likely true. Then there are the guides. Some guides are good, providing carefully documented historical information. Some pass on local traditions as historical fact. Some like to embellish their stories. Some may want to sound knowledgeable even when they aren't sure. Many of the ancient visitors to Rachel's Tomb were faced with the same problems that modern tourists have: dependence upon guides, the blurring of many sites, memories that conflate and connect with stories taught from childhood. For this reason, it is essential that these ancient witnesses be treated with a critical eye.

The result of this chaotic process of early manuscript making includes some things one would expect, but also a number of surprises. One of these surprises is that some of the most frequently cited sources are really not that reliable. Another surprise is related to the distribution of testimonies over time. Rather than being content with half a dozen or even a full dozen witnesses, we have tried to compile as many sources as possible. During the Roman and Byzantine era, when Christians dominated, there was really not much attention given to Rachel's Tomb in Bethlehem. It was only when the Muslims took control that the shrine became an important site. Yet it was rarely considered a shrine exclusive to one religion. To be sure, most of the witnesses were Christian, yet there were also Jewish and Muslim visitors to the tomb. Equally important, the Christian witnesses call attention to the devotion shown to the shrine throughout much of this period by local Muslims, and then later also by Jews. As far as the building itself, it appears to be a cooperative venture. There is absolutely no evidence of a pillar erected by Jacob. The earliest form of the structure was that of a pyramid typical of Roman period architecture. Improvements were made first by Crusader Christians a thousand years later, then Muslims in several stages, and finally by the Jewish philanthropist Moses Montefiore in the nineteenth century. If there is one lesson to be learned, it is that this is a shrine held in esteem equally by Jews, Muslims, and Christians. As far as authenticity, we are on shaky ground. It may be that the current shrine has physical roots in the biblical era. However, the evidence points to the appropriation of a tomb from the Herod family. If there was a memorial to Rachel in Bethlehem during the late biblical era, it was likely not at the current site of Rachel's Tomb.

Early Christian Period

In 333 c.e., a pilgrim known only by the name of his home in Bordeaux was the first person to record having seen Rachel's Tomb in Bethlehem. This was a period of major transition for Bethlehem. Jews had been expelled first from Jerusalem and then Judea. The makeup of the church gradually had changed from Jewish-Christian to Gentile-Christian. Political rule from Rome was being replaced by Byzantine Greek. Newcomers, like the Bordeaux pilgrim, began the long trek to see the holy sites; and scholars, like Origen, Eusebius, and Jerome, began collecting literary works and recording biblical helps for the growing church in the Greek and Latin speaking world.

A century prior to the Bordeaux pilgrim, the biblical scholar Origen had moved from Alexandria, Egypt, to Caesarea on the Palestinian coast, where he worked in the newly established Christian library to interpret biblical texts. Origen is credited as the first Christian to mention Rachel's tomb though his fragmentary work is available only through Eusebius.[1] There is no evidence that Origen actually saw the monument or even had an interest in visiting the biblical sites—though he was close enough to make that journey to Bethlehem if he wanted.[2] He was primarily a textual scholar. One of the biblical tools that he helped to create was called *Onomasticon*, an alphabetical listing of biblical place names with descriptions. Later, Eusebius, the early fourth-century scholar, historian, and bishop of Caesarea, issued his own *Onomasticon*, simply revising Origen's text. Then Jerome followed in the late fourth-century, translating the work into Latin. One must be careful then in citing all three sources. In reality, they represent a single source repeated under different names.

Under the place name *Ephratha*, the *Onomasticon* mentions the presence of Rachel's tomb in Bethlehem. Presumably Origen's only source was the Genesis 35 text. It reads: "Ephratha: (Gen 35, 16. 19). The region of Bethlehem, the city of David, in which the Christ was born. Of the tribe of Benjamin. On the way Rachel was buried, five miles from Jerusalem, in the hippodrome. The tomb is shown still today. And the father of Bethlehem was called Ephratha, as in Chronicles."[3] Origen and Eusebius say nothing about where the tomb was located or whether it included a monument that one could visit. There is only the information available from the biblical text,

---

[1] Justin Martyr in discussing the slaughter of innocents cites the Genesis tradition that Rachel had been buried in Bethlehem but says nothing about an existing tomb. Interestingly, Justin proposes that the reference to Ramah in the Jeremiah lament of Rachel must refer to a contemporary city in Arabia. Justin, *Dial. C. Tryph.* 78. PG 6.657–60.

[2] E. D. Hunt, *Holy Land Pilgrimage in the Late Roman Empire, A.D. 312–460* (Oxford: Clarendon Press, 1982) 92–93.

[3] Eusebius, *Das Onomastikon der biblischen Ortsnamen*, ed. by Erich Klostermann (Hildesheim: Georg Olms Verlagsbuchhandlung, 1966) 82.10-14. *Ephratha* (Gen. 35, 16.19) *xōra Bēthleem tēs poleōs Dauid, eph hēs ho Xristos egennēthē. Phulēs Beniamin. Hēs pros tē hodō ethapsan tēn Raxēl, apo sēmeiōn d' tēs Hierouslēm, en tō kaloumenō Hippodromō. Deiknutai to mnēma eis eti nun. Kai ho patēr tou Bēthleem ekaleito Ephratha, hōs en paraleipomenais.*

including the note that it is there "still today." The reference to the *hippodrome* betrays the scholar's methodology since this is a mistranslation by the Septuagint of Genesis 48:7. There simply is no evidence for a hippodrome near Bethlehem. So T. D. Barnes has noted, "By its very nature the *Onomasticon* has less relevance to the Palestine of Eusebius' own day than to biblical times."[4] It is true that one also finds the expression, "The tomb is shown." The passive voice suggests the possibility of local tradition, yet one must be careful about the reliability of such statements. In the entry under *Bethlehem*, one finds, "there one is shown the tombs of Jesse and David,"[5] although the actual tomb of David is located in Jerusalem.

The report of the Bordeaux Pilgrim has a totally different character, documenting what he actually saw rather than reflecting on biblical texts. Known as the *Itinerary of the Bordeaux Pilgrim*, it presents only the basics, "Four miles from Jerusalem, on the right of the road to Bethlehem, is the tomb in which was laid Jacob's wife Rachel."[6] The information here is much more specific. It is located four miles from Jerusalem—a very accurate description when considering the modern Rachel's Tomb—and its position is near the main road on the right. Missing from the report is any hint whether the pilgrim actually stopped to visit the tomb or any physical description of the monument. There is nothing about who was responsible for the upkeep of the tomb or who looked after it.

The writing of Jerome is still of a different character in that he had come from Rome in 386 to reside in Bethlehem while he carried out his scholarly work. He wrote at a time when the value of pilgrimage was actively debated. To be sure, the spiritual riches of the biblical record were equally available to Christians in faraway lands. So while Jerome encouraged pilgrimage, the value of such visits was that it pointed the pilgrim back to the biblical texts.[7] He had the advantage of being in a position where he could visit many of the sites himself, yet he continued to rely heavily on earlier written sources

---

[4] T. D. Barnes, "The Composition of Eusebius's *Onomasticon*," JTS, n.s. 26 (1975) 412–15, quote from 413.

[5] Eusebius, *Onomasticon*, 42.12.

[6] "*Item ab Hierusalem euntibus Bethleem milia quatuor super strata in parte extra est monumentum, ubi Rachel posita est uxor Iacob.*" *Itinerarium Burdigalense*, P. Donatus Baldi, *Enchiridion Locorum Sanctorum* (Jerusalem: Tupis PP. Franciscanorum, 1955) 96.1. Wilkinson, *Egeria's Travels*, 22–34.

[7] See Jerome, Letter 58, *Patrologia Latina*, vol. 29, ed. by Jacques-Paul Migne (Paris, 1844–1864) 401; Hunt, 90–102.

like those of Origen and Eusebius. As an example, his Latin translation of the *Onomasticon* entry for *Ephrata* includes several additional details, which are printed in italics: "Ephrata in the region of Bethlehem, the city of David, in which Christ was born. *It is in the tribe of Judah, granted that many generally appraise it wrongly* in the tribe of Benjamin, near the road where the tomb of Rachel is, five miles from Jerusalem in this place which is called Hippodrome *by the Septuagint. We read* Ephrata also in the book of Chronicles, *as was stated above*."[8] Where there was clearly a mistake—the reference to the tribe of Benjamin—he offered a correction. Yet it is puzzling that he does not recognize the mistake in the term *hippodrome*—first connected with the Rachel story in the Septuagint translation of Genesis 48:7. The expression in the biblical text, "still some distance" (*kbrt*) to go to Ephrath, was interpreted as the distance of running a horse or a hippodrome.[9] Strangely, Jerome persists in the misinformation about the hippodrome even though as a resident he must have known better. Regarding Rachel's Tomb, Jerome provides no additional information from what he received from Eusebius. It is located near the road, five miles from Jerusalem. Missing from Jerome's translation, however, is the comment, "The tomb is shown still today."

Did Jerome have firsthand information about Rachel's Tomb in Bethlehem? There is one passage that might suggest that he did. In 404 he wrote a lengthy letter to commemorate the death of the Roman noblewoman Paula who had followed Jerome to Bethlehem and spent the last twenty years of her life there. Sections 8–14 (out of 34 sections) describe her lifelong pilgrimage to various biblical sites including Rachel's Tomb in Bethlehem. Jerome writes, "She [Paula] proceeded to Bethlehem stopping on the right side of the road to visit Rachel's Tomb. (Here it was that she gave birth to her son, destined to be not what his dying mother called him, Benoni, that is the 'Son of my pangs,' but, as his father in the spirit prophetically named him, Benjamin, that is 'the Son of the right hand'). After this she entered into the cave where the Savior was born. . . ."[10] Here he mentions the location

---

[8] Jerome, *Onomasticon*, 83.12–16. "*Efratha region Bethleem ciuitatis Dauid, in qua natus est Christus, est autem in tribu Iudae, licet plerique male aestiment in tribu Beniamin, iuxta uiam, ubi sepulta est Rachel, quinto miliario ab Ierusalem in eo loco, qui a Septuaginta uocatur Hippodromus. Legimus Efratham et in Paralipomenon libro, sicut dictum est.*"

[9] The same interpretation is found in the Testament of Joseph.

[10] Epistle 108.10. S. L. Greenslade, *Early Latin Theology: Selections from Tertullian, Cyprian, Ambrose, and Jerome*, in Library of Christian Classics, V (Philadelphia: The Westminster Press, 1956) 348–82, esp. 355. Also CSEL 55, 316; PL 22, 284. Baldi, 100.1–2. "*Perrexit Bethlem et in*

of the tomb "on the right side of the road" consistent with the statement of the Bordeaux Pilgrim, but no other information is given. Jerome notes in the letter that it took him all of two nights to dictate it. He neither made use of notes from Paula, nor does he suggest that he accompanied her on these visits. S. L. Greenslade concludes from a comparison of this letter with passages in the *Onomasticon* and earlier itineraries, such as Egeria and the Bordeaux Pilgrim, that this does not represent the actual pilgrimage of Paula. Rather, Jerome composed this fictional itinerary from earlier literary sources.[11] When the phrase *in parte extra* (on the right side) is found in both Jerome and the Bordeaux Pilgrim, one needs to suspect dependence. A listing of the pilgrim along with Origen, Eusebius, and Jerome need not mean four separate sources. In later years, the situation will continue as pilgrims rely on the *Onomasticon* for their reports.

To complicate the matter, Jerome mentions one other tomb in his *Onomasticon* that is pertinent to the issue of Rachel's Tomb. In the paragraph on *Bethlehem*, Eusebius had noted briefly only the distance of six miles from Jerusalem, its proximity to the Hebron road, the tombs of Jesse and David, and the origin of the name in Chronicles. Following a close translation of this short paragraph, Jerome inserts a comment about Migdal Eder and then this comment about the tomb of Archelaus: "But near the same Bethlehem, one is shown the tomb of Archelaus, king of Judea, which is the beginning of the path to our cells and the turning point from the public road."[12] Here Jerome is adding to the received text on the basis of personal experience, as he makes clear with his note about "the path to our cells." The main route from Jerusalem to Bethlehem had been fixed for centuries, if not millennia. One traveled south along the watershed of the Judean hills about five miles where a fork in the road continued south to Hebron and diverted to the east for a mile to Bethlehem. This would have been the main route that Jerome had frequented on his way to his cell in the monastery near Nativity Church that he and Paula had helped establish in Bethlehem. Likely, the tomb of Archelaus had been pointed out to Jerome as he hurried back to Bethlehem.

---

dextra parte itineris stetit ad sepulchrum Rachel, in quo Beniamin non, ut mater vocaverat moriens, Benoni, hoc est filium doloris mei, sed, ut pater prophetavit in spiritu, filium dexterae procreavit. Atque inde specum salvatoris ingrediens. . . ."

[11] S. L. Greenslade, 347.

[12] Jerome, *Onomasticon*, 45.1-3. ". . . *sed et propter eandem Bethlehem Regis quodam Judaeae Archeolai tumulus ostenditur, qui semitae ad cellulas nostras e via publica divertentis principium est. . . ."*

The descriptions of Rachel's Tomb in the two Jerome texts and that of Archelaus' Tomb in a third text provide some interestingly similar details. The tombs are located along the main road.

"on the right side of the road"   —Rachel (Letter about Paula)
"near the road . . . five miles from Jerusalem" —Rachel (*Onomasticon* 83)
"the turning point from the public road"   —Archelaus (*Onomasticon* 45)

Of course, the Genesis text had long established that Rachel was buried "on the way."

So one would expect the *Onomasticon*, derived primarily from Scripture, to locate Rachel's Tomb by the main road. Yet the details, *fork in the road, five miles from Jerusalem*, and *on the right side*, all are clearly compatible with the modern Rachel's Tomb. One can only wonder if Jerome was actually aware of two separate tombs in Bethlehem. Were there tombs of both Rachel and of Archelaus? Jerome leaves us with a puzzling situation.

The quantity of writing left by Jerome is amazing. He had the potential for providing much helpful detail on Rachel's tomb, and yet all we have are three short statements. We are left with the impression that the monument associated with Rachel was not really important to Jerome. This is especially the case when reading a document like Jerome's 386 letter to Marcella in which he describes in detail the many biblical sites to be explored, not just in Bethlehem, but in all the Holy Land.[13] Page after page of sites are included. Then toward the end comes a beautiful line, "We shall hasten, if not to the tents, to the monuments of Abraham, Isaac and Jacob, and of their three illustrious wives." This, of course, is a reference to the Machpelah tomb in Hebron where the six are buried together (Gen 49:31), yet not a word about illustrious Rachel and her tomb. So his confusion may not be all that surprising.

Unfortunately, Jerome's contemporaries are completely silent on the matter of Rachel's tomb. Egeria of Spain had undertaken a pilgrimage in 381 to 384, but the section about Bethlehem is missing. Her detailed report about the Jerusalem liturgy cites the role of Bethlehem clergy and the various ceremonies associated with Bethlehem, but none extend to Rachel's tomb. So it was with the Armenian Eustathios. In 341 Aeteria wrote about

[13] Jerome, Letter 46, in Philip Schaff, ed., *A Select Library of the Nicene and Post-Nicene Fathers of the Christian Church*, vol. 6 (New York: Charles Scribner's Sons, 1909).

Bethlehem the year before Jerome's arrival (385) and said nothing.[14] Nor did S. Paulinus Nolanus in 403.[15] It seems that Rachel's tomb was not really considered that important in Bethlehem. Again, it should be stressed that the current Rachel's tomb is not located in an obscure place. It is situated just off the main Jerusalem-Hebron road, a route that has likely been followed by travelers for five millennia or more. Even today the road is the preferable route from the West Bank north, the alternative to the East through Wadi Nar considered much more difficult. The tomb is situated at the very point of a fork in the road where travelers turn off to Bethlehem. In the days before travel by motorized vehicles, the site would have provided a natural resting place before the final leg to Bethlehem. Therefore, the omission by so many contemporaries of Jerome is most unexpected.

It doesn't change in the following two centuries or so. Eucherius (430) in a letter to Faustus mentions Bethlehem and the way from Jerusalem to Hebron, but not Rachel's Tomb.[16] Theodosius (518) writes an extensive "Topography of the Holy Land," also with detail concerning the route from Jerusalem to Hebron, yet surprisingly omits any reference to Bethlehem, including Rachel's tomb.[17] Sophronius (580–635), who served as Patriarch of Jerusalem, wrote beautiful poetry about the Church of the Nativity in Bethlehem and other sites, but not about Rachel's tomb.[18] Finally, this is the period of the first known Christian map, the Madaba map, which includes numerous holy sites, especially around Jerusalem.[19] Bethlehem is listed, the regional name Ephratha, and Ramah, but not Rachel's tomb.

The only references to Rachel's tomb during this time are questionable at best. One is a short description of a dream Peter the Iberian had about a Jerusalem pilgrimage. Peter had come to Palestine in the mid-fifth century to take up the monastic life, most of which he spent as Bishop of Maiumas in Gaza. Shortly after Peter's death in 491 at Mar Saba monastery east of Bethlehem, John Rufus undertook to write his biography, including mention that Peter was often criticized for never having made a pilgrimage to the holy sites around Jerusalem. So John Rufus wrote about an imaginary

[14] Baldi, *Enchiridion*, 103.

[15] Ibid., 104.

[16] John Wilkinson, *Jerusalem Pilgrims Before the Crusades* (Warminster, UK: Aris & Phillips Ltd., 2002) 94–98; Baldi, *Enchiridion*, 105.

[17] Baldi, 107; Wilkinson, *Jerusalem Pilgrims*, 103–16.

[18] Baldi, 105, 107, 109.

[19] Wilkinson, *Jerusalem Pilgrims*, 152–56.

pilgrimage to Jerusalem that occurred in a dream of one of Peter's followers. It includes a listing of twelve churches but offers no detail except their location in a clockwise cycle beginning and ending in Jerusalem. He describes that fictional itinerary as follows: "After that [the house of Lazarus] he took the road which goes from there till he came to holy Bethlehem. After praying there he went to Rachel's tomb. After praying there, and in the other churches and sanctuaries along the road, he went down to Siloam, and from there up to Holy Sion, where he finished his holy circuit, since he had worshipped the Savior in all the places."[20] The unusual route taken, the reference to "praying" at Rachel's Tomb, and the inclusion of it among all the "churches and sanctuaries" are not realistic for this period. It was likely included merely to fill out this "holy circuit."

A second reference contained in the report of an actual pilgrimage gives misleading material. The Piacenza Pilgrim (570) includes travels through Constantinople, Syria, and Egypt, as well as extensive reports on Palestine. While describing the various holy sites along the Jerusalem-Hebron road, he identifies a place called Ramah at the third-mile marker from Jerusalem. He writes, "On the way to Bethlehem, at the third milestone from Jerusalem, lies the body of Rachel, on the edge of the area called Ramah."[21] Of course, Ramah had always previously been located north of Jerusalem.[22] Yet here the pilgrim was informed that Rachel's body lay in the grave.

One might excuse the short three-mile figure as an inaccurate guess, but he gives further details that show his confusion. "There I saw standing water which came from a rock, of which you can take as much as you like up to seven pints. Every one has his fill, and the water does not become less or more. It is indescribably sweet to drink and people say that Saint Mary became thirsty on the flight into Egypt, and that when she stopped here this water immediately flowed. Nowadays there is also a church building there."[23] The Piacenza Pilgrim reports a large rock in the middle of the road which spewed forth water explained as a miracle from the Virgin. While not related to the gospel nativity accounts, this detail is fascinating because it parallels the story of Jesus' birth in *Qur'an* 19. This rock has also been associated with

---

[20] Ibid., 101.

[21] Ibid., 142; Baldi, 108; "*Via, quae ducit Bethlem, ad tertium miliarium de Hierosolima iacet Rachel corpore, in finis loci, qui vocatur Rama.*"

[22] The location here corresponds with the Madaba Map.

[23] Wilkinson, *Jerusalem Pilgrims*, 142.

the Mar Elias Monastery and the newly discovered Kathisma church[24] just to the east of the Jerusalem-Hebron road, still a significant distance north of today's Rachel's Tomb. The Piacenza Pilgrim simply does not know the location of Rachel's tomb. Interestingly, his report seems more to be identifying the site known today as Ramat Rachel, half-way between Jerusalem and Bethlehem. The Hebrew *Ramah*, of course, means "height" and Ramat Rachel was aptly named because of its location on a significant hill. Excavations there in the 1950s uncovered a fifth-century church.[25] This may indeed be the Ramah mistaken by the Piacenza Pilgrim. John Wilkinson agrees with this assessment: "The effect of the book is patchy. Passages, which read like records of personal experience contrast with others which seem factual and dry . . . or from books."[26] The unreliability of this pilgrim's account can also be shown by his willingness to accept a tradition placing the tombs of David and Solomon just outside Bethlehem.

The confusion of the Piacenza Pilgrim and the silence of his contemporaries are all the more striking because these are the centuries when Bethlehem flourished more than at any other time in its history. Following the visit of Constantine's mother Helena in 326, the Church of the Nativity was constructed and a large influx of foreigners flocked to Bethlehem. It has been estimated that over one hundred monasteries, like Chariton and Mar Saba, sprang up in the surrounding countryside and within the city.[27] Even the Roman Emperor Justinian was struck by Bethlehem's importance in the sixth century and dedicated funds to fortify the walls and to embellish the town through the construction of churches, including the rebuilding of the Church of the Nativity. This attention, however, did not seem to extend to Rachel's tomb. The era of Byzantine Rule did not treat this monument favorably. It was not until after the arrival of the Muslim Caliph Omar that reports about Rachel's Tomb resume.

---

[24] Stephen J. Shoemaker, "The (Re?)Discovery of the Kathisma Church and the Cult of the Virgin in Late Antique Palestine," *Maria*, 2 (2001) 21–72. This church has only been excavated beginning in 1997 following discoveries from the widening of the Jerusalem-Hebron road and the establishment of a large building complex at Abu Ghneim/Har Homa.

[25] Y. Aharoni, "Ramat Rachel," *Encyclopedia of Archaeological Excavations in the Holy Land*, vol. IV, ed. by Michael Avi-Yonah (Englewood Cliffs, NJ: Prentice Hall, 1976) 1000–09. Aharoni mistakenly identified that church as the Kathisma.

[26] Wilkinson, *Jerusalem Pilgrims*, 13.

[27] Mitri Raheb and Fred Strickert, *Bethlehem 2000: Past and Present* (Heidelberg: Palmyra, 1998) 77–87.

First, one other observation should be made. It is worth noting that this is the same period (fifth through seventh centuries) when one sees the ascendancy of the cult of Mary in Jerusalem. This is evident through the Church of the Assumption in Jerusalem and the Church of the Nativity in Bethlehem, and along the road between them is the Church of the Kathisma. Seemingly, this new role for Mary leaves little room for the recognition of the earlier mother figure Rachel. The Jewish matriarch symbolized suffering in childbirth. Yet it was the Virgin Mother's son who walked the *Via Dolorosa*, while the Virgin herself became exempt from suffering, assumed into heaven as recognized in the annual August 15 celebration.

One thing that is totally missing from the few references to Rachel's Tomb during this era is a physical description. In spite of the Genesis report that the tomb was related to the pillar erected by Jacob and that it was still standing "to this day," no one undertook to describe it. It will not be until the Muslim era that the first physical description is offered. Arculf, a pilgrim from Gaul in 670, confirms our judgment about a lack of interest in Rachel's tomb during the first six centuries of the church, saying that he found it in poor condition.[28] His other comments are equally important. The tomb had no adornment. While Arculf surely admired the architectural embellishments all over Jerusalem and Bethlehem, as far as this monument goes, it was nothing special. Arculf also corroborates the location of the tomb on the right side of the Jerusalem-Hebron road where the fork heads east to Bethlehem.

Perhaps the most important contribution of Arculf comes in his three-word description: *lapidea circumdatum pyramide*. The actual sepulcher was "surrounded by a stone pyramid."[29] This detail will be repeated by others in later centuries:

---

[28] "*Rachel in Effrata, hoc est in regione Bethlem . . . in eadem regione iuxta via humatam refert Rachel. Est quaedam via regia, quae ab Helia contr meridianam plagam Chebron ducit, cui viae Bethlem vicina VI milibus distans ab Hierusolyma ab orientali plaga abhaeret. Sepulchrum vero Rachel in eadem viae extremitate ab occidentali parte, hoc est in dextro latere, habetur pergentibus Chebron cohaerens, vili operatione collocatum et nullam habens adornationem, lapidea circumdatum pyramide. Ibidem et nominis eius titulus hodieque monstratur, quem Iacob maritus super illud erexit,*" Baldi, 110.7; Lombardi, "H. Farah–W. Farah," 341, fn. 39.

[29] Wilkinson gives a rather strange translation here, "protected by a stone rail," Wilkinson, *Jerusalem Pilgrims*, 187. However, this is not supported by the Latin.

Cuius adhuc pyramis a transeuntibus videri potest (John of Wurzburg, 1165);[30]
Ubi etiam pyradmis eius nomini assignata consistit (Theodericus, 1172);[31]
Hic autem titulus est pyramis alta (Felix Fabri, 1480–83).[32]

The tomb of Rachel was built as a pyramid. Such a description is totally incongruous with the Genesis report of Jacob erecting a stone pillar and construction practices of later days. Of course, one thinks of the earlier Egyptian funerary monuments. However, this style is characteristic of the Hellenistic-Roman era, occurring as early as the Maccabean tombs erected by Simon in 142 B.C.E. (1 Macc 13:28).[33] The well-known Tomb of Cestius in Rome from the first century B.C.E. was influential in the spread of this pyramid form throughout the empire. In Jerusalem it is best represented by the tomb of Bene Hezir, popularly known as the tomb of Zachariah, in the Kidron Valley[34] and is also known from the tomb of Queen Helena of Adiabene, buried in Jerusalem in the mid-first century C.E.[35] In other words, the style of the monuments points to an origin in the first century B.C.E. or first century C.E.

This is, in fact, consistent with Jerome's report of the tomb of Archelaus at this very location. Archelaus, the son of Herod the Great, had been named tetrarch of Judea from his father's death in 4 B.C.E. to 6 C.E., when he was deposed to Lyon in southern France. His burial in the early- to mid-first century C.E. on this high point in the Judea hills would have provided a picturesque setting with the Herodium off in the distance. The Hellenistic-Roman architectural style would have been fitting for this son of Herod, who was raised and educated in Rome and who spent his latter years in such an important Roman center as Lyon. There is nothing to suggest Semitic origins—such as the *matzevah* erected by Jacob—as one would expect for the tomb of Rachel.

Why does one find contradictory information concerning a tomb near the Bethlehem turnoff on the road from Jerusalem? In one source, Jerome calls it the tomb of Archelaus. In other reports, it is named the tomb of Rachel.

---

[30] Baldi, 131.

[31] Ibid., 132.

[32] Ibid., 150.

[33] Lombardi, 342.

[34] N. Avigad, "Jerusalem," *Encyclopedia of Archaeological Excavations in the Holy Land*, vol. II, ed. by Michael Avi-Yonah (Englewood Cliffs, NJ: Prentice Hall, 1976) 628–31.

[35] Josephus, *Antiquities* 20.95.

One is struck by the phonetic similarities between the names Archelaus and Rachel (with the hard semitic "ch"). This may account for the transformation from the tomb of Archelaus to the tomb of Rachel. After several centuries, Archelaus had lost significance for the local people of Bethlehem and, with newcomers populating the area, he was all but forgotten. However, there was increased interest in biblical texts as prophesy about Jesus as the literary texts were explicated and illuminated. Especially after the arrival of Matthew's Gospel, Rachel was associated with the Bethlehem infancy story. One can imagine visitors such as the Bordeaux Pilgrim passing by the monument at the side of the Jerusalem-Hebron road and hearing the explanation of his guide—not unlike modern tourists who comprehend explanations only partially. Thus "Tomb of Archelaus" was heard as "Tomb of Rachel." This was apparently the case when the Bordeaux Pilgrim visited Jerusalem's Sheep pool and called it "Bethsaida" rather than "Bethesda."[36] It is quite possible as well that such confusions were made by local residents of later generations who had misheard the explanation from their elders. Thus we find multiple reports coexisting alongside each other, as at the time of Jerome. In time there was no reason to correct the name back to "Tomb of Archelaus," so the name "Tomb of Rachel" prevailed.

The transformation during this period appears to be one only of name. There is no ownership of Rachel's Tomb on the part of the local population as is evident from both the silence among witnesses and from Arculf's report of deteriorating conditions. What was once a political monument did not automatically become a religious monument with the change of name. During the early Christian period it was symbolic of a distant memory from the past.

---

[36] Bordeaux Pilgrim, line 589; Wilkinson, *Egeria's Travels*, 29. Like many pilgrim reports there is also a lack of critical analysis. Just a couple of sentences after his mention of Rachel's Tomb, the Bordeaux Pilgrim reports the location of the tombs of David and Solomon also in Bethlehem, 598.

CHAPTER 7

Islam and the Age of Crusades

The First Muslim Period

The Muslim period began with the arrival of the Caliph Omar in Jerusalem in 638. His rule was characterized by an era of cooperation among Christians and Muslims. His agreement with the Christian Patriarch Sophronius is well-known: [The inhabitants] "shall have security for their lives, their children, their goods, and their churches, which shall neither be pulled down nor occupied."[1] Archaeology confirms that there was no destruction. It was a peaceful transition. Omar was accompanied by several Christian tribes from Arabia who settled in the Bethlehem area. Therefore, reports of Christian pilgrims continued throughout the time of Muslim rule.

Interest in pilgrimage was evident by the publication of new guidebooks. Some time before the planning of the Dome of the Rock began in 692, Epiphanius the Monk wrote the first edition of a guidebook on "The Holy City and the Holy Places." In it he comments briefly about the Bethlehem area: "To the south of the Holy City, two miles along the road, is the tomb of Rachel. And six miles away in that direction is Holy Bethlehem where Christ was born. . . ."[2] He goes on to describe the Church of the Nativity and various monasteries. With regard to Rachel's Tomb, the report is again not helpful, giving no detail of description and placing the tomb too far to the north.

Perhaps the most important pilgrim of this period was Bishop Arculf (mentioned briefly above) from Gaul in the 670s, who includes a rather significant report about Rachel's Tomb. Arculf himself did not leave a journal of his two-and-a-half year journey, but soon after his return to Europe he met

---

[1] Wilkinson, *Jerusalem Pilgrims*, 17.

[2] Ibid., 209; Baldi, 117, *hai hotikon meros tēs hagias poleōs hōs apo miliōn duo parastrata esti tēs Raxēl ho taphos. Kai palin hōs apo miliōn heks estin hē hagia Bēthleem.*

Adomnan, the Abbot of Iona, who was in the process of writing the book *On the Holy Places*. This book, which was completed before 688, made use of literary sources such as Jerome, Eucherius, and others, but also included many long quotations from Arculf. This is the case in his report on the tomb:

> The Book of Genesis speaks of Rachel being buried at Ephrata, which means, in the neighborhood of Bethlehem, and the *Liber Locorum* [of Jerome] says she is buried in that neighborhood, "near the road." I further questioned Arculf about this road, and he replied, "There is a highway which leads south from Aelia to Hebron. Bethlehem is not far to the east of this road, six miles from Jerusalem. Rachel's tomb is at the end of this road and on the west of it, that is, on your right as you go towards Hebron. It is of poor workmanship, having no adornment, and covered by a stone pyramid. Today they point out an inscription giving her name, which Jacob her husband erected over it."[3]

Unlike his contemporary Epiphanius, Arculf locates the tomb precisely on the right side at the fork where the Bethlehem road leaves the main route to Hebron, consistent with the current Rachel's Tomb in Bethlehem and with the report of the Bordeaux Pilgrim three centuries earlier. The confirmation from Jerome, mentioned by Adomnan, is somewhat vague—"near the road." However, an inscription of Rachel's name confirms the eyewitness character of Arculf's report.

Most important, Arculf gives the first physical description of the tomb. It is "unadorned" (*nullam habens adornationem*) and "of poor workmanship" (*vili operatione collocatum*). This agrees completely with the picture we have seen in the previous centuries where there is very little attention given to the tomb. The third part of his description reads in Latin, *lapidea circumdatum pyramide*. As mentioned earlier, John Wilkinson mistranslates this as "surrounded by a stone rail." However, the presence of the word *pyramid* seems to be most significant in understanding the original structure.

A short time later in 702, the Venerable Bede composed his book *The Holy Places*, in which he includes this short note, "Bethlehem is to the east of the highway which leads from Aelia to Hebron, and to the west is the tomb

---

[3] Wilkinson, *Jerusalem Pilgrims*, 186–87. "*Rachel in Effrata, hoc est in regione Bethlem . . . in eadem regione iuxta via humatam refert Rachel. Est quaedam via regia, quae ab Helia contr meridianam plagam Chebron ducit, cui viae Bethlem vicina VI milibus distans ab Hierusolyma ab orientali plaga abhaeret. Sepulchrum vero Rachel in eadem viae extremitate ab occidentali parte, hoc est in dextro latere, habetur pergentibus Chebron cohaerens, vili operatione collocatum et nullam habens adornationem, lapidea circumdatum pyramide. Ibidem et nominis eius titulus hodieque monstratur, quem Iacob maritus super illud erexit.*" Baldi, 110.7.

of Rachel, which has even today her name inscribed on it."[4] Bede never traveled to Palestine but composed his work in the library using Adomnan as well as other sources. Thus Arculf's report about the location and the inscription with Rachel's name was preserved also in this work. Because of the reputation of Bede, this book became one of the most read books on the Holy Places.

By the mid-eighth century, the situation began to change for the Christian Church. A severe earthquake in 746 destroyed numerous church buildings from Jerusalem to the Sea of Galilee. This was followed by a change from Umayyad to Abassid rule. Archaeologists at the Church of the Kathisma along the Hebron Road have noted a destruction layer at this time that resulted in the remodeling of that building into a mosque. There is no archaeological or literary evidence about any effects on nearby Rachel's Tomb.

An early ninth-century report suggests that the tomb could have been affected. In writing a comprehensive chronology of the church in 810, George Synkellos, who had served the Patriarch in Constantinople for two decades, made use of written sources such as Julius Africanus, Eusebius, and others. At a single point in his narrative—summarizing the story of Jacob and his family from Genesis up to the death of Rachel—he adds a personal note, "In my journeys to Bethlehem and what is known as the Old Larva of blessed Chariton, I personally have passed by there frequently and seen her coffin lying on the ground."[5] Presumably, Synkellos had made a number of extended stays at Chariton's monastery to the south of Bethlehem and thus offers his own observation from repeated experience. His description could well point to local destruction.

Yet there is another line of evidence that complicates the picture. For those in Palestine, worship continued to be formalized around the established shrines and churches. A late seventh or early eighth-century Jerusalem calendar designates six different Holy Days centered on Bethlehem sites. Special festivals were held at the Church of the Nativity on December 24, 25, and May 31. The Church of the Kathisma, located a short ways north

---

[4] Wilkinson, *Jerusalem Pilgrims*, 223. Baldi, 113.4; "*Via regia, quae ab Helia Chebron ducit, ab oriente Bethleem, ab occidente sepulchrum Rachel habens titulo nominis eius usque hodie signatum.*"

[5] William Adler and Paul Tuffin, trans. and eds., *The Chronology of George Synkellos: A Byzantine Chronicle of Universal History from the Creation* (Oxford: University Press, 2002) 153.

on the Jerusalem-Hebron road, hosted liturgies on August 13 and December 3. Finally, on July 18 on the road to Bethlehem at Rachel's Tomb, an annual memorial service was held.[6] One would assume that some sort of church structure or at least an altar would be present for the liturgy to be said, yet no physical remains support this idea. Several centuries later, a well-valued Georgian translation of the church calendar mentions two days of commemoration: first, a commemoration of the saint on February 20 "at the tomb of Rachel"; then a memorial service on July 18 "on the road to Bethlehem in the church of Rachel."[7] The transformation had been made to a religious shrine. Still, there is surprisingly no information about Rachel's Tomb for the later ninth and tenth centuries.

The next pilgrim report occurs in the early eleventh century by a certain presbyter named Jachintus who undertook a long-awaited pilgrimage focusing on Bethlehem and Jerusalem. His is one of the most detailed descriptions of the Church of the Nativity and the Church of the Holy Sepulchre. He notes also that the city of Bethlehem had been destroyed with only a few houses standing. In reporting his journey from Bethlehem to Jerusalem, he says, "At the half-way point in the journey, which is next to a Christian cemetery is the tomb of Rachel, and it is the same distance on—two miles—from Rachel's Tomb to the Holy City Jerusalem."[8] Again, the description of the distance is puzzling since it suggests the possibility of confusion with one of the churches closer to Jerusalem. The mention of a cemetery, however, is important in view of the large cemetery that surrounds Rachel's Tomb today. Since Jachintus describes it as a Christian cemetery, it would seem that the reported church building near this site had by this time been destroyed.

It is also at this time that we find the first evidence of Jewish devotion to the Bethlehem monument. During the seventh through the eleventh centuries, there were also Jewish pilgrims to the Holy Land. As Moshe Gil notes, "Jewish pilgrimage went on continuously, as long as external circumstances permitted."[9] From the fragmentary manuscripts discovered in the Cairo

---

[6] *Kalendarium Hieroslymitanum saec. VII–VIII.* Baldi, 112; "*18 Jul. In via ad Bethlehem ad sepulchrum Rachelis, eius memoria.*"

[7] Gérad Garitte, *The Calendrier palestino-georgien du Sinaiticus*, 34 (Brussels: Society of Bollandistes, 1958) 162, 282.

[8] Wilkinson, *Jerusalem Pilgrims*, 271. In his first edition in 1977, Wilkinson had dated Jachintus to the mid-eighth century.

[9] Moshe Gil, *A History of Palestine, 634–1099*, trans. by Ethel Broido (Cambridge: Cambridge University Press, 1992) 631.

Geniza an unknown person writes a letter to a cousin: "Almighty God may grant that you go up to Jerusalem and see the tomb of Eleazar, the gates of mercy and the place of the altar and the Mount of Olives and Rachel's Tomb, may she rest in peace, and the graves of our ancestors, may they rest in peace."[10] Of course, the recipient has not yet visited the Holy Land, but the letter assumes that the named sites are accessible, likely from reports of other returning pilgrims. At the same time it must be noted that there are other Jewish pilgrim reports from this era that mention Jerusalem and Hebron, but not Rachel's Tomb.

From the beginning of the Umayyad period, Muslim visitors and pilgrims also made their way to Jerusalem, some in connection with the *Hajj* and others simply to show their devotion to the Holy Places.[11] It was not long before Bethlehem was part of the Muslim itinerary. In 985, the Muslim geographer al-Muqaddasi wrote *Description of Syria and Palestine* on the basis of his travels. So he writes: "Beit Lahm is a village about a league from Jerusalem, in the direction of Hebron. Jesus was born here, whereupon there grew up here the palm tree; for although in this district palms are never found, this one grew by a miracle. There is also a church, the equal of which does not exist anywhere in the country around."[12] In 1047, the Persian poet Naser-e Khosraw also visited Bethlehem, referring to this as a place "belonging to the Christians" where there "are always numerous pilgrims."[13] He comments that he passed the night there. By the thirteenth century, the Muslim writer Yakut comments that "Muslims have never ceased to visit Bait Lahm in pilgrimage."[14] Like both Christian and Jewish pilgrims of the period, many of the Muslim writers pass over Rachel's

---

[10] Gil tentatively dates the letter to the eleventh century. The name Abü'l-Fadl on the verso may be that of the author. The letter is found in the Taylor Schechter Collection, University Library, Cambridge. Quoted in Gil, section 830, page 626.

[11] Amikam Elad, *Medieval Jerusalem and Islamic Worship: Holy Places, Ceremonies, Pilgrimage* (Leiden: Brill, 1995) 62. See also Hunt Janin, *Four Paths to Jerusalem: Jewish, Christian, Muslim, and Secular Pilgrimages, 1000 b.c.e. to 2001 c.e.* (Jefferson, NC: McFarland & Co., 2002) 69–85.

[12] Muhammed al-Mukaddasi, *Description of Syria, including Palestine* in *The Library of the Palestine Pilgrims' Text Society*, vol. III (London: Palestine Exploration Fund, 1886) 50. His mention of the palm tree refers to *Qur'an* 19.25.

[13] Naser-e Khosraw, *Book of Travels*, trans. by W. M. Thackston, Jr. (Albany: State University of New York Press, 1986) 53.

[14] Yakut 1.779, quoted by Guy Le Strange, *Palestine under the Moslems: A Description of Syria and the Holy Land from a.d. 650 to 1500* (London: Alexander P. Watt, 1890) 300.

Tomb. However, 'Ali of Heart notes that "between Jerusalem and Bethlehem is the tomb of Râhîl, mother of Joseph."[15]

The Crusades: 1099–1185

During the twelfth century, as expected, the literary record concerning Rachel's Tomb reaches an apex. While previously references averaged one, or at best two, per century, now the written comments average better than one per decade. Naturally, some of these are by Western Europeans,[16] the Germans Johannes of Wurzburg and Theodoricus, a geographical work, and several traveler guides. Yet the surprise of the Crusader period is that the list of witnesses also includes a Christian abbot from Russia, the Greek Orthodox priest John Phocas from Crete, a Muslim, and several Jewish rabbis.[17]

After an entire millennium in which the pyramid tomb remained virtually unchanged, the Crusader witnesses point to structural changes. Johannes of Wurzburg (1165)[18] still was able to refer to the pyramid, but, in the words of Rabbi Benjamin of Tudela who stopped in Bethlehem on an eight-year pilgrimage (1166–73),[19] the tomb of Rachel "is covered by a cupola, which rests upon four pillars," and John Phocas (1185) wrote that it "is a roofed building with a square vaulted structure."[20] Presumably, the renovations that incorporated the pyramid into the new structure were undertaken by the Latin Christian community.

Characteristic of this period is a tradition that linked the current structure of the tomb to the story of Jacob. The pyramid apparently consisted of

[15] Quoted by Le Strange, 299.

[16] Nicole Chareyron, *Pilgrims to Jerusalem in the Middle Ages* (New York: Columbia University Press, 2005).

[17] John Wilkinson with Joyce Hill and W. F. Ryan, *Jerusalem Pilgrimage, 1099–1185* (London: The Hakluyt Society, 1988).

[18] "*Milliario a Bethlehem, via, quae ducit Jerusalem, Chabrata, locus, in quo, cum Benjamin pepperisset Rachel, occubuit, ibique a viro suo Jacob tumulata quiescit, cujus tumulo superposuit Jacob dedecim lapides non modicos in testamentum duodecim filiorum suorum; cujus adhuc pyramis a transeuntibus videri potest.*" Baldi, 131.7; Lombardi, fn. 45.

[19] Teddy Kollek and Moshe Pearlman, *Pilgrims to the Holy Land: The Story of Pilgrimage through the Ages* (New York: Harper & Row, 1970) 118.

[20] "*Urbs vero Bethleem a sancta civitate sex fere mille passibus distat . . . Inter monasterium [Mar Elias] et Bethleem, Rachelis sepulchrum, structura quatuor fornicibus tholi instar in fastigiatum cacumen desinentiis, opertum; locus ille trianguli formam efficit.*" Baldi, 133.1; Wilkinson, Hill, and Ryan, 332; Lombardi, fn. 50.

twelve stones, and Jacob had twelve sons. When Genesis 35 said that Jacob erected a pillar in Rachel's honor, it really meant that he erected a twelve-stone pyramid. The earliest witness to this tradition is the *Work on Geography* dated to 1128–37: "A mile from Bethlehem on the road which leads to Jerusalem is Chabratha, the place in which, when Benjamin had died, Rachel died for sorrow. There she was buried by Jacob, and over the tomb the twelve stones placed by Jacob still exist today."[21] The use of the name *Chabratha* indicates that this is a report based on the Septuagint and traditions gathered from scholars such as Jerome.[22] However, the note that the twelve stones "still exist today" points to recent pilgrim reports. So also the Muslim geographer Muhammad al Idrisi in 1154 describes the tomb in similar words: "Bait Lahm is the place where the Lord Messiah was born, and it lies six miles distant from Jerusalem. Half-way down the road is the tomb of Rāhīl, the mother of Joseph and Benjamin, the two sons of Jacob—peace be upon them all. The tomb is covered by twelve stones, and above it is a dome vaulted over with stone."[23] The tradition seems to have spread widely so that it is repeated by Christian visitors, Johannes of Wurzburg (1165) and Theodericus (1172).[24] The similarity would suggest that the keepers of the shrine, like modern-day guides, had at this time developed a standard recitation composed of common elements, some true and some mere legend.

In time a number of variations are recorded. According to the report of Rabbi Benjamin of Tudela (1166–73) there are only eleven stones, not twelve: "From Jerusalem it is two parasangs to Bethlehem, called by the Christians Beth-Leon, and close thereto, at a distance of about half a mile, at the parting of the way, is the pillar of Rachel's grave, which is made up of eleven stones, corresponding with the number of the sons of Jacob. Upon it is a cupola resting on four columns, and all the Jews that pass by carve their names upon the stones

---

[21] "Work on Geography," Wilkinson (1988), 198. The pilgrim here, remembering Rachel's name for her son (Benoni, "Son of Sorrow"), thought that mother and son both died during the birth. This inaccuracy is another example of what happens as pilgrims visit and record their experiences at religious shrines.

[22] Jerome, *L. Loc.* 173.5. Earlier, this twelfth-century work refers to the nearby town as Ephrata, founded by the Jebusites, but that Jacob himself renamed it Bethlehem, meaning house of bread. Wilkinson (1988), 197. Clearly, the author misspeaks in the text quoted above concerning the death of Benjamin.

[23] Wilkinson (1988), 227.

[24] "*Ubi etiam juxta locus, qui dicitur Chabratha, ubi Rachel uxor Jacob, cum Benjamin peperisset, defuncta est. Qua ibidem sepulta, Jacob xii lapides super ipsius tumulum congessit, ubi etiam pyramis ejus nomini assignata consistit.*" Baldi, 132.2.

of the pillar."[25] Clearly, the rabbi's report is based on close observation since it describes also features such as the four columns and cupola. Likewise, he notes the practice of leaving graffiti on the stone, the names of Jewish visitors.

Further variations explain the difference in the number of stones in a way typical of Jewish midrash. It was not only Jacob who erected the pillar, but also his sons helping him. Twelfth-century Rabbi Jacob ben R. Nathaniel Ha Cohen thus notes in his report that Benjamin was excluded: "Like this also is the grave of our mother Rachel, in Ephrath, a tower built of hewn stones with four doors. There are eleven stones on her grave, for they say that Benjamin was small and could not bring his stone and the top stone was erected there by our father Jacob."[26]

Similarly, the report of the visit of Rabbi Petachia of Ratisbon between 1170–87 repeats this detail: "The rabbi then came to Rachel's grave, at Ephrath, half a day's journey from Jerusalem. Upon her grave are eleven stones according to the number of the eleven tribes; and because Benjamin was only born at her death there is no stone erected for him." As Rabbi Petachia expands on the tradition, he notes a detail totally uncharacteristic for an ancient tomb in Bethlehem: "They are of marble. The stone of Jacob, however, consisting of one piece of marble, above all of them, is very large, a load for many persons." Then the rabbi adds a rumor suggesting conflict between Christian and Jewish communities of this time: "A mile from hence are the priests who took away the large stone from the grave and placed it in a building for strange service. In the morning, however, it was seen on the grave as before. This was repeated several times, until at last they abstained from carrying it away." In reports from the early middle ages, it was noted that Rachel's name had been inscribed on the tomb. Later, Benjamin of Tudela noted the practice of leaving graffiti. Now Petachia notes a variation of this custom, "On the stone is engraved the name of Jacob."[27] This tradition about the twelve stones continues in various forms.

---

[25] He also mentions that there were two Jewish residents of Bethlehem, dyers by profession. Michael A. Signer, ed., *The Itinerary of Benjamin of Tudela: Travels in the Middle Ages* (Malibu, CA: Joseph Simon Pangloss Press, 1983) 86, revising earlier editions edited by Marcus Nathan Adler in 1907 and A. Asher in 1840.

[26] Others date this account to the thirteenth through the fifteenth centuries, though Adler places it in the twelfth century. Adler, 98.

[27] He reached Damascus between the time that Saladin had captured Damascus in 1174 and before Jerusalem. The record was composed by Rabbi Judah the Pious bar Samuel on the basis of Petachia's notes. Elkan Nathan Adler, ed., *Jewish Travelers in the Middle Ages: 19 Firsthand Accounts* (New York: Dover Publications, Inc., 1987) 88.

Two centuries later Sir John Maundeville (1356) notes (contrary to the details of the Genesis story) that Jacob "caused twelve great stones to be placed over her, in token that she had borne twelve children."[28]

With the resurgence of Christian institutions under the Crusaders, it is not surprising that visitors occasionally mention Rachel's Tomb in context of the other churches along the Jerusalem-Hebron road. The "Seventh Guide" (1160) mentions the Church Monastery of Saint Elias a short distance to the north,[29] though John Phocas notes it had been destroyed in an earthquake and was currently being rebuilt under the direction of a Syrian abbot. Daniel the Russian Abbot (1106–08), however, shows some confusion, pointing on each side of the tomb to a monastery and church of the Holy Mother now destroyed and also the place of the Kathisma, though only the stone and not the church are mentioned.[30] The "Second Guide" (1170) also shows confusion, listing the memorial of Rachel before "the place where Elijah is venerated" on the road from Jerusalem to Bethlehem.[31] Interestingly, this guide's unique reference to "the Mound of Rachel" could possibly point to a tradition, not about the tomb but the name Ramah, which means "height." In his travels north of Jerusalem, Daniel visits biblical Ramah,[32] noting however that this was still considered the region of Bethlehem and that this is the location where King Herod killed the babies at the time of Jesus' birth—perhaps a sign that the alternative northern tradition of Rachel's Tomb was still recognized. The "Work on Geography," however, places Ramah two miles west of Bethlehem and locates the graves of the innocents three miles south of Bethlehem.[33]

With such a wealth of sources on Rachel's Tomb during the twelfth century, one must balance the reports by what is missing. There is no description of activities by those visiting the tomb or of rituals followed by the local Christian community. Rachel's Tomb can only be considered a minor shrine. Interestingly, there are more pilgrim reports that totally omit mention of Rachel's Tomb than those who do refer to it.[34]

---

[28] Sir John Maundeville, "Bethlehem" in Thomas Wright, ed., *Early Travels in Palestine* (London: Bohn, 1848) 164.

[29] "Seventh Guide (1160 C.E.)," Wilkinson, Hill, and Ryan, 236.

[30] "Daniel the Abbot: Jerusalem Pilgrimage," Wilkinson, Hill, and Ryan, 147; Baldi, 127.

[31] "Second Guide (1170 C.E.)," Wilkinson, Hill, and Ryan, 241.

[32] "Daniel the Abbot," Wilkinson, Hill, and Ryan, 151.

[33] "Work on Geography," Wilkinson, Hill, and Ryan, 197.

[34] John Wilkinson (Wilkinson, Hill, and Ryan) compiles the testimonies of nineteen literary works during this period. Yet thirteen of them do not even mention Rachel's Tomb.

The Second Muslim Era

With the end of Crusader control of Jerusalem in 1187 and diminishing Christian influence, Rachel's Tomb passed over to Muslim control. It became popular for Christians during this period to refer to all Muslims as Saracens. Specifically, Egyptian Mameluks ruled for most of the next three centuries, and the attitude between various religious groups was positive.[35] Gradually, tensions did develop between Muslims and Christians. When Felix Fabri arrived in Ramlah in 1484, he was presented with a list of ethical guidelines for Christian pilgrims when interacting with Muslims. Among these were the following warnings:

> **Article 2:** No pilgrim ought to wander along about the holy places without a Saracen guide, because this is dangerous and unsafe. . . .
>
> **Article 7:** The pilgrims must proceed to visit the holy places in an orderly manner. . . .
>
> **Article 22:** Let the pilgrim beware of entering mosques. . . .
>
> **Article 23:** Let the pilgrim especially beware of laughing to scorn Saracens who are praying. . . .[36]

However, Rachel's Tomb was a shrine open to all faiths as is evidenced by the large number of Western Christians who report on visits to Rachel's Tomb:

> Burchardius of Mount Zion (1283);[37]
> Fr. Antonius de Reboldis (1327–30);[38]
> Jacob of Verona (1335);[39]
> Ludolphus de Sudheim (1335);[40]
> Fr. Niccolò da Poggibonsi (1345);[41]

---

[35] Kollek and Pearlman, 121.

[36] Hunt Janin, "Appendix V: Instructions for Christian Pilgrims, c. 1484," *Four Paths,* 223–24.

[37] "*Prius tamen occurrit sepulcrum Rachel, ad dextam, iuxta viam.*" Baldi, 138.1.

[38] "*Veniendo de Bethleem, juxta viam est sepulcrum Rachelis uxoris Jacob, mirabilius sepulchrum, quod unquam viderim. Non credo per XX paria bovum possent unum de lapidibus illis, qui sunt ibi, trahere sed nec movere.*" Baldi, 140.1.

[39] "*Inter Bethleem et Jherosolymam, magis prope Bethleem, in via, est sepulcrum Rachel.*" Baldi, 141.9.

[40] "*Inter Bethleem et Ierusalem sunt tria miliaria, in qua via est sepulchrum Rachel et una ecclesia que Gloria in excelsis est vocata. . . .*" Baldi, 142.6.

[41] "*Partendosi altri da ditto monistero [Sant' Elia], e andando verso Bethelem, presso a un miglio, ad mano destra, in nuno campo, presso alla via, si è una tomba tonda, con tre porte*

Sir John Maundeville (1356);[42]
Nicolaus of Marthono (1394–95);[43]
Grethenios (1400);[44]
Johannes Poloner (1422);[45]
Felix Fabri (1480–84);[46]
Francesco Suriano (1485);[47]
Pietro Casola (1494);[48]
Sir Richard Guyleforde (1506).[49]

The comments of all these visitors are quite positive. Sir John Maundeville was impressed with the countryside, describing the way from Hebron to Bethlehem as "a very fair way, by pleasant plains and woods."[50] Canon Pietro Casola confirms the care taken by the local residents to develop the area: "In

---

d'intorno; e dentro si è una grande sepoltura sopra terra, alta VII piedi. E qui Iacob patriarca sì seppelli Rachel sua moglie, e in testimonio di XII figlioli c'avea, sì gli puose sopra XII grandi pietre, et ancora appare. . . ." Baldi, 144.2.

[42] "From Bethlehem to Jerusalem it is but two miles . . . And in that way is the tomb of Rachel, the mother of Joseph the patriarch, who died immediately after she was delivered of her son Benjamin; and there she was buried by Jacob, her husband, and he caused twelve great stones to be placed over her, in token that she had borne twelve children." Wright, *Early Travels in Palestine*, 164.

[43] "*Accedentes versus Jerusalem, per medium mileare invenimus quamdam magnam tumbam fabricatam, in qua stetit et mortua fuit illa valens mulier Raccel; et per duo milearia invenimus domos ubi stetit sanctus Elyas propheta. . . .*" Baldi, 146.6.

[44] "*Bethleem est un village fortifie au midi de Jerusalem, a sept verstes environ. A mi-chemin se trouve le couvent de Saint Elie le prophete . . . Sur ce meme chemin, se trouve le tombeau de Rachel, mere de Joseph.*" Baldi, 147.1.

[45] "*Deinde ad dextram prope viam, que itur in Hebron, est sepulchrum Rachelis, . . . quod per sarracenos ornate est constructum et ad austrum versum habentes ibi sepulturam eorum, et dicitus locus Chabrata.*" Baldi, 148.1.

[46] "*Hic autem titulus est pyramis alta, de lapidibus albis quadratis et politis fabicata, et est hodie pulchra capella. . . .*" Baldi, 150.3.

[47] "*Luntano da queste fonte, mezo miglio, è la casa di Helias, de la qual fo facto uno monasterio, habitato de Greci et officiato. Da questo monasterio, sino alla sepoltura di Rachel è mezo miglio: in honor de la quale e per reverential, il Saraceni hano edificato lo suo monumento cum una tribuna su quatro colonne. . . .*" Baldi, 151.2.

[48] M. Margaret Newett, trans., *Canon Pietro Casola's Pilgrimage to Jerusalem in the Year 1494* (Manchester: Manchester University Press, 1907).

[49] "And there also we passyd faste by the sepulcre of Rachell, the wife of the sayd Jacobe." Henry Ellis, ed., *Pylgrymage of Sir Richard Guyleford to the Holy Land, A.D. 1506* (London: Camden Society, 1851).

[50] Wright, 162.

my opinion, the road from Jerusalem to Bethlehem is the most beautiful we saw in those parts, there are so many beautiful things there—grapes, figs, olives . . . Farther on, near to Bethlehem, I saw the sepulcher of Rachel, the wife of the Patriarch Jacob, who died in childbed. It is beautiful and much honored by the Moors."[51] Casola confirms that the tomb had now become an important Muslim shrine.

Sometime, possibly in the fourteenth century, the tomb underwent further remodeling, although it is difficult to determine the exact nature of those changes. One of the earliest Christian visitors of this period, Antonius de Reboldis speaks of the "more beautiful sepulcher," which Niccolò da Poggibonsi measured as standing seven feet tall. Felix Fabri still describes the original pyramid structure. Fabri, however, also refers to a beautiful chapel (*pulchra capella*) which likely means that Christians were welcome also for prayer, yet Johannes Poloner and Francesco Suriano both credit the changes in the shrine to the Saracens. So, while the Crusader Christians had undertaken the first renovations of the shrine, the Muslims contributed to its building, adorning and beautifying the monument.

Already by the early eleventh century, Christians were burying their dead in a cemetery surrounding the tomb. Now in the fifteenth century, Johannes Poloner reports that Muslims, too, buried their dead around the tomb and especially to the south—a practice that continues to the present time.

The Ottoman Empire, ruling from Turkey, had expanded to include the Holy Land by 1516 and would continue until World War I. They were known for their centralized power and lack of respect for the local population and their concerns. Under the Ottomans the walls and fortifications of the Christian town of Bethlehem were dismantled. Yet in the reports of pilgrims, such as Richard Torkington (1517)[52] and Boniface of Stephanis (1552–64),[53] there is no indication of any changes regarding visits at the shrine.

At the end of the sixteenth century we receive the first visual representation of Rachel's Tomb through the sketches of Franciscan Father Bernadino

[51] Newett, *Canon Pietro Casola's Pilgrimage*, 262.

[52] "Nott far thens we might se the place in which Jacobb the patriarke dwellyd and ther also we passyd fast by the Sepulcre of Rachell the wyff of the seyd Jacobe." W. J. Loftie, ed., *Ye Oldest Dearie of Englysshe Travell: Being Hitherto Unpublished Narrative of the Pilgrimage of Sir Richard Torkyington to Jerusalem in 1517* (London: Leadenhalle, 1857) 46.

[53] "*Prope etiam est Domus Jacob Patriarchae, in qua Rachel ei mortua fuit . . . Progredientes haud multum a Domo Jacob, ad dextram iuxta viam, est sepulcrum Rachelis dilectae uxoris ipsius Jacob Patriarchae. In hac via non longe a sepulcro Racehl est cisterna.*" Baldi, 153.4-5.

Amico. Amico spent five years in Palestine from 1593 to 1597 visiting historic sites, drawing the facades, and making careful plans of buildings. After returning to Rome, he enlisted the engraver Antonio Tempesta to complete his works for publication. In 1610, the book of etchings was published under the name *Trattato delle Piante & Immagini de Sacri Edifizi di Terra Santa*, which is translated as *Plans and Images of the Sacred Edifices of the Holy Land*.[54] For the first time, accurate pictures were available in Europe for important biblical sites, including Rachel's tomb.

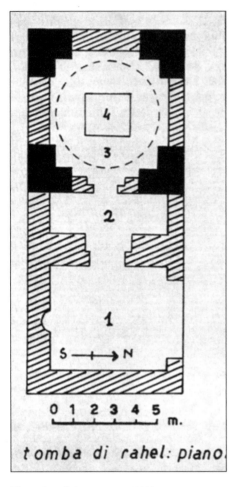

Floor plan of Amico—year 1610

The plan shows two structures. The larger one on the right contains a round, aboveground monument that his own notation identifies as "Sepolchro." The structure itself appears to have square dimensions with four pillars creating four arched openings and a dome centered above the actual tomb. To the left is a much smaller structure with a single arch described as a resting place for visitors. A short wall surrounds the compound with a small stairway leading up to the main structure. Amico described his visit to the tomb as follows:

This design is the tomb of Rachel near Bethlehem, one mile out on the Jerusalem side, and it is about 60 steps off the road to the west. And it seems that time, the consumer of all things, has here lost her power, for it is intact, as if had been made [*sic*] but today; the tomb according to what people say, has a

---

[54] A second edition with etchings of Jacques Callot was published in 1620.

surface of such a material that even iron cannot hurt it. I did not measure it, but from what I could judge the wall is four palms, the pilaster five square, and between one and the other ten. The arch, which looks like a little chapel and is marked with the letter B, is a place, in the center of which there is a basin built into the lower part of the wall, which basin the Muslims keep full of water almost always for the service of wayfarers. (And of these basins there are numberless ones throughout the country, where there is shortness of water, and they are legacies for their souls in conformity with their sect.) And the place is held in much veneration, and they do not wish that the Christians put a foot inside. Hence I could not measure it, but I have represented it as best I could to preserve a record of such an antiquity.[55]

Amico's comment that Christians were not allowed marks a critical change. Under the Ottoman government an attitude of exclusivity has prevailed. Thus it is not surprising that the number of pilgrim reports drops at this time.[56]

Drawing of Amico—year 1610

[55] T. Bellorini, E. Hoade, and B. Bagatti, *Fra Bernardino Amico, Plans of the Sacred Edifices of the Holy Land* (Jerusalem, 1953) 62.

[56] Janin also notes the disapproval of pilgrimages by Protestant reformers such as Luther and Calvin as a factor in the diminished pilgrim trade, 149.

The next renovation takes place in 1615 at the hands of Mohammed Pasha of Jerusalem, an Ottoman-appointed official.[57] By walling up the arches, the resulting structure resembled the common Muslim funerary shrines called *weli* that dot the Middle East landscape.

For the next two centuries we are left with the single testimony in 1697, from Henry Maundrell, the chaplain of the British Levant Company in Aleppo, Syria, who spent two months in Jerusalem. His journal became the most popular guidebook of the era with no less than seven English editions and several translations published within the next fifty years.[58] Concerning Rachel's Tomb he wrote: "Rachel's Tomb. This may probably be the true place of her internment, mentioned in Gen. XXXV.19; but the present sepulchral monument can be none of that which Jacob erected; for it appears plainly to be a modern and Turkish structure.[59]

[57] Linda Kay Davidson and David M. Gitlitz date the renovations to 1615 in *Pilgrimage: From the Ganges to Graceland* (Santa Barbara, CA: ABC-Clio, 2002) 511. Howard R. Berlin, "Vignettes on the Banknotes of the Palestine Currency Board," http://www.drberlin.com/palestine/vignette.htm. Lombardi's date of 1560 precedes Amico's open-arch drawing and thus is too early, 246.

[58] Janin, 154–56.

[59] Wright, 456.

CHAPTER 8

The Modern Age: Contributions and Control in the Nineteenth and Twentieth Centuries

The Age of Exploration and Research

When Napoleon attacked Egypt in 1799, his motives were purely for conquest. The Napoleon attacks moved up the coast to the city of Acre until he was finally defeated in 1802. This marked a new era for European involvement in the Middle East. The Ottoman Empire had proven vulnerable and Palestine seemed up for grabs. The first reaction from within was a consolidation of forces by Egypt so that by 1831 the Egyptian Muhammad Ali Pasha had occupied Palestine, threatening Ottoman stability. For ten years, his son Ibrahim Pasha ruled Palestine with a central and modern administration that was open to contacts with the West. In 1838, the British Consulate was established in Jerusalem, soon followed by France, Russia, Prussia, Austria, Spain, Greece, Sardinia, and the United States.[1] While France threw its support behind Egyptian rule, British Foreign Officer Lord Palmerston preferred resumption of Ottoman control as a window for further British influence in the region.[2] Eventually an agreement was reached at the London Conference

[1] James Finn, the British Consul during the 1840s and 1850s, records his memoirs in *Stirring Times, or Records from Jerusalem Consular Chronicles of 1853–1856*, 2 volumes (London: C. Kegan Paul, 1878); see especially vol. 1, 84–100. The British, along with the Prussians, were responsible for the first Protestant schools and hospitals. The United States Consul in Beirut continued to look after concerns for the entire region until 1857 when a consulate was established in Jerusalem.

[2] Sir Charles Webster, *The Foreign Policy of Palmerston 1830–1841, Britain, the Liberal Movement and the Eastern Question*, vol. 2 (New York: Humanities Press, 1969) 753–76.

of 1841 whereby Muhammad Ali and his successors were allowed sole control over Egypt, while the Turkish Sultan regained authority over Palestine. The price for the Ottomans was the acceptance of a number of reforms, including the land reform act of 1856 and concessions to Christians for a measure of self-rule. The Ottomans followed with a series of statements concerning religious toleration, some carried out in practice and others virtually ignored. Over the coming decades, Western influence grew significantly in the Holy Land.

The result was a resurgence of visitors from the West throughout the nineteenth century. This included traditional pilgrims but also Protestant visitors who desired to get in touch with biblical lands. Still others came for the purpose of exploration and research, many of them with a more secular attitude and many with critical questions.

There were some from the West who found it difficult to resonate with the life and culture of the Middle East, including its religious shrines. Such was the American Mark Twain, who did not show much interest when visiting the tomb in 1867. After a detailed report about Mar Saba monastery, the Church of the Nativity, Shepherd's Fields, and the Milk Grotto, he hardly mentions this short stop: "We got away from Bethlehem and its troops of beggars and relic-peddlers in the afternoon, and after spending some little time at Rachel's tomb, hurried to Jerusalem as fast as possible."[3] While others such as the sixteenth-century visitor Richard Torkington reported that "we passyd fast by" the tomb, our knowledge of Mark Twain suggests that his "some little time" betrays his questioning attitude and lack of patience at such commemorative sites.

For some visitors the question of authenticity of these many biblical sites was in question. A German woman named Ida Pfeiffer betrays her skepticism by the use of quotation marks around the title "Rachel's Tomb." It seems that she, too, did not stop to walk around on her 1842 visit. After an hour and a half horse ride from Jerusalem past Mar Elias and other sites, she briefly notes, "On the right hand we passed 'Rachel's grave,' a ruined building with a small cupola."[4] It did not seem to impress her. The building appeared in a state of ruin even though, as we shall soon see, major renovations had been recently carried out. Pfeiffer did not inspect the shrine but was content to pass by without stopping.

---

[3] Mark Twain, *The Innocents Abroad* (New York: Oxford University Press, 1996) 602.

[4] Madame Ida Pfeiffer, *Visit to the Holy Land, Egypt, and Italy*, trans. by H. W. Dulcke, 1842; online at http://www.gutenberg.org/files/12561/12561.txt.

For Jesse Amos Spencer in 1850, however, the edifice reminded him of the "hundreds of tombs of Mohammedan saints in various parts of the country."[5] For C. W. M. van de Velde during his 1852 visit, however, the tomb "makes no small appearance, with its white plastered dome, which has been often renewed, as travelers inform us."[6] His greater concern is how the present tomb fits with the geography of the 1 Samuel 10 account that locates Rachel's Tomb north of Jerusalem.[7] He approaches the dilemma with a modern critical mind.

Another visitor, Mrs. G. L. Dawson Damer of Britain, also raised the question of authenticity, but answered in the affirmative: "The spot is, I believe, correctly chosen as the place of her internment, but the building itself does not appear of an ancient construction."[8] When she passed by Rachel's Tomb on December 4, 1839, she had already explored Greece, Turkey, and Egypt, and thus could contrast this small structure with the antiquities of other lands. Others would note specifically that the style was typical of the contemporary Muslim funeral shrines known as *welies*, not what one would expect for a structure from the biblical period.

The visits for this period thus often give attention to detail in describing the structure. Such was the case with British Diplomat William Turner who visited Rachel's Tomb in 1817. He wrote:

> At a quarter past nine we left St. Elias, and riding along low mountains, by roads of stone, at twenty-five minutes before ten stopped at a building, which is called the tomb of Rachel, which is about half a mile north of Bethlehem. It is a small square building, with a dome at the top, which though it has been often repaired, is said by the Jews, who pay it great veneration, to be excessively ancient. The entrance is, by a door not above three feet high. The tomb within (which is white-washed, and covered with Jewish names) is of the shape ∩ and is ten feet three inches long, four feet ten inches broad, and about nine feet high. A little to the right of the tomb the Turks have constructed a small fabric of stone to pray on, for they also have a great veneration for this tomb. It stands on a small hill, which like the mountains round, is planted

[5] Jesse Amos Spencer, *The East: Sketches of Travel in Egypt and the Holy Land* (New York: George P. Putnam, 1850) 369.

[6] C. W. M. van de Velde, *Narrative of a Journey through Syria and Palestine in 1851 and 1852*, vol. II (London: William Blackwood and Sons, 1854) 10.

[7] Ibid., 50–53.

[8] Mrs. G. L. Dawson Damer, *Diary of a Tour in Greece, Turkey, Egypt, and the Holy Land*, vol. 2 (London: Henry Colburn, Publisher, 1841) 2.

with olive trees. After stopping here a quarter of an hour, we continued our road to Bethlehem.[9]

Turner's interjection, "is said by the Jews," suggests that his observations have been informed by Jewish worshipers who were present at the site. The monument indeed is a composite, having "been often repaired," and one can distinguish portions constructed by the Ottoman Turks. Still, his language, "is called the tomb of Rachel" and "is said by the Jews," suggests that he may not have been completely convinced.

One of the first Americans to visit the tomb was John Lloyd Stephens, who in 1836 took along "a Christian boy" to point out the sites. While expressing more of a sense of awe and wonder, Stephens demonstrates the new critical spirit, raising the question "whether it be her tomb or not." He writes:

> The first was the tomb of Rachel, a large building, with a whitened dome, and having within it a high, oblong monument built of brick and stuccoed over. I dismounted and walked round the tomb, inside and out, and again resumed my journey. All that we know in regard to this tomb is that Rachel died when journeying with Jacob from Sychem to Hebron and that Jacob buried her near Bethlehem; whether it be her tomb or not, I could not but remark that, while youth and beauty have faded away and the queens of the East have died and been forgotten and Zenobia and Cleopatra sleep in unknown graves, year after year thousands of pilgrims are thronging to the supposed last resting place of a poor Hebrew woman.[10]

This was the beginning of the age of modern archaeology. Sometime during the 1820s, in the process of some repair work, workers began digging down at the foot of the monument and were surprised not to find a cavity where they expected the actual grave of Rachel. In a makeshift archaeological dig, they explored further to find no such cavity. However, they did find an uncommonly deep cavern some distance from the tomb which apparently satisfied their curiosity for the original resting place of Rachel. This was not part of an official archaeological report but was included from the local memory by Rabbi Joseph Schwarz who lived in Jerusalem during the mid-nineteenth century. Schwarz, who published his study in 1850, says that this exploration took place about twenty-five years earlier.[11]

---

[9] William Turner, *Journal of a Tour in the Levant*, vol. 2 (London: J. Murray, 1820) 235.

[10] John Lloyd Stephens, *Incidents of Travel in Egypt, Arabia Petraea and the Holy Land*, reprint edition (Mineola, NY: Dover Publications, 1996) 339.

[11] Rabbi Joseph Schwarz, *A Descriptive Geography and Brief Historical Sketch of Palestine*, trans. by Isaac Leeser (Philadelphia: A. Hart, 1850) 110.

In 1838, the well-known archaeologist Edward Robinson paid a visit to Rachel's Tomb as part of a general survey of biblical sites that he documented and published, bringing a new enthusiasm to readers in the West. Something, however, had happened to Rachel's Tomb as well as other biblical sites. On January 1, 1837, a major earthquake rocked the region, destroying a number of complete villages and doing damage to old stone buildings.[12] Robinson is the first of several visitors to note the effects on this shrine. His volume has all the marks of a scientific journal, noting even his arrival at Rachel's Tomb at 4:25 in the afternoon followed by his visit to Mar Elias monastery at 4:55. It was long enough to make several observations while jotting down a few notes:

> Someways up the general acclivity, where here rises towards the northeast from Wady Ahmed, stands the Kubbet Râhîl, or Rachel's Tomb, which we reached at 4.25. This is merely an ordinary Muslim Wely, or tomb of a holy person; a small square building of stone with a dome, and within it a tomb in the ordinary Muhammedan form; the whole plastered over with mortar. Of course the building is not ancient; in the seventh century there was here only a pyramid of stones. It is now neglected and falling to decay; though pilgrimages are still made to it by the Jews. The naked walls are covered with names in several languages; many of them in Hebrew.[13]

Following these observations, he does raise the question of "the general correctness of the tradition" about Rachel, concluding that it is authentic because of its agreement with the Genesis account and because of citations by the Bordeaux Pilgrim and Jerome. In footnotes he estimates the age of the current structure and provides further documentation.

Further geographic surveys and historical reports listed Rachel's Tomb in their catalog of biblical sites. These include the 1872 survey by Conder and Kitchener:

> Kubbet Rahîl (Mu).—A Modern Moslem building stands over the site, and there are Jewish graves near it . . . The Kubbeh is now a square building, with a court on the east. The original building (as represented in some of the older views) was open, with four arcades (one on each face) supporting the

---

[12] Rev. John F. Lanneau, "Letter from Jerusalem: The Earthquake in Syria," *Adams Sentinel* (Gettysburg, PA, June 12, 1837). According to Joseph Schwarz, 407, fifteen hundred Jews in Safed lost their lives to that catastrophe.

[13] Edward Robinson, *Biblical Researches in Palestine, Mount Sinai and Arabia Petraea*, vol. 1 (Boston, 1841) 218.

dome. These have been filled in except on the east, where a second chamber has been built on. The original square building measures 23 feet side, the arcades having a span of 10 feet. The height is approximately 20 feet, not including the dome, which rises another 10 feet. The chamber added to the east measures 13 feet east and west, by 23 feet north and south externally. The covered court, east of this again, has a window and mihrab on the south, and a double window on the east. On the north is a low wall. The court measures about 23 feet square, and is used as a praying-place by Moslems. The inner chambers, entered by a door, of which the key is kept by the Jews, are visited by Jewish men and women on Fridays. The inmost chamber under the dome contains a cenotaph of modern appearance.[14]

Precise scientific measurements are provided and an attempt is made to distinguish the various phases of building. In the paragraphs that follow, the surveyors also raise the question of authenticity and answer in the affirmative, listing as evidence a selection of historical citations.

With the great influx of travelers, there arose a need for good critical guidebooks. In 1876, Karl Baedeker produced one of the first modern critical guidebooks that became the standard for visitors in the late nineteenth century. He included the following excerpt on Rachel's Tomb:

After 9 minutes a road diverges to the right, leading to Hebron and the Pools of Solomon (p. 253). To the right here stands an insignificant building styled the Tomb of Rachel (Arabic: *Kubbet Rahil*). The dome of the tomb closely resembles those of the innumerable Muslim welies (p. 35), and the whitened sarcophagus is apparently modern. The entrance is on the N. side. The tomb is revered by Muslims, Christians and Jews, and is much visited by pilgrims, especially of the last-named faith. The walls are covered with the names of these devotees. The tradition appears to agree with the Bible narrative. Rachel died on the route to Ephratha (Bethlehem), in giving birth to Benjamin, and was buried "on the way" (Gen. xxxv. 19). Throughout the whole of the Christian period the tradition has always attached to the same spot, and for many centuries the supposed tomb was marked by a pyramid of stones, of which the number was said to have been twelve, corresponding with the twelve tribes of Israel. The monument seems to have been altered in the 15th cent., since that time it has been completely restored. A serious objection to the genuineness of the tomb, however, is founded on the passage 1 Samuel

[14] Capt. C. R. Conder and Capt. H. H. Kitchener, *The Survey of Western Palestine: Memoirs of the Topography, Orography, Hydrography and Archaeology*, vol. III (London: Palestine Exploration Fund, 1872) 129.

x.2, where the boundary between Judah and Benjamin could not, for many reasons, have passed this way, it is more probable that the tomb lay on the N. side of Jerusalem.[15]

Unlike earlier guides, Baedeker provides much more detail from a critical perspective. So the "supposed" tomb is likely historically inaccurate, giving way to the strong evidence for Rachel's Tomb in the northern tradition.

Baedeker's critical guide is in stark contrast to visitors of the Middle Ages who had often approached the tomb only in a devotional sense and not with a critical eye. This latter view still continued among evangelicals in the nineteenth century. For William Rae Wilson, who traveled to the Holy Land from London in 1823, the Bible was his guide. His diary for the fifth of February states that, while making his way from Jerusalem to Bethlehem, he fell in dismay when his servant dropped his Bible on the road. With his trip delayed to retrieve the lost Bible, Wilson had to hurry past Rachel's Tomb, but he entered into the written text a list of pertinent Bible passages that for him brought the monument to life.[16]

For visitors like Wilson, another kind of guidebook was in order, such as the one prepared by the Irishman Josias Leslie Porter. First serving as a missionary in Damascus in 1849, his travels extended into Galilee and Jerusalem over the next decades. In 1858, he published his guide to the Holy Land as part of the popular *Murray's Handbooks Series*. "It is one of the few shrines which Muslims, Jews, and Christians agree in honouring, and concerning which their traditions are identical," he writes concerning Rachel's Tomb.[17] He describes the building as "a small white square building, surmounted by a dome" and he provides the Genesis passages for the reader to meditate on during the visit. Although this is an era of the rise of biblical criticism, Porter conflates the contrasting biblical traditions. In referring to the nearby village of Beit Jala he asks, "Is not this the Zelzah mentioned by Samuel in sending Saul home after anointing him king at Ramah?"[18] Later in his section on Kirjath-jearim, he sketches out what for him must be the southern border of

[15] Karl Baedeker, *Jerusalem and Its Surroundings: Handbook for Travelers* (London: Dulau and Co., 1876).

[16] William Rae Wilson, *Travels in Egypt and the Holy Land* (London: Longman, Hurst, Rees, Orme, and Brown, 1823) 210–12.

[17] Josias Leslie Porter, *A Handbook for Travellers in Syria and Palestine*, Part I (London: John Murray, 1858) 74.

[18] Ibid.

Benjamin—"a crooked one it is true," he notes—beginning north of Jerusalem at Kirjath-jearim, cutting south along the edge of Beit Jala and Rachel's Tomb, and then heading northeastward to the Jordan River.[19] In 1886, Porter, now the president of Queen's College in Belfast, published another introduction for pilgrims, focusing on Jerusalem, Bethany, and Bethlehem. Much is word-for-word from his handbook three decades earlier. His question quoted above about Zelzah is now formulated as a statement and the reader is instructed about the Bible passages that "will be read on the spot." Still, he is impressed in the way that Muslims, Christians, and Jews were able to share this tomb.[20]

The guidebooks conveyed a similar message to hundreds of Westerners during the mid 1800s. Their goal was to connect the visitor with the biblical story. Certainly there is a different kind of piety for the Protestants of Western Europe and the United States when compared to earlier Orthodox, Armenian, and Catholic pilgrims. So in most of the modern diaries and journals, there is a silence when it comes to the element of a Christian experience of worship and prayer.

Not so for Rev. Moses Margoliouth who visited in 1848. For his May 12 visit to Rachel's Tomb in the company of a Mr. Woodstock and two missionaries of the London Jewish Society, Mr. Nicolayson and Mr. Synianki, he describes how "we chanted, in a melancholy strain, the words of Jeremiah, quoted by St. Matthew: 'A voice was heard on high, lamentations and bitter weeping; Rachel weeping for her children.'"[21] Only then did they proceed to Bethlehem.

Another message that often comes through is that Rachel's Tomb was a living monument where the local population found respite and quiet from the daily routine. This was underscored already in the 1817 visit of William Turner who offered both a physical description of the site and observations about those who came there for prayer. Edward Robinson had noted that Jews continued to make pilgrimage to this site and to leave their mark in graffiti in Hebrew characters. Conder and Kitchener called attention to the *mihrab* where Muslims said their prayers.

---

[19] Ibid., 285.

[20] J. L. Porter, *Jerusalem, Bethany, and Bethlehem* (London: Nelson, 1886) 114–16.

[21] Rev. Moses Margoliouth, *A Pilgrimage to the Land of My Fathers* (London: Richard Bentley, 1850) 377–78, 401.

Mrs. Damer's 1839 diary noted a funeral taking place at the tomb on the day of her visit. Intrigued by the rituals of the large number of participants, she wrote: "An Arab funeral was taking place close to it, attended by about fifty wild and starved-looking Arabs. The only ceremonial appeared to consist in each individual contributing a stone towards raising a mound, which had gained considerable elevation when we passed it a few hours afterwards, on our return from Bethlehem."[22] Others comment on the cemetery as a visible sign of the importance of this monument to the local community. Rev. Daniel Garver, who made the trip by horseback on November 27, 1857, like many before him, summarized in his journal the Genesis story and recounted other biblical references. Then he continued: "This spot is regarded with veneration by all classes of people and it is esteemed a great honor to be buried near the dust of the patriarch's wife. Hence all around we see Jewish and Mohammedan graves. A small stone building, surmounted by a dome is erected over her grave."[23]

One visitor from the mid-nineteenth century left a visible representation that managed to connect the ancient monument with contemporary adherents to the shrine. William Henry Bartlett was an artist who, intrigued by the descriptions of Edward Robinson, visited the biblical sites to record his impression both on canvas and on paper. His 1842 painting has been described as a realistic depiction of the tomb several decades before the first photograph.[24] Bartlett's painting shows in typical fashion a domed main cubical chamber and an arched side room on the south with a small vestibule in the front. Described in his prose as a "Turkish mosque," the tomb stands in open country with the village of Beit Jala on a hillside in the distance. Yet the scene is one of warmth with contemporary travelers, an Arab mother and child on a camel guided by her husband, approaching the sacred space where others rest outside and yet another stands in the doorway. It is a living shrine, not merely a monument of stone. Bartlett's own prose notes that the individuals captured on canvas were indeed present on the day of his visit, inspiring him to make mental connections

[22] Damer, 2.

[23] Rev. Daniel Garver, "Visit to Hebron and Bethlehem," *Ohio Repository*, Canton, OH, July 7, 1859; online at http://www.shalomjerusalem.com/jerusalem/jerusalem27_1858-59.html.

[24] Rechavam Zeevy, "Introduction to Reprint," W. H. Bartlett, *Walks about the City and Environs of Jerusalem* (Jerusalem: Canaan Publishing House, 1974), first published in London in 1844.

with their ancestors in the biblical era. In reading this account, it is impossible to avoid the conclusion that such a visit for the Western pilgrim was indeed a religious experience. Bartlett's *Walks about the City and Environs of Jerusalem* became quite influential during the nineteenth century both as an illustrated introduction to the biblical stories for churches in England and as a guidebook among visitors to the Holy Land. It became quite apparent through works like these that Rachel's Tomb was a shrine that was shared by Christians, Muslims, and Jews alike.

Finally, we have a rather lengthy report of American travelers to the Holy Land at the end of the nineteenth century. A certain B. W. Johnson wrote a travelogue describing his visit to Bethlehem:

> After Jerusalem and Nazareth there was no place that we were so eager to see; hence when Mr. Crunden announced that we were to take an afternoon drive to Bethlehem, the boys raised a shout of joy.
>
> "But can we make a visit in an afternoon?" asked Will. "How far is it?"
>
> "We surely ought to," replied Bayard. "It is only six miles south of here, on the road to Hebron."
>
> "O, yes," retorted Will. "I will suspect you have just got that out of Baedeker; I saw you studying up a moment ago."
>
> We were not going on horseback. We were going to vary our usual style of travel by taking our first drive in Palestine. Hence, just after noon a lot of rickety-looking carriages were drawn up near the Jaffa Gate, for our party. . . .
>
> Three horses, all harnessed abreast, were hitched to each other, and a driver who looked like a Bedouin, handled the whip and lines. As we found after we had started, their great delight was to race, and to try to drive around each other. I believe that we passed other carriages, and were also driven around by others, a dozen times. . . .
>
> Driving rapidly over the plain, gazing on either hand on hills, plains, valleys, and places which have been the scenes of sacred story, we paused about a mile from Bethlehem at a fountain by the roadside, shaded with trees, under which stands a curious Mohammedan mosque. "What place is this?"
>
> "This," was the reply of our Dragoman, "is the Tomb of Rachel."
>
> There is something very touching in the simple Bible story of her death . . . [Jacob] refers very tenderly to the story of his loss: "As for me, when I came

from Padan, Rachel died by me in the land of Canaan in the way, when yet there was but a little way to Ephrath, and I buried her there in the way of Ephrath; the same is Bethlehem" (Gen. 48.7).

The pillar placed here by the mourning old patriarch has long since passed away, but Jew and Mohammedan and Christian are agreed that it is the spot where the mother of Joseph and Benjamin was buried. How real old Jacob and his family seem to us as we read the Bible story and see them weeping over their beloved dead. Human hearts thirty-five hundred years ago were much the same as now, and human sorrows have always been the same. . . .[25]

In many ways, the focus in this report is clearly on the hard physical stones characterized here as "a curious Mohammedan mosque." Yet Mr. Johnson's empathy for human grief and sorrow helps to explain his recognition of the shared nature of this shrine. Human hearts in Johnson's day were no different than in the day of Jacob and Rachel. Sorrows have been the same. So it was that pilgrims and locals alike, adherents of all three monotheistic religions, found Rachel's Tomb accessible, located as it was along the side of the road.

The Jewish Contribution

This historical survey demonstrates that the ever-developing Rachel's Tomb has been the product of many hands, first the Greco-Roman architect who erected the pyramid structure probably in the first century c.e.; then the Christian builder who erected pillars and a dome in the twelfth-century Crusader structure; then Muslim renovations under the Saracens in the thirteenth century and by Muhammed Pasha of Jerusalem in 1615. It is only appropriate that the next changes be undertaken by Jews.

To be sure, Jewish interest in the Bethlehem monument went a long way back in history. This is clear from the accumulations of midrash and from the visits of pilgrims like Rabbi Benjamin of Tudela and Rabbi Petachia of Ratisbon. Clearly, there were many other unnamed Jewish visitors over the centuries, just as there were Christians and Muslims. Three Jewish pilgrims in particular can be named from the first three centuries following the Crusades. Samuel ben Samson visited the tomb in 1210 shortly after

[25] B. W. Johnson, *Young Folks in Bible Lands* (St. Louis: Christian Publishing Co., 1892), excerpts from chapter 12.

the Muslims recaptured Jerusalem. "On our way to Hebron we came to the sepulcher of our mother Rachel. Journeying on from that tomb, we found the sepulcher of Nathan the Prophet, where there is a mosque."[26] He only mentions the tomb in passing, but the attribution to Rachel as "our mother" clearly shows an attitude of devotion. In 1334, Isaac ben Joseph ibn Chelo is the first to note the practice of the Jerusalem Jewish community of visiting the tomb on the eve of Yom Kippur: "On the eve of the day of the great pardon they all resort to the tombs of Rachel and of Nathan the Prophet to perform their devotions there. I have visited these two tombs. The first is a monument composed of twelve stones, surmounted by a cupola also of stone. I have prayed for you and for myself on the sepulcher of our mother Rachel."[27] From his letter back to family in Italy in 1488, Rabbi Obadiah Jaré da Bertinoro notes that prayer was acceptable also for the occasional Jewish visitor: "On Tuesday morning, the 13th of Nisan, we left Hebron, which is a day's journey distant from Jerusalem, and came on as far as Rachel's tomb, where there is a round, vaulted building in the open road. We got down from our asses and prayed at the grave, each one according to his ability."[28] Such accounts underscore the open attitude of the Muslim caretakers of Rachel's Tomb during this period.

The comments of Amico a century later that spoke of Muslim exclusivity must be weighed carefully. Perhaps they marked a change of policy under the Ottomans. Perhaps the issue centered more on Amico's activities of measuring and drawing the tomb. To be sure he mentions nothing of a visit for the purpose of prayer and devotion. Yet even assuming limited access to the tomb by Christians—perhaps Jews were given more access than Christians—in the early Ottoman period, that policy did not last.[29]

Gradually, Ottoman control over Palestine waned and the Turkish rulers became more concerned about protecting the center of their crumbling empire. Through the later Ottoman period the attitudes of local Muslims

---

[26] Adler, 104.

[27] Ibid., 135–36.

[28] He emigrated from Italy to Palestine in 1487. This selection comes from a letter written in 1488, the first of three letters from Palestine. Adler, 234.

[29] Linda Kay Davidson and David M. Gitlitz are totally misleading in stating, "After they [Muslims] took control of the Holy Land, they did not allow others to visit the tomb until 1615, when the pasha of Jerusalem made repairs to the structure and gave Jews the right to its exclusive use," in *Pilgrimage: From the Ganges to Graceland* (Santa Barbara, CA: ABC-Clio, 2002) 511.

became much more tolerant of others. There were, of course, exceptions to the rule. Bethlehemites still talk about an eighteenth-century Arab Sheik who was known to harass them on a regular basis, yet it was the Muslim village of Fagour five miles to the south that came to the aid of the still exclusively Christian town of Bethlehem. As a result, Muslims were invited to settle in the southwest section of Bethlehem for the first time. Such actions point to a new era of openness between Christians and Muslims in the area around Rachel's Tomb.

The seventeenth century, however, was marked by a decline in Jewish settlement in Palestine.[30] The difficulties of the Jerusalem Jewish community were publicized when the Messianic pretender Shabbetai Tzevi visited Jerusalem in 1662.[31] Yet by the time of the death of the Baal Shem Tov in 1760, a new wave of Hasidic pilgrimages increased, especially on chartered ships during the summer months.[32] It was about this time that a record appears concerning Jewish interest in the upkeep of Rachel's tomb, though it comes as a negative report. A letter dated 27 Av 5519 (March 1756) notes a dispute between the Jerusalem Jewish community and the Istanbul Jewish Committee for the Jews of Palestine. When Elijah Samnun of Jerusalem had used committee funds to fix a wall at Rachel's Tomb, the Istanbul committee questioned whether this expenditure was proper in view of the many pressing needs of the Jerusalem community. The letter from Istanbul instructed that Samnun repay the sum of five hundred *kurus* from his own pocket.[33]

A significant change occurs with the arrival of Western Jews. Among them was Moses Montefiore, who is credited by an inscription within the tomb with the next major renovation. A successful London entrepreneur, Montefiore (1784–1883) was well known for his philanthropic work and his tireless efforts and travels to support world Jewry. Having a special place in his heart for Jerusalem and its Jewish population, he made no less than eight trips to the Holy Land, documented by diaries written by Montefiore himself and his wife Judith. The Montefiores' first voyage to the Middle East lasted nearly ten months from May 1, 1827, to February 20, 1828, including eight days in the Holy Land (October 16–23). Most of their

---

[30] Jacob Barnai, *The Jews in Palestine in the Eighteenth Century: Under the Patronage of the Istanbul Committee of Officials for Palestine*, trans. Naomi Goldblum (Tuscaloosa, AL: University of Alabama Press, 1992) 54.

[31] Gershom Scholem, *Sabbatai Sevi: The Mystical Messiah* (New York: Littman, 1997).

[32] Barnai, 27, 37.

[33] Ibid., 120, 251.

visit was restricted to Jerusalem, but on Friday, October 19, when Moses Montefiore was consumed with business in Jerusalem, Judith took a day trip to visit the Church of the Nativity in Bethlehem. Along the way she encountered Rachel's Tomb as recorded in her private diary:

> The road was rocky; but fig, olive, and mulberry-trees adorned many of the hills, and the declivities were covered with a gay harvest of the most beautiful wild flowers. After an hour's ride we came to Rachael's tomb, which stands in a valley on the right, near to which is a well at present without water. We dismounted to view this most interesting monument of sacred history. It is formed of four square walls, with Gothic arches bricked up, and is covered by a dome-roof.

With this initial visit, Lady Montefiore began her love affair with Rachel's tomb. Her language is nothing but positive, describing the tomb in an almost idyllic setting of fruit and olive trees and wildflowers. The description of the building is similar to that of earlier visitors: the dome-roof and the bricked-up arches. There is not a hint of any deteriorating condition. She continues:

> On entering I was deeply impressed with a feeling of awe and respect, standing, as I thus did, in the sepulcher of a mother in Israel. The walls of the interior are covered with names and phrases chiefly in Hebrew and other Eastern characters; but some few English are to be found among them, and to these I added the names of Montefiore and myself. My feelings of gratitude on this occasion were not a little increased by a knowledge of the circumstance, that only six European females are said to have visited Palestine in the course of a century.[34]

Along with her youthful idealism Lady Montefiore provides an emotional response, pointing to a living monument that continues to instill feelings of awe, respect, and gratitude. It was not merely an edifice to gaze at, but a shrine to enter and pray. Like Robinson, she notes the graffiti on the wall, evidence that the shrine was still used by Muslims and Jews alike. In her

---

[34] Judith Montefiore, *Private Journal of a Visit to Egypt and Palestine: 1827* (London: 1836) 206. This 322-page 1836 edition was privately printed and circulated only in narrow circles. In 1975, a one-hundred-page selection was photocopied and published: Israel Bartal, ed., Judith Montefiore, *Private Journal of a Visit to Egypt and Palestine: 1827* (Jerusalem: Yad Izhak Ben Zvi, 1975). In this edition, the selection quoted occurs on page 83. Bartal notes that "unlike other diaries and writings, it was not tampered with by translators nor by others who sought to alter it." Bartal, "Introduction," 1. The official diaries of the Montefiores would be edited and published six decades later.

final comment Lady Montefiore gives a reminder about the role of women in this era. Few European women had visited this site. Even though she was a well-educated woman and a person of stature in her own right, her role is that of Montefiore's representative. Along with her own name, she inscribes also that of her absent husband.

The Montefiores' second trip to the Middle East in 1839 included a more extensive itinerary from Galilee in the north to Hebron in the south. Here we no longer have Judith's own report, but the published and edited excerpts from the Montefiore diaries:

> *Friday, June 14*: With feelings of deep regret we left the Mount of Olives for Hebron, and after three hours' journey reached Rachel's Tomb. Seeing that it was greatly out of repair and going fast to ruin, Lady Montefiore gave directions for an estimate for its restoration to be made. Half way to Hebron we rested for an hour near a fortress and a great reservoir.[35] Our route lay through a mountainous country, little cultivated. On the summit of a mountain at some distance we saw the tombs of Nathan the prophet and Gad the seer. About an hour's ride from Hebron we were met by the representatives of the Hebrew community. . . .[36]

On this visit both Moses and Judith were present as part of a trip from Jerusalem to Hebron, and one senses a different tone. The journey from Jerusalem takes three times as long, the landscape is uncultivated, and the tomb lies in ruins.[37] Of course, the January 1, 1837, earthquake had intervened.[38] There is no description of the tomb and no sense that this is an active religious site. While an inscription inside the current structure credits Moses Montefiore with remodeling the tomb, it seems that it was his wife, Lady Judith Montefiore, who had a special place in her heart for this monument. This is substantiated by the 1839 entry: "Lady Montefiore gave directions for an estimate for its restoration to be made."[39] Moses Montefiore is present, but not a word records his impressions or even his actions.

[35] Likely Solomon's pools.

[36] L. Loewe, ed., *Diaries of Sir Moses and Lady Montefiore* (in two volumes), vol. 1 (Chicago: Belford-Clarke Co., 1890) 182.

[37] This final assessment is in agreement with Robinson, 218.

[38] Rev. John F. Lanneau, "Letter from Jerusalem: The Earthquake in Syria," *Adams Sentinel* (Gettysburg, PA, June 12, 1837).

[39] George Collard very briefly mentions this visit ("stopping en route at Rachel's Tomb where Lady Montefiore gave orders for its restoration") in *Moses, the Victorian Jew* (Oxford: The Kensall Press, 1990) 87.

In reality, there is surprisingly little about Rachel's Tomb in the two-volume edited summary of the Montefiore diaries. Although they passed this way on several visits going from Jerusalem to Hebron, only in 1839 is there a report of stopping at the tomb, and then it is for only a relatively short period of time, perhaps an hour or so. Even Judith's 1827 entry is omitted from the later edited collection. There are no reports in the diaries concerning the completion of the tomb, nor is there any mention in Montefiore's 1925 biography.[40]

The diaries do record, however, that later during the 1839 visit, the Montefiores traveled to Alexandria, Egypt, where on July 13, Montefiore met with the Mohammad Ali Pasha to discuss a list of projects. These included rebuilding the wall of Tiberias; land acquisition to help Jews in Safed economically; and proposals for improvement in human rights. He offered to transfer a sum of one million English pounds to carry out these projects and perhaps others unmentioned.[41] Rachel's Tomb, which would have been considered relatively minor, was not mentioned specifically in the list of projects. Yet presumably Muhammad Ali, who now controlled Palestine, held ultimate responsibility for any improvements just as it was the local Pasha who carried out the renovations of 1615.

This, of course, was an extremely volatile time in Palestine. Although Montefiore's visit was facilitated by his close connections with the British government and their newly established consul in Jerusalem, the situation would soon change. During Holy Week 1840, in Damascus, there was a strange disappearance of a Christian priest. With growing anti-Semitism, the Christian community blamed the Jews of Damascus in the age-old accusation of the Passover blood libel, claiming it to be a ritual murder. Ibrahim Pasha, the Egyptian governor now in control also of Palestine and Syria, was too eager to accept this explanation, and Jews were rounded up and imprisoned in hope of a confession. Perhaps this would have been only a regional issue had Montefiore not recently completed his visit to the region. His dismay over this event, probably more than any other, pushed him to greater activism on behalf of Jews in the Middle East as throughout the world. At his prompting, British, as well as American pressure, brought about the

---

[40] Paul Goodman, *Moses Montefiore* (Philadelphia: The Jewish Publication Society of America, 1925).

[41] Loewe, *Diaries*, I, 196–203.

release of the Jewish detainees.[42] He subsequently met with British Foreign Secretary Lord Palmerston, whose London conference of 1841 led to the withdrawal of Egypt from Palestine. Palmerston then wrote to the Ottoman Sultan, who was now back in control of Palestine, encouraging him to allow a greater role for Jews in Palestine as a way of keeping the Egyptian Pasha in check.[43] Presumably this train of events played a significant role in Montefiore securing permission for the renovation of Rachel's Tomb.

The date of Montefiore's renovations of Rachel's Tomb is made clear by Rabbi Joseph Schwarz who resided at this time in Jerusalem. He stated: "In the year 5601 [1841], Sir Moses Montefiore, of London, caused the same to be entirely renovated, furnished it with a cupola, and an entrance hall, so that at present it is a quite handsome building."[44] The actual renovations centered on the completion of a vestibule adjacent to the tomb itself. This second room was now enclosed with an open, arched entryway. A *mihrab* was added in the south wall for Muslims who wished to pray. The cupola, however, had already been a well-recognized feature of the tomb and likely underwent repair work. As noted earlier, William Henry Bartlett captured the newly renovated tomb on canvas in 1842.[45] It was shortly after this that photography was introduced to the Middle East. An external view of the remodeled tomb is available in an 1866 photo—the first photo on record. Compared with the numerous photos and paintings of the early twentieth century, one can easily see that there were few changes over the next century. The familiar, quaint, stone structure in an idyllic roadside setting was now fixed.

Surprisingly, the Montefiore diaries fail to mention visits to Rachel's Tomb on subsequent journeys. On their third trip, there is no report of travel south of Jerusalem. On their fourth trip in September 1855, after meeting the governor of Jerusalem concerning several other projects, including the building of a windmill outside Jerusalem, the diary mentions only their passing directly from Jerusalem to Hebron.[46] In the end, however, there is clear evidence for Judith Montefiore's attachment to the tomb.

---

[42] Abigail Green, "Rethinking Sir Moses Montefiore: Religion, Nationhood, and International Philanthropy in the Nineteenth Century," *The American Historical Review*, 110:3 (June 2005), online: http://www.historycooperative.org/journals/ahr/110.3/green.html.

[43] Lloyd Geering, "Who Owns the Holy Land?" *The Fourth R*, 15:3 (2002).

[44] Schwartz (1850), 110.

[45] W. H. Bartlett, *Walks about the City and Environs of Jerusalem* (Jerusalem: Canaan Publishing House, 1974), first published in London in 1844.

[46] Montefiore, *Diaries*, II, 54–55.

First photo of Rachel's Tomb—year 1866. Photo provided by Historic Print and Map Company.

When she died in 1862, her husband erected for her a mausoleum near the Ramsgate Synagogue in London. He had thought of burying her in Jerusalem but instead modeled her London tomb after the Bethlehem Rachel's Tomb.[47] According to one report, Moses Montefiore considered making further renovations shortly before his death in 1885, but it is not clear whether anything more was carried out.

Montefiore's role with regard to Rachel's Tomb must be considered in view of his general attitude toward human rights and religious freedom. During his visit to the Pasha in Egypt in 1839, his request for Jewish human rights fit into the larger British program of emancipation of all enslaved and oppressed peoples. Through his efforts, Christians as well as Jews improved their standing in the Middle East. Later, through his intervention for all minorities in Morocco, he was praised for demonstrating "new proof of the universal principles of the religion of which you are such a brave champion."[48] His contributions at Rachel's Tomb must be considered in

[47] Goodman, 157; Collard, 137.
[48] Green.

view of such an open attitude. This is quite clear from the fact that a *mihrab* remained in the south wall and that Muslims continued to be welcomed for prayer and for the burial of their dead in the surrounding cemetery.

Many writers emphasize Ottoman prejudice against minority religions during this period. The Crimean War fought from 1853 to 1856 was also evidence of attitudes of rigidity and obstinacy among the Holy Land's Christians. Yet there were signs of hope. On April 7, 1856—just one week after the announcement of peace—the Sultan's Edict of Toleration was read in Jerusalem. In many ways Jerusalem was already advanced in comparison to other sections of the empire. Often this was dependent upon the attitude of the Ottoman-appointed Pasha in Jerusalem. In 1845, the Pasha had offered a "profession of equality for all religions in the administration of local government."[49] Yet the Ottoman Sultans frequently changed the officeholders and the early 1850s were marked by several elderly and impotent pashas. However, in February 1855, a progressive pasha named Kiamil Pasha took office. He occasionally attended Christian worship services and made groundbreaking concessions concerning two religious sites that had previously been open only to Muslims: the *Haram* of Jerusalem with its Dome of the Rock and the Tomb of the Patriarchs in Hebron. That March he arranged special permission for the visiting king and queen of Belgium to be the first non-Muslims to set foot inside the Dome of the Rock.[50] Also, in July 1855 he made no less a concession for Moses and Judith Montefiore as the first Jewish visitors to the Dome of the Rock, and he presented Moses with a *firman* from the Sultan to build the first Ashkenazi synagogue in Jerusalem, as well as to sell land for Montefiore's economic projects.[51] Later the Prince of Wales was the first non-Muslim admitted to the Tomb of the Patriarchs,[52] and by Easter 1856 large numbers of pilgrims were admitted to the Dome of the Rock in Jerusalem.[53] As a sign of the new religious cooperation, a Muslim Durweesh, the guardian of the sepulcher of Zebulun in Galilee, together with the Rabbis of Safed, submitted a request to Montefiore to help with repairs at that patriarchal tomb.[54] This is the context in which Rachel's Tomb was shared during the middle nineteenth century.

[49] Finn, *Stirring Times*, vol. 1, 201.

[50] Finn, vol. 2, 228.

[51] Ibid., 325–35.

[52] Ibid., 338.

[53] Ibid., 413.

[54] Ibid., 339.

With regards to Rachel's Tomb itself, a wealth of information is available through the diaries and memoirs of James Finn, the British Consul to Jerusalem from 1850 to 1862. The Finn family frequently camped in tents along the highway north of Mar Elias and made family outings to Artas to the south. His records include both informal observations while passing by the tomb and summaries of an official nature. As British Consul, Finn had special responsibilities with regard to the Jewish population. Already in April 1841, Foreign Secretary Lord Palmerston had instructed Finn's predecessor to support Jews in oppression.[55] There were surely humanitarian and political motives. However, this also was the age of John Darby and a new era of Evangelical thinking about the Jews and their role in the Holy Land. In 1808, the British had established *The London Society for Promoting Christianity among the Jews*, whose president was Palmerston's own son-in-law, Lord Ashley, the Earl of Shaftesbury.[56] Elizabeth Anne Finn, the wife of the British Consul, was the daughter of a lifelong missionary of the same *London Society*. Whatever their motives, the British helped to facilitate the immigration of European Jews during the mid 1800s. Prior to Finn's time, the majority of Jerusalem Jews were Sephardic. By the end of Finn's tenure in Jerusalem, the number of Ashkenazi Jews equaled Sephardic Jews.[57] A significant number of them were elderly Russian Jews who came to Jerusalem on a one-year visa with the desire of dying in the Holy Land but then extended their stay under British protection.

In his memoirs, Finn demonstrates a sympathetic attitude toward Jews praying at the tomb. On one occasion (August 1855), he encountered such a recent immigrant along the road:

> Farther on, beyond the convent of Mount Elias, I overtook a very poor and fanatic-looking Jew (Ashkenaz), with prayer-books under his arm, proceeding to Rachel's Tomb to offer up his devotion. Just before him, and also walking, was the junior secretary of the Latin Patriarch, with clerical dress and a very broad hat; he was of course an European. The contrast between the proud step of the one, and the humble downcast look of the other, was most

[55] Ibid., vol. 1, 106–07.

[56] Geering, "Who Owns the Holy Land?" According to Mrs. Finn, "Thanks to Lord Ashley and Lord Palmerston, the British consuls were instructed to befriend in every possible way the Jews in Jerusalem and Palestine, who had no kind of European protection," Elizabeth Anne Finn, *Reminiscences of Mrs. Finn* (London: Marshall, Morgon and Scott, 1929) 34.

[57] Arnold Blumberg, *A View from Jerusalem, 1849–1858: The Consular Diary of James and Elizabeth Anne Finn* (Rutherford: Farleigh Dickinson University Press, 1980) 44–45.

remarkable. At Rachel's sepulcher I found a large assemblage of Ashkenazim, it being the last day of the month, on which day the Jews are in the habit of going thither for prayer. The Jews were thankful to be able to visit this spot as well as other graves—such as that of Simon the Just—north of Jerusalem, on stated occasions, for religious observances.[58]

Such an attitude did not go unnoticed. The key for coexistence between the newcomers from Europe and the longtime residents of the land was a posture of humility. This still came through on joyous occasions, as Finn noted:

> On the road homeward I found Jews assembling at Rachel's Sepulchre, and on my enquiring the reason they told me that Rabbi Nissim was sending out a great and beautiful *menorah* candlestick, or chandelier, to burn there in honour of 'our mother Rachel';—the companies thickened as I advanced. There were some Spanish (Sephardi) as well as German (Ashkenaz). The women were carrying oranges (plentiful at this season) and bottles of wine in handkerchiefs, and the lads were singing in chorus and clapping hands. At length came the honored candle-stick, covered with muslin. They told me that fifty candles were to be lighted. Some of the Jews were also carrying candles, vowed by themselves, to be lighted there, painted with wreaths of green and spotted with gold leaf. They were all in great glee and in best attire, it being Passover week. Some Armenian pilgrims were passing on the way to Bethlehem, and, of course, despised the Jews.[59]

Here it may be significant that Ashkenazi and Sephardic Jews had integrated in this annual Passover visit to the tomb. Although there was joy and celebration, there are also signs of respect and sensitivity. Perhaps this is how one should understand the mention of oranges purchased from the local Muslims and the wine bottles wrapped in handkerchiefs so as not to offend. On another occasion, when Finn observed a number of Bethlehem Muslims who were burying one of their dead near the tomb, he commented how they frequently carried water from Bethlehem to refresh the Jewish worshipers.[60] Generally, Muslims and Jews managed to get along fairly well in sharing the tomb of Rachel.

To be sure, there were plenty of points of friction between the various religious communities. One such episode is noted in Finn's diary for March 23, 1852: "A Mossulman appeared in the office and complained of an English

[58] Finn, *Stirring Times*, vol. 2, 37–38.

[59] Ibid., 235.

[60] Ibid., 38.

Jew—who had hired his Donkey to Rachel's tomb and returned without it. A few hours afterwards the donkey was found by a Fellah (The Jew then was requested to give a present of a few piasters to the founder [*sic*] and a few more to the owener [*sic*] for the loss of his time in looking after it (both parties were contented)."[61] This is likely simply a case of cultural insensitivity since the culprit is identified as a "British Jew" who didn't see to it that a borrowed donkey was returned. Yet with mediation the matter was quickly settled.

There were other issues that were more complex. Finn notes that in the early 1850s the Taamri tribe from east of Bethlehem required an annual fee of fifty pounds "for not injuring the Sepulchre of Rachel."[62] Relations with the Taamri, whom he called "wild Arabs" in contrast to the peaceful, settled Muslims in the Bethlehem area, apparently consumed a good deal of the consulate's time. This particular Bedouin tribe controlled the area from the Dead Sea to Bethlehem and, under the leadership of Shaik Hhamdan, was known to cause problems on a regular basis for the Christian community of Bethlehem.[63] The residents of Bethlehem solved the conflict through the help of another Muslim clan that settled alongside the Christians in Bethlehem. Finn's approach, however, was to "buy" protection from Shaik Hhamdan. This resulted generally in safe travel conditions for tourists who wished to visit the area.[64] However, when traditional life was disrupted there were often problems. Such was the case for expatriate John Meshullam, who settled south of Bethlehem at Artas, transforming pasture land into fenced gardens, removing access of precious sources of water from their flocks. Finn was frequently called upon to intervene and resorted to arrest and imprisonment to establish law and order. An entry in Finn's diary shows how this problem persisted while a weak pasha was in power in early 1855: "January 19, 1855—We also required the apprehension & imprisonment of Shaik Hamdan [*sic*] of the Taamri for extorting money with his sword drawn, from Jews at Rachel's sepulcher yesterday."[65] Following the

---

[61] Blumberg, 103.

[62] Other Bedouin groups extracted fees from the Jews for safe travel along Jaffa Road, for respect over graves near the village of Siloam, and for the right to pray at the Western Wall. Finn, vol. 1, 119. By way of comparison, Finn's own annual salary at this time was eleven times the amount the Taamri received. Finn, 98.

[63] Blumberg, 90, 101, 115, 141.

[64] Finn usually paid a fee of one pound per person. Elizabeth Anne Finn, 59.

[65] Blumberg, 185.

installation of Kiamil as Pasha of Jerusalem, the matter was finally settled several months later as Finn noted in his diary: "May 25, 1855—Shaikh Hhamdan of the Taamri warned not to exact any more tribute from Jews at Rachel's Sepulchre."[66] According to Finn's wife, "Ever after the Jews came and went in peace; they were never attacked again."[67] There were also occasions of ruffians acting as troublemakers at the tomb. Yet as the following entry in Finn's memoirs shows, it was the peaceful local Muslims that kept the troublemakers in check:

> It happened about this time on a similar occasion, some men of the village of Cufeen, on the Hebron Road—a very rough and thievish set—came by on the road and saw the Jews at Rachel's sepulcher at their prayers; they began to curse and were preparing to plunder and strip them. Some of the Bethlehem Moslems, who were in the habit of bringing the Jews water to drink on these occasions in return for backsheesh, were at the moment engaged in burying their dead near the spot; they at once called out to the would-be robbers of the Jews, 'Leave them alone; they are under English protection!' The thieves desisted, and went on their way.[68]

When considering that Finn's memoirs and diaries cover a period of over a decade, these few incidents do not seem to warrant a general picture of chaos and harassment with regard to Rachel's Tomb.[69] Even during periods of general unrest, such as occurred after the death of the Jerusalem pasha in early 1855, regular worship went on at Rachel's Tomb: "Though the peasantry were in a restless condition, the Jews were in no way molested. On the contrary, they were left in safety and undisturbed."[70]

From the descriptions of Conder, Baedecker, and others noted above, we have a picture of Jews and Muslims sharing the worship space at the tomb. The local Christian community, however, no longer seemed to have an attachment as they did prior to the Ottoman period. As for Jewish practice, the tomb was frequented on Fridays, the new moon, and Passover. Earlier

---

[66] Ibid., 194.

[67] Elizabeth Anne Finn, 73.

[68] James Finn, 38.

[69] In contrast, David S. Landes has taken Finn's single comment about Arabs extracting protection money for Rachel's Tomb as characteristic for this period, in "Palestine before the Zionists," *Commentary* (February 1976) 52. This in turn was noted uncritically in Joan Peters, *From Time Immemorial—The Origins of the Arab-Jewish Conflict over Palestine* (New York: Harper & Row, 1984) 181.

[70] Finn, *Stirring Times*, vol. 2, 235.

we read of the joyous celebration of both Sephardic and Ashkenazi Jews for Passover in the year 1855. A letter from a Jerusalem Jew named Pinchas, son of Hayim, describes the emotional prayer that took place on his visit to the Tomb in 1864:

> On the eve of the first day of Iyar, about sixteen of us went to the grave of our mother Rachel. We recited the afternoon and evening service, ate and drank in good fellowship, and rose up at midnight for the prayers of *Hazot* and *Tikkun Rachel*, as is our custom. Suddenly I began to weep so uncontrollably that I fell into a stupor, during which I heard a roaring noise and saw before me Pinhas, the son of Rabbi Meir Apt. 'Know you not,' he said 'that Shlomele Radomsker is deathly ill?' Whereupon I broke into such bitter tears that my soul almost departed my body.[71]

Pinchas, a Hasidic Jew, wrote this letter because he had been unaware of the illness of Rabbi Shlomo of Radomsk until this was revealed to him in a vision at the tomb. As a result, the community was convinced that the prayers at Rachel's Tomb were a contributing factor in the rabbi's recovery. These kinds of experiences added to the prestige of this religious shrine for Jews both in Jerusalem and the diaspora.

As an enclosed structure, we now begin hearing about the key for the tomb. Possession of the key means control. This is a significant aspect of religious shrines. One of the more interesting parallels concerns the key for the Church of the Holy Sepulcher in Jerusalem, where the key was long ago entrusted to two Muslim families because the various Christian factions did not trust each other with this symbol of control. Up until the mid-nineteenth century, possession of the key for Rachel's Tomb had been entrusted to various Muslims from the Bethlehem area, the last of these being Osman Ibrahim al Atayat.[72] As noted in Conder and Kitchener's 1872 survey, however, Moses Montefiore secured control of the key of Rachel's Tomb for the Jews. This was a significant move since there were no Jews living in the vicinity of Bethlehem or the tomb. Caretakers were therefore appointed, one from the Sephardic community and another from the Ashkenazi community. The Sephardic Joshua Burla served for nearly sixty years until his death in 1929. The Ashkenazi Jacob Freiman, the beadle of the newly built Hurvah synagogue in Jerusalem began in the nineteenth century, and then

---

[71] Dresner, 193.
[72] See 1929 report of British Commission in next chapter.

his son Solomon Freiman followed up through World War II.[73] The key was kept in old city Jerusalem. Visits to the tomb would thus be accompanied by the rabbi himself. Even the key later took on symbolic value so that it was loaned out to women in labor to place under their pillow while giving birth.[74] As for the shrine itself, it would continue to be a holy place for Muslims, Jews, and Christians.

Twentieth Century: From Cooperation to Exclusivity

For an entire millennium it had been the practice of visitors to leave their mark on Rachel's Tomb, writing their names on the monument or on the walls as a kind of holy graffiti. This practice was later formalized with regular guest books kept by the guardian of the tomb. Often visitors wrote comments and even prayers in their own languages. At other times the guardian Solomon Freiman made entries as if writing in a diary. No one knows for certain when this practice began. Only two of the books from the pre-1948 era survive, one from the mid-1930s and the other from the mid-1940s.[75] Samuel Dresner has included eighteen of these entries in his volume on Rachel. Five of Freiman's entries are included here:

> January 21, 1936—Two pilgrims came today, one a Jew, the other a Muslim. The Jew prayed fervently and shed tears over the exile. The Muslim too wept and prayed according to his custom. Both lit candles and went on their way.

> Nov. 14, 1944—The grave was open all night commemorating the anniversary of Rachel's death. About fifty people were present: Hasidim, kabbalists, Sephardim, westerners, Kurdim, and Bukharim. They wept and prayed for the welfare of the people Israel in exile . . .

> January 15, 1945—A black soldier, Joseph son of Moses of Johannesburg, visited the grave of our mother Rachel a second time. Yesterday he came with a group of Christian black soldiers and bought three books of psalms, a mezuzah, and a packet of earth, but did not reveal that he was a Jew.

---

[73] Dresner, 196.

[74] http://www.jewishmag.com/2mag/Israel/israel.htm.

[75] Susan Sered notes that she attained access to these books through Freiman's son. She notes that entries occur in numerous languages, but the guard frequently made notations in Hebrew. Susan Starr Sered, "Rachel's Tomb: Societal Liminality and the Revitalization of a Shrine," *Religion* 19 (1989) 27–40, see especially fn. 11, pp. 39–40.

May 3, 1945—Four Egyptian Arabs and one woman measured the grave with string for an omen. One recited psalms and other prayers in Arabic.

June 17, 1945—From six in the morning until five in the evening several hundred Arabs mourned the death of their sheik, whose body was placed in the outer court for several hours where the lamentation was fearful. I have never seen its like.[76]

Such comments demonstrate the shared nature of the tomb, even up to the end of World War II. According to Dresner, this was in part due to the open attitude of Freiman, who spoke fluent Arabic and who welcomed Arabs and Jews alike. Such entries also demonstrate the similar nature of human needs and the appealing character of Rachel in meeting those needs.

Israeli anthropologist Susan Starr Sered has undertaken a more detailed study of these diaries, seeing the entries as a window into life at the tomb, its visitors, their concerns, and their prayers. Her study was restricted to the actual comments and prayers of Jewish visitors. One can only be touched by the poignant words of an unnamed visitor on December 28, 1944: "I ask Rachel Our Mother to grant mercy and salvation to the Jewish nation as a whole. To our soldiers who are heroically and valorously fighting in the Occupied Countries [of Europe]—all the best and they should return speedily, healthy and unharmed, to their homes. And to all the daughters of Israel who, for the good of our people, sit in [British] detention camps and prisons—speedy release and all the best."[77] Here Sered recognizes a major transformation in the tomb from one decade to the next: "Through the mid-1930s Rachel's Tomb was a minor Jewish, Christian, and Muslim shrine, not associated with any special concerns or sought out by any particular population."[78] With many more visitors arriving in the 1940s than the 1930s, at a time of social upheaval, the shrine began to play an increasingly important role for Jewish visitors.

As expected the shrine had always played a role in fertility rituals. Thus, a simple request from April 3, 1944, is typical: "Rachel Our Mother, I beg Your Highness to pray for me, that I will have a male child this year."[79] Other requests for good health are common. Yet the dramatic increase in entries is linked to the political situation in Europe. Another wrote, "Rachel,

---

[76] Dresner, 197–201.
[77] Sered (1989), 27.
[78] Ibid., 28.
[79] Ibid., 34.

Rachel, Mother of the Israeli Nation, for how much longer will the tears of Israel be shed in vain? Arise, arise from your sleep."[80] Prayers connect the exile of Jeremiah's day with the modern situation: "Rachel, Rachel! For how long shall we continue being scorned by the nations? For how long shall we be without a homeland?"[81] In addition to such laments, the book also records visits from individuals who managed to escape the holocaust in Europe, such as thirty-six immigrant Polish children who came to light candles.[82] Later there is a reference to a curtain from a Polish synagogue that was draped over the tomb of Rachel.[83] Sered concludes that these external events played an important role in the transformation of the shrine to the cause of Jewish nationalism.

In addition to her study of the guest books from the 1930s and 1940s, Sered also carried out field work at Rachel's Tomb in 1982 in order to understand the prayers and rituals practiced by modern devotees. She notes that, in a male-dominated religion, this shrine has grown in importance as a spiritual refuge for women. It is a place today where women seek help through intercession in matters of marriage, pregnancy, and childbirth. She notes the common practice of lighting oil lamps and candles in spite of a prominent sign, "Forbidden to Light Candles!"

In recent years one of the more popular rituals involves tying a red string around the wrist as something of a charm to assist in fertility. During a visit to the tomb, women will wrap the red string around the tomb seven times—a practice Sered has been able to document as early as the 1930s. She describes the enactment of this ritual as something of a complicated process: "The string-wrapping ceremony tends to turn Rachel's Tomb into a bit of a circus. The area right around the tomb on the women's side of the shrine is usually crowded with women pressing up right next to the tomb. The wrapper must pass the string above the heads of, or between, other women. Then she has to pass the string around the men's side without actually walking through. She will usually throw the ball of string over the heads of the men, to a friend standing on the other side of the tomb."[84]

---

[80] Entry from early 1945. Ibid., 33.

[81] Entry from February 7, 1946. Ibid., 32.

[82] Entry from March 16, 1943. Ibid., 33.

[83] Entry from April 26, 1945. Ibid., 34.

[84] Susan Starr Sered, "Rachel's Tomb and the Milk Grotto of the Virgin Mary: Two Women's Shrines in Bethlehem," *Journal of Feminist Studies in Religion*, 2.2 (Fall 1986) 7–22, quote from pp. 11–12.

Sered notes that this is primarily an Ashkenazi custom, though other Jews are also taking up the practice. Most recently it has been popularized by Madonna, who has taken an interest in studying mystical Judaism. When the popular singer visited Rachel's Tomb several years ago, she created quite a commotion.

Women often bring a newborn child to the tomb in thanksgiving for a successful childbirth. They kiss the tomb, they pray, and they weep, as Rachel was known to do. Sered summarizes the ritual of prayer as follows:

> The typical woman enters the courtyard surrounding the building, washes her hands, kisses the mezuzah on the door, and then tries to get close enough to the tomb to touch it. Then she will take a prayer book or a book of Psalms (whether or not she knows how to read) and pray. After that she will probably kiss the tomb, talk to Rachel for a while, kiss the book, and put it down. She might then stay in the room for a time and give money to the women collecting for charity. When she leaves she will put money in the box for donations for the upkeep of the building and once again she will kiss the mezuzah. Sephardic women often back away from the tomb and out the door before turning and walking away. Older women will hold their hands in the direction of the grave, "catching" some of its power.[85]

Sered sees the biblical Rachel, one who struggled with real-life problems of family, quarrels, jealousy, and infertility, as one with whom it is natural for women to identify.

This latter period also marks a growing institutionalization of the shrine. In 1944, a Hasidic rabbi declared that men and women must stand on separate sides of the tomb. In 1945, Rabbi Herzog (the chief rabbi of Palestine) appointed certain women to light Sabbath candles each week at the tomb and suggested the installation of an eternal light in memory of Holocaust victims. Certain days also became marked for special visits, especially the day commemorating Rachel's death on the eleventh of Heshvan, in the autumn, and also the day before new moons. More and more, large groups of people began visiting the tomb rather than just individual devotees.[86] The image of Rachel's Tomb has recently emerged as a favorite on mezuzahs, amulets, menorah lamps, and walls of synagogues.[87] Such changes mark an overall transformation to a shrine primarily Jewish in character.

---

[85] Ibid., 14.
[86] Ibid., 36.
[87] Dresner, 186.

In more recent decades, Sered notes that the nationalistic prayers have diminished while fertility concerns have moved to the forefront. Nevertheless, the transformation has been complete. Today this is a shrine exclusively for Jewish women.

CHAPTER 9

The Politicization of Rachel's Tomb

When the crusaders undertook a renovation of Rachel's Tomb in the twelfth century, were there political motivations? What about the Muslims after they regained control a century later? It is difficult to differentiate such motivations since religion and politics have often been intertwined in societies throughout history. Certainly the Emperor Constantine's contribution to the building of Christian monuments carried political overtones. Yet Rachel's Tomb was not included in Constantine's building program, and the shrine remained neglected for a number of centuries. When Muhammad Pasha of Jerusalem undertook a rebuilding of Rachel's Tomb in the seventeenth century, the connection was clearly more evident. For a time, at least, it appeared to result in a more exclusive attitude about Rachel's Tomb. Even for Montefiore, whose attitude was one of religious tolerance, one must recognize from the timing of his renovations that they had political ramifications.

In recent years, however, a major change has taken place. There is no question that the status of the tomb is linked closely to political decisions.

Status Quo—1852

The starting point for all discussions of religion and politics in the modern dispute is the 1852 *firman* of the Ottoman Sultan Abdul Mejid—an agreement popularly known as the *Status Quo*.[1] The context of this ruling was the struggle taking place for foreign control of holy places, especially among the French, Italians, and Russians, in relation to the Crimean War. The *Status Quo* in effect guaranteed that there would be no changes in the balance of religious influence from the way things were in 1852, thus the

---

[1] Capitulations had been made by the Ottoman government in 1604, 1637, 1673, 1740, and 1757 to regulate the practices by various religious groups in Jerusalem.

name *Status Quo*. That particular agreement was in reality only concerned with Christian sites and particularly those in Jerusalem: The Church of the Holy Sepulchre; the convent of Dayr al-Sultan; the Sanctuary of the Ascension; and the tomb of the Virgin Mary in Gethsemane.[2] Within time the list was extended also to include sites in Bethlehem: The Church of the Nativity, the Milk Grotto, and the Shepherd's Field.[3]

With the dissolution of the Ottoman Empire after World War I, the League of Nations passed on responsibility for Palestine to the British. Article 13 of the Mandate makes clear the responsibility with regard to holy places: "All responsibility in connection with the Holy Places and religious buildings or sites in Palestine, including that of preserving existing rights and of securing free access to the Holy Places, religious buildings and sites and the free exercise of worship, while ensuring the requirements of public order and decorum, is assumed by the Mandatory."[4] Article 14 specified that the British were to undertake a study and define the rights connected to the holy places and to the various religious communities. This study was carried out by L. G. A. Cust, District Officer of Jerusalem with the assistance of Abdullah Effendi Kardus, former District Officer of the Bethlehem subdistrict and published in 1929 as *The Status Quo in the Holy Places*.[5] The list of sites under the *Status Quo* was expanded to include also Jewish and Muslim sites, including Rachel's Tomb.

The document begins with a short physical description: "The present Tomb consists of an open ante-chamber and a two-roomed shrine under a cupola containing a sarcophagus. The building lies within a Moslem cemetery, for which it serves as a place of prayer. The keys of the actual shrine are in the possession of the Jews, one for the Sephardic Community, and another for the Ashkenazic. The Tomb is a favorite place of Jewish pilgrimage, especially during the month of Elul and the Tishri festivals when large crowds visit it."[6] The most significant part of this opening statement is the fact that both Jews and Muslims considered the site as holy and that both actively worshiped there. At the same time, an important distinction is

---

[2] Michael Dumper, *The Politics of Sacred Space: The Old City of Jerusalem in the Middle East Conflict* (London: Lynne Rienner Publishers, 2002) 108.

[3] Ibid., 20.

[4] R. Lapidot and M. Hirsch, *The Arab-Israeli Conflict and Its Resolution: Selected Documents* (Dordrecht, Netherlands: Kluwer Academic Publishers, 1992) 28.

[5] L. G. A. Cust, *The Status Quo in the Holy Places* (Jerusalem: Ariel Publishing House, 1980).

[6] Ibid., 47.

made that will have critical implications throughout the rest of the twentieth century and down to the present day. For the Jews, who did not live in the vicinity—the closest being five miles away in Jerusalem—the shrine was primarily a pilgrimage site. For the Muslims it was a place of prayer primarily for those who lived in the neighborhood. This is where they buried their dead. Presumably these differences made it possible for the day-to-day sharing of the tomb.

That is not to say that there were not disagreements between the two religious communities. In fact, both sides disagreed concerning the question of ownership. First, Cust gave the Jewish argument: "The Jews claim possession of the Tomb as they hold the keys and by virtue of the fact that the building which had fallen into complete decay was entirely rebuilt in 1845 [*sic*] by Sr. M. Montefiore. It is also asserted that in 1615 Muhammad, Pasha of Jerusalem, rebuilt the Tomb on their behalf, and by *firman* granted them the exclusive use of it."

Then Cust recorded the Muslim argument: "The Moslems, on the other hand, claim the ownership of the building as being a place of prayer for Moslems of the neighborhood, and an integral part of the Moslem cemetery within whose precincts it lies. They state that the Turkish Government recognized it as such, and sent an embroidered covering with Arabic inscriptions for the sarcophagus; again, that it is included among the Tombs of the Prophets for which identity signboards were provided by the Ministry of Waqfs in 1328 A.H. [= 1898 c.e.]. In consequence, objection is made to any repair of the building by the Jews, though free access is allowed to it at all times."[7] Because of these conflicting claims, Cust did not make a final judgment, but left that to a future decision to be made by the Holy Places Commission. However, he did offer several observations that contradicted the Jewish claim of exclusive ownership. First, he noted that the keys to the tomb had remained in Muslim hands until recent times. The last Muslim guardian in fact had been Osman Ibrahim al Atayat, who handed over the keys to the Jews in the mid-nineteenth century, presumably at the time of the restoration by Montefiore. Second, he noted that the antechamber included in Montefiore's restoration was especially designed for Muslim prayer. Therefore, the argument of exclusive rights was essentially undercut by the British investigation. As far as the claim of a 1615 *firman* granting exclusive rights, he offers neither confirmation nor denial.

---

[7] Ibid., 47.

The report also took into consideration recent practice at the tomb with regard to repairs. In 1912, Jews were granted permission to repair the main room of the shrine, funded by Marcus Adier, brother of the chief Rabbi of England, using Jewish laborers. However, they were not allowed to extend their repairs to the antechamber.[8] A similar cleaning and whitewashing was undertaken soon after the British Mandate went into effect. However, controversy followed when additional repairs were proposed by the Chief Rabbinate in 1921. The Municipality of Bethlehem rejected the Jewish request when the *Waqf* claimed their own right to undertake the same repairs. The British High Commission then intervened to rule that only the government would undertake repairs until the matter of counter-claims was resolved. However, after strong Jewish protest, the government decided that repairs were not necessary at that time.[9] In 1925, when the Sephardic community argued that the structural condition of the tomb was dangerous, the British denied the Jewish request to undertake these repairs and instead instructed the public works department to carry out necessary repairs. These included repointing the walls and cementing the exterior of the dome. However, Jewish authorities refused the government-appointed workers the key to carry out repairs on the interior of the tomb.[10]

The British Holy Places Commission accepted the *Status Quo* report, but never ruled on the counterclaims of Muslims and Jews. Rather, the British preferred to focus on this particular shrine as a model of a shared site. The British Mandate thus recognized the rights to worship of both Muslims and Jews. As a public demonstration of this support they issued a postage stamp in 1932 featuring a photo of Rachel's Tomb with the word "Palestine" in both Arabic and Hebrew.[11]

British Mandate Stamp

[8] Ibid., 47.

[9] Ibid., 48.

[10] Ibid., 48.

[11] Nabil al Shaath and Hasna Reda Mekdashi, *Palestinian Stamps (1865–1981)* (Beirut: Dar al-Fata al-Arabi, 1981) 7–8.

U.N. Partition and Aftermath

With the establishment of the United Nations Special Committee on Palestine, discussion concerning the holy places continued to play an important role. According to the partition plan adopted by the United Nations on November 29, 1947, Jerusalem was to be established as an international city. Because of the unique role the city played in the life of three religions, Judaism, Islam, and Christianity, U.N. Resolution 181 thus included a section concerning the holy places, guaranteeing free access to all, and another section designating special powers to be granted the governor of Jerusalem with respect to these holy places. The borders of this shared Jerusalem were to be expanded to include also the holy sites of Bethlehem, thus also Rachel's Tomb. Of course, this never came to be. The war of 1948 led to a divided and politicized Jerusalem. The U.N. General Assembly passed Resolution 194 on December 11, 1948, with a significant portion of the document calling for U.N. supervision of the sharing of religious sites. With the armistice of 1949, Bethlehem, along with Rachel's Tomb, was incorporated into the West Bank of the Hashemite Kingdom of Jordan. Therefore, after a period of time in the mid-1940s when Jewish activity at Rachel's Tomb had reached unprecedented heights, the shrine fell back into Muslim control. Clause 8 in the 1949 armistice stated that Jordan would ensure free access for Jews to holy places. To be sure, the Jordanians would point out that Jews were not excluded from Rachel's Tomb for the period from 1949 to 1967. However, the border between Israel and Jordan remained impassable and, for all practical purposes, Jews felt excluded.

Israeli Control

Following the Six-Day War in June 1967, Jerusalem and the West Bank, along with Bethlehem and Rachel's Tomb, fell into Jewish hands. U.N. Resolution 242 designated the area as occupied territory and called for a return to Arabs hands—a position that remains the platform for all peace negotiations even to the present day. However, the Israeli government began its own unilateral actions. On June 7, 1967, Israeli Prime Minister, Levi Eshkol announced that the Ministry of Religious Affairs would appoint a council of religious clergymen to oversee the newly acquired religious sites. However, this was never really carried out. Eshkol also instructed his Minister of Justice to annex Rachel's Tomb to Jerusalem. However, it was Defense Minister Moshe Dayan who argued, and prevailed, that Rachel's Tomb needed to be treated with special sensitivity as a religious site.[12] On June 27, 1967, the Israeli Knesset passed the Protection of Holy Places Law. It stated:

> 1. The Holy Places shall be protected from desecration and any other violation and from anything likely to violate the freedom of access of the members of the different religions to the places sacred to them or their feelings with regard to those places.
>
> a. Whosoever desecrates or otherwise violates a Holy Place shall be liable to imprisonment for a term of seven years.
>
> b. Any person who does anything likely to impair freedom of access to a Holy Place or to hurt the feelings of anyone to whom a place is sacred, shall be liable to imprisonment for a term of five years.
>
> 2. This law shall add to and derogate from any other law. The Minister of Religious Affairs is charged with the implementation of the law, and he may, after consultation with, or upon the proposal of, representatives of the religions concerned and with the consent of the Minister of Justice, make regulations as to any matter relating to such implementation.[13]

This particular law is consistent with the Hague Convention statements concerning cultural and religious property and also with Article 27 of the Geneva Convention. It should be noted that Israel has not signed Article 16 of the Geneva Protocol II which prohibits any act of hostility against cultural property or its use in any military effort,[14] a statute that has had important implications in recent years.

While the 1967 Israeli law applies to numerous religious sites, especially in Jerusalem, it does guarantee the freedom for all to worship at Rachel's Tomb in Bethlehem and protects the tomb from violent activity and harassment. Control of Rachel's Tomb was turned over to the chief rabbinate. Many Israelis, such as the well-respected former mayor of Jerusalem Teddy Kollek, continued to speak of Rachel's Tomb as a site considered sacred also to Muslims.[15] Yet the tomb gradually became a holy place exclusively for Jews. The role of the Minister of Religious Affairs is key in the interpretation and implementation of Israeli law. By 1977, the Likud party had managed to dominate the government, and the militant Jewish settler movement, Gush Emunim, gained more influence.

---

[12] Uzi Benzimann, *Jerusalem, A City without a Wall*. Nadav Shagai, "Rachel's Tomb: Beyond or Within?" *Haaretz* (2002).

[13] Quoted in Dumper, 19.

[14] Ibid., fn. 7, 36.

[15] Kollek and Pearlman.

With the peace process of the 1990s, sacred places such as Rachel's Tomb were treated with all seriousness. The interim agreement signed by Yitzak Rabin and Yasser Arafat on the White House lawn on September 28, 1995, again restated the basic principal: "Both sides shall respect and protect the religious rights of Jews, Christians, Muslims, and Samaritans concerning the protection and free access to the holy sites as well as freedom of worship and practice."

According to the Oslo Accords, the West Bank was to be divided initially into three areas:

+ Area A was comprised of Palestinian cities where there was full withdrawal of Israeli military and political control.
+ Area B was territory where Palestinians and Israelis would share governance until a gradual withdrawal of Israeli forces was complete.
+ Area C was made up of settlements and state land that remained completely under Israeli control.

Originally, Prime Minister Rabin had decided to place Rachel's Tomb under Area A. Following pressure from religious groups, a last-minute change was made.[16] With regard to Rachel's Tomb, the interim agreement offered a special section designating its treatment as part of Area B:

> Without derogating from Palestinian security responsibility in the City of Bethlehem, the two sides hereby agree on the following security arrangements regarding Rachel's Tomb which will be considered a special case during the Interim Period:
>
> 1. While the Tomb, as well as the main road leading from Jerusalem to the Tomb as indicated on map No. 1, will be under the security responsibility of Israel, the free movement of Palestinians on the main road will continue.
>
> 2. For the purpose of protecting the Tomb, three Israeli guard posts may be located in the Tomb, the roof of the Waqf building, and the parking lot.
>
> The present situation and existing practices in the Tomb shall be preserved.[17]

In December 1995, Israeli forces withdrew from the city of Bethlehem, designated as Area A. Rachel's Tomb and the territory around it were designated as Area B. In reality, the Israeli government did not recognize the

---

[16] Shagai, "Rachel's Tomb."

[17] "Annex I, Article V: Security Arrangements—West Bank," Interim Agreement on the West Bank and Gaza Strip (Oslo II), September 28, 1995.

shared control over Rachel's Tomb. For all practical purposes it was treated as Area C, exclusive territory of Israel.

A short time later in February 1996, the Israeli government began a two-million-dollar, eighteen-month facelift of Rachel's Tomb, including a thirteen-foot high security wall and an adjoining military post. When the project was complete, the celebration took place on the day commemorating Rachel's death, November 11, 1997. However, it was more than a religious ceremony. One of the main speakers was Israeli Defense Minister Yitzhak Mordechai, who addressed the worshipers while soldiers clutching automatic rifles guarded the area. Another speaker was Deputy Religious Affairs Minister Yigal Bibi who called for the adjacent Jerusalem-Hebron road to be closed to Palestinian traffic.[18] Throughout the process of building and on the day of dedication, the local Palestinian community attempted peaceful demonstrations to protest the transformation of the site into a fortress, but to no avail.

Several years later when the al-Aqsa Intifada broke out, the area around Rachel's Tomb became a center for clashes between Palestinians and Israeli soldiers. Because of the withdrawal of the Israeli army from Area A since 1995, this was the closest place where Bethlehem youth might confront soldiers. As was noted in the introduction, the result was a number of Palestinian youth injured and killed by Israeli gunfire outside the religious shrine.

In August 2002, the Israeli government announced yet another change. Rachel's Tomb was no longer to be considered part of Bethlehem but was being annexed to Jerusalem. The transition was complete from Area A to Area B, and now to Area C. This was not an easy task because Palestinian businesses and residential areas were located on all sides of the tomb. On September 13, the Israeli newspaper *Haaretz* published an editorial referring to this action as a land "grab." It said:

> The security cabinet's decision to add the Rachel's Tomb compound to the Jerusalem "security envelope" cannot be described as anything other than full annexation of the compound. Ostensibly, this is a military solution meant to guarantee the safety of people at prayer and the tourists who visit the historic site that has been at the center of many attacks during the intifada.

> According to the plan, a wall will be built around the compound, linking it to the Jerusalem municipal jurisdiction. The plan includes diverting the access

---

[18] Dina Kraft, "Thousands Worship at Fortified Tomb," AP Wire Service (November 11, 1997); Steve Rodan and Margot Dudkevitch, "Rachel's Tomb reopens after renovations," *The Jerusalem Post* (November 12, 1997) 2.

road to Bethlehem, and construction of a new bypass road that will link up to Jerusalem. There is no dispute about the need to guarantee the safety of holy sites in a manner that allows prayer without endangering lives. But there is a substantial difference between security and exploiting security needs to conduct a political grab that unilaterally creates new facts on the ground.

"Grab" is the precise definition of the security cabinet decision. The compound is not within the boundaries of the state of Israel and has never been annexed to it.

The Oslo II agreements designated the area as Area A, under full Palestinian security and civil control, but under pressure of the religious parties, its status was changed and it was designated Area C, under full Israeli control. Once again, it appears that it was not security concerns behind the current decision, but pressure by religious parties and the ambitions of the mayor of Jerusalem. . . .

The decision to annex Rachel's Tomb should be returned to the file of subjects to be raised during negotiations, if indeed Israel is seeking the world's understanding in its fight against terrorism.[19]

This was the period in which plans for the new dividing wall between the West Bank and Israel were being disseminated, and early construction had begun in the northern West Bank. On February 17, 2003, Israel's military commander for the West Bank, Moshe Kaplinski, issued notices to Palestinians residing in the neighborhood of Rachel's Tomb, announcing the confiscation of 3.5 acres of land for an extension of the new wall that would place the shrine on the Jerusalem side of the wall—virtually excluding it from Bethlehem. In an interview with the *Jordan Times* Bethlehem Mayor Hanna Nasser said that the notice applied only to the land upon which the wall would rest. In reality the confiscation would include over one thousand acres with several dozen homes, shops, and restaurants.[20] Since that time, the construction of the wall has continued as planned.

At the same time, Israeli Defense Minister Benjamin Ben-Eliezer and the Civil Administration approved the purchase of a number of buildings around Rachel's Tomb. By the fall of 2003 a newly established yeshiva was

---

[19] Editorial, "Grabbing Rachel's Tomb," *Haaretz* (September 12, 2002).

[20] Palestinians Protest Bethlehem Land Grab," *The Jordian Times* (February 19, 2003). James Bennet, "New Wall Sharpens Arab-Israel Divisions," *The New York Times* (February 18, 2003).

meeting in one of the buildings under the direction of a radical group called Shavei Rachel and with the permission of new Defense Minister Shaul Mofaz. On October 25, 2004, an article in *Haaretz* reported that two Jewish families had moved into a house, establishing yet another Jewish settlement and creating the first Jewish presence in Bethlehem in centuries. The paper reported: "Right-wing activists and people involved with the yeshiva were preparing to ultimately bring 10 families to live there and transform it into a settlement near the holy site, on the northern outskirts of Bethlehem, to provide a basis for a Jewish hold in that region. . . . Activists from the Shavei Rachel group, who are involved in the move, said that the site had undergone renovations throughout the past year and that the building was connected to the grave compound with the approval, aid and knowledge of the army and the political echelon."[21] On February 3, 2005, the Israeli High Court ruled against a petition filed by the community of Bethlehem against the annexation of Rachel's Tomb. This was followed six weeks later by an Israeli Cabinet decision to continue with the construction of the wall dividing Rachel's Tomb from Bethlehem.[22] Throughout 2005, construction on the wall continued uninterrupted. By Christmas 2005, *Christian Science Monitor* correspondent Joshua Mitnick concluded, "Near the entrance of Bethlehem, the neighborhood around Rachel's Tomb—the traditional burial spot of the Old Testament matriarch—has become a ghost town."[23]

These developments show the continued politicization of Rachel's Tomb. The rights of Muslims and Christians to worship in freedom were no longer respected. The power of the modern state made exclusive Jewish worship the only possibility.

[21] Nadav Shagai, "Two Jewish families move into house near Rachel's Tomb," *Haaretz* (October 25, 2004).

[22] Michael Jansen, "If the Palestinian-Israeli Conflict is to be Resolved," *The Jordan Times* (March 23, 2005).

[23] Joshua Mitnick, "Christmas behind Israel's Walls," *The Christian Science Monitor* (December 22, 2005) 6.

Epilogue

Today Rachel's Tomb plays a very important role for Jewish women. Young mothers and would-be mothers find Rachel a willing listener to concerns about conception and childbirth. Mother Rachel shares their tears and accepts their prayers of thanksgiving. In a world where men often dominate religious institutions, such a shrine for women is indeed refreshing.

Who could even think of questioning the sincerity and the validity of the religious fervor of that young Hasidic Jewish woman who sat beside me ten years ago in a Palestinian taxi from the Damascus gate to Bethlehem to pray to mother Rachel? Yet, as was noted in the prologue, something is not right with the current picture. When some are accepted and others rejected, when some throw stones and others are shot by high-powered rifles, when a humble shrine is turned into an impregnable fortress, then something's not right. How odd it is to use that word *impregnable* for a religious shrine? This is Rachel, after all. It doesn't fit her story.

Our survey of biblical Rachel reminds us that Rachel's story is one of vulnerability and rejection, one of struggle and longsuffering, one of tears and deep emotion, yet always one of faithfulness, hope, and patience. Rachel was always on the way.

That character is a reminder of the words of Hebrews 11 that "faith is the assurance of things hoped for, the conviction of things not seen." The stones and mortar are at best only an aid in connecting with the divine essence of the universe that gives meaning and hope to life. To turn them into anything more totters on the edge of idolatry, no less than the *terafim* Rachel once stole from her father's house. The on-the-way designation of Rachel's burial—along with the uncertainty of the place name Ephrath and the ambiguity of the Hebrew *kbrt* (yet some distance from)—results in the impossibility of ever locating the actual tomb of Rachel. In all probability it was not the current Rachel's Tomb outside Bethlehem, but rather somewhere in the north. Having said that, one must be careful not to diminish in any way the religious importance of the Bethlehem shrine, to discredit the prayers that are offered inside, to humiliate any worshipers, or to disrespect the historic building. Still, questions of authenticity do undercut the political motivation often used to manipulate and transform such a religious site into an exclusive nationalistic shrine—this includes political motivations from all sides.

Stones and mortar, like pieces of real estate, do often get in the way. That's why religious leaders frequently today call attention to the living stones. It was not the stone erected by Jacob that gave meaning to the exiles of Jeremiah's day, but the living tears of a long-dead ancestress. Rachel was a real human being. Her suffering relates to all human suffering. Her tears provide comfort and hope for all. Our survey of later religious writers demonstrates without a doubt that Rachel was held in the highest esteem by generations of Jews, Muslims, and Christians alike. To say that Rachel belongs exclusively to one religion is to be like a child who claims that mother liked him or her best. Rachel weeps for all her children. As the rabbis noted, Rachel was buried on the way to be accessible to all who passed by.

During the past two millennia, the shrine of Rachel in Bethlehem has witnessed changes in government, migrations of peoples, and religious change. How appropriate that the current structure is a combined effort by the hands of Christians, Muslims, and Jews, making use of an already existing shrine likely first erected by the family of Herod or perhaps some unknown aristocratic family. Yet rarely in that history did the builders claim ownership. It did happen at times. Human beings tend to act that way. However, our survey shows a long train of visitors from all faiths who generally recognized and showed respect for the diversity of prayers among the local population. Our conclusion is that exclusive attitudes were an exception to the rule. Rachel's Tomb was seen as a shrine to be shared.

As for the future of Rachel's Tomb, one would hope we will learn from the past. The diary entry of the shrine's guardian, Solomon Freiman, for January 21, 1936, provides such a formula:

> Two pilgrims came today, one a Jew, the other a Muslim. The Jew prayed fervently and shed tears over the exile. The Muslim too wept and prayed according to his custom. Both lit candles and went on their way.[1]

These two unnamed individuals visited Rachel's Tomb because they were on their way. Like Rachel they were likely on-the-way characters faced with

---

[1] Dresner, 197.

the struggles and concerns of daily life. Like Rachel they shared their tears and their prayers. Like Rachel they walked in faith and lived in hope, lighting candles as they went on their way.

This episode from the recent past was possible because Rachel's Tomb was accessible and welcoming to all. Is that scenario possible for the future? Is it possible to dismantle the barricades and cut the barbed wire? Is it possible to put away the weapons of separation and the attitudes of exclusivity? Is it possible for the politicians to step back and the devotees of Rachel to kneel humbly in the forefront?

Many will likely say that a shared religious shrine is no longer possible. Many will say that changes over the past generation cannot be reversed. Meanwhile, Rachel weeps for her children. Rachel weeps because we are all her children. Rachel weeps because we all are hurting and desperately in need of healing. Rachel weeps because we have forgotten her story: Rachel, always on the way, always at risk and vulnerable to the hostile forces around her, always living with the hope that the impossible will become possible.

Jeremiah lived in a day when the possible seemed impossible, when military power and might ruled, and when religious dreams seemed fruitless and without purpose. In that situation, not unlike today, Jeremiah penned that poignant lament of Rachel weeping for her children. For those who say "impossible," Jeremiah reminds us that the lament was surrounded with words of hope and promise. For those who shake their heads at the failed solutions of the recent past, he points to something new.

> For the Lord has created a new thing on the earth;
> A woman encompasses a man. (Jer 31:22)

That is something new. A woman surrounding a warrior. At that Rachel would surely shed tears of joy.

APPENDIX

Ephrath and Bethlehem

How clear is it that the term "Ephrath" must refer to Bethlehem? As a place name Ephrath only occurs in Genesis 35 and 48. Elsewhere one finds Ephrathah, an adjectival form meaning "fertile." An appealing suggestion is that Ephrathah would refer to any fertile region, a designation that would be appropriate for Bethlehem, but other locations as well. The biblical evidence, however, points to a number of other possibilities, from a clan name to a variation of a tribal designation. The complexity of this usage makes any certainty about the origins of the name in Genesis questionable.

From Micah 5:2, one would gather that Ephrathah is a late designation for Bethlehem. Interestingly, this designation rarely occurs in early references to Bethlehem. This is clear from the earliest mention of the name Bethlehem in the fourteenth century B.C.E. Amarna letters from Egypt, where Bethlehem is known well enough that the name Bethlehem stands by itself. In the early Judges 19 text, where a Levite was treated without hospitality and his concubine was raped, Bethlehem is introduced merely as "in Judah" to distinguish it from another Bethlehem in the tribal territory of Zebulun (Josh 19:15). Likewise, in the early story of Samuel's visit to Bethlehem to choose David as the successor of Saul, there is no need for further explanation. Samuel goes to "Bethlehem" (1 Sam 16:4). David's father Jesse is identified simply as "the Bethlehemite" (1 Sam 16:1). A little later when Saul seeks out David to play the lyre in his palace, he is identified as "the son of Jesse the Bethlehemite" (1 Sam 16:18).

Then the reader comes to the famous episode of Goliath, the Philistine warrior. To the complete surprise to the reader, David is introduced as if there had been no chapter 16—a sign of an insertion: "Now David was the son of an Ephrathite of Bethlehem in Judah named Jesse, who had eight sons . . ." (1 Sam 17:12). This statement has all the signs of an insertion from a different source.[1] Although David has been introduced to Samuel and the court of Saul—and most important to the reader—the impact of the story is based on the unexpected fact that the youngest son, the one out tending the sheep, will be chosen to lead. As for the town, it is described once again as Bethlehem in Judah, but Jesse is described as an Ephrathite, presumably his clan name.

The post-exilic book of Ruth also presents Ephrathah as a clan name connected with Bethlehem. Elimelech, the father-in-law of Ruth the Moabite (in her first marriage), is described as an Ephrathite (Ruth 1:2). Upon Ruth's arrival in Bethlehem and her marriage to Boaz, Naomi's kinsman, she receives a blessing to become like Leah and Rachel—an oddity that Rachel is not distinguished from Leah if indeed she does have a special place in Bethlehem: "May the Lord make the woman who is coming into your house like Rachel and Leah, who together built up the house of Israel. May you produce children in Ephrathah and bestow a name in Bethlehem" (Ruth 4:11).

Just a few verses later the reader is told that Ruth and Boaz had a son Obed and that Obed was to be the father of Jesse (Ruth 4:17). The genealogy that concludes the book (Ruth 4:18-22) presents the same ten generations that occur in Matthew 1 from Judah's son Perez to David. The generations are as follows: Judah > Perez > Hezron > Aram > Aminadab > Nashshon > Salmon > Boaz > Obed > Jesse. There is no explanation about where the clan Ephrathah fits in.

Another chronology, however, offers an explanation. The books of Chronicles are a revision of the books of Samuel and Kings, written from a priestly perspective about 350 B.C.E. One of the main priestly concerns was to record the ancient genealogies. 1 Chronicles chapters 2–4 highlight the family tree of Judah. The fact that Judah, the fourth-born son of Jacob, occurs first reflects the post-exilic importance of the tribe of Judah. Within this genealogy (1 Chr 2:9-12), one finds the same ten names as occur in Ruth 4:18-22.

Surprisingly, there is also special attention to Caleb (1 Chr 2:9, 42-55; 4:4), the individual who helped in spying out the land in the time of Moses (Num 14). In that text Caleb is described as a member of the tribe of Judah and the son of Jephunneh (Num 13:6; 14:6). In Numbers 32:12, however,

---

[1] See also evidence of a parallel story in 2 Samuel 21:19 when a man named Elhanan kills Goliath.

in crediting Caleb and Joshua for their faithfulness, Caleb is referred to as a Kenizite, one of the pre-Israelite peoples living in Canaan (Gen 15:19). The book of Joshua continues this latter tradition referring to him as the son of Jephunneh, but a Kenizite (Josh 14:6, 14). Because of his work in spying out the land, Caleb was allowed to live among the tribe of Judah and given the land around Hebron (Josh 14:13-15; 15:13-19). In 1 Chronicles 2:9, however, Caleb is portrayed as a member of the tribe of Judah, the great-grandson of the patriarch Judah and son of Hezron, who is known in the other genealogies as the father of Ram.[2]

Caleb is of special importance to this study for three reasons. First, Caleb seems to be from a place called Ephrathah. At least, his father was reported to have died in Caleb-ephrathah (1 Chr 2:24). Second, Caleb's second wife was named Ephrath (1 Chr 2:19) or Ephrathah (1 Chr 2:50; 4:4). Third, among Caleb's descendants are individuals named Hebron (1 Chr 2:42), Bethlehem (2:50), Kiriath-jearim, Beth-gader (identified with Gedor, Josh 15:58), and possibly also Tekoa (1 Chr 2:24).[3] Here it would seem that the name Ephrathah has a southern origin. The name of Caleb's second wife would seem to be related to this clan name, which in turn raises questions about the connection to the Ephrathah clan of Bethlehem. Many commentators suggest that this information cannot be accepted as historically accurate, but is only helpful to understand geographical changes of re-settlement following the exile.[4] For descendants of Caleb and Ephrathah, this would mean settlement in the central area of the country including Bethlehem and Kiriath-jearim, a town of Benjamin located even to the north of Jerusalem (Josh 18:14). One thus might assume a movement of the Ephrathah clan from south to north.

There are entirely too many difficulties to accept the genealogy of Caleb in 1 Chronicles 2–4 as accurate. As is often the case, a writer uses older material and makes revisions to fit his purpose. 1 Chronicles connects the origin of the clan Ephrathah to Caleb, yet the connection to Bethlehem was already present in Micah 5:2; 1 Samuel 17:12; and Ruth 1:2 and 4:11, and thus not dependent on the creative hand of the Chronicler. Is it possible then to find in 1 Chronicles a kernel of truth about the origins of the clan

---

[2] Along with Ram and Caleb (or Chelubai), a third son of Hezron is Jerahmeel who likewise was the ancestor of a non-Israelite group residing in the far south of Israel (1 Sam 27:10; 30:29).

[3] Lamonette Luker, "Ephrathah," *Anchor Bible Dictionary*, vol. 2, 557–58.

[4] Roddy Braun, 1 Chronicles, *Harper's Bible Commentary*, 345.

Ephrathah? The key verse would seem to be 1 Chronicles 2:24, which has the strange reference to a place named Caleb-ephrathah.[5] Here the Septuagint translation renders the verse quite differently. Since the RSV followed the Septuagint at this particular verse and the NRSV followed the Hebrew text, they can be compared side by side:

> After the death of Hezron, Caleb went in to Ephrathah, the wife of Hezron, his father, and she bore him Asshur, the father of Tekoa (1 Chr 2:24 RSV as LXX).

> After the death of Hezron, in Caleb-ephrathah, Abijah wife of Hezron bore him Asshur, father of Tekoa (1 Chr 2:24 NRSV as MT).

The Greek Septuagint translation (LXX) is clearly late, coming in the second or first centuries before the Common Era. Issues of scribal interpretation or the improvement of the text must always be taken into consideration. Yet in this particular case, it is significant that the Vulgate translation is quite similar to the Septuagint. This means that the Hebrew text used by Jerome when he translated the Bible into Latin (fourth century c.e.) was similar to the Hebrew text used by the translators of the Greek Septuagint five hundred years earlier. It is the Hebrew text (MT) from the Middle Ages then that is likely corrupted.

According to the Septuagint reading of 1 Chronicles 2:24, Ephrathah was the wife of Hezron in his old age. Thus the clan name Ephrathah likely was originally associated with Hezron, the ancestor of Jesse and Boaz. However, there is still a problem in dating this tradition since it does not appear in early texts about Bethlehem. One needs to be careful about absolutes. One cannot say with certainty that the Ephrathah-Bethlehem link was only a post-exilic development. Neither can one say with certainty that the tradition of placing the clan of Ephrathah at Bethlehem goes back to patriarchal and matriarchal times or even to the time of the E writer of the Pentateuch. As far as probabilities, one can say that the importance of the clan Ephrathah arose during the time of the later monarchy, especially as the traditions about David were gathered and as the longing increased for a new king like David. By the time of 1 Chronicles those traditions were linked to Caleb and geographically expanded not only to include Bethlehem but also the territory from Tekoa and Gedor in the south to Kiriath-jearim

---

[5] The name Asshur (1 Chr 2:24) is likely the same as Hur (1 Chr 2:19, 50), identified as the son of Caleb. Luker, vol. 2, 557–58.

in the north, within the traditional territory of the tribe of Benjamin. This tradition seemed to move northward.

However, there are traditions which suggest the opposite. In three relatively early texts the term Ephrathite designates people from Ephraim, north of the tribe of Benjamin (Judg 12:5; 1 Sam 1:1; 1 Kgs 11:26). Most translations simply read Ephraim, although Ephrathite is found in the King James Version. Luker refers to this usage as an "etymological coincidence."[6] The same form in Hebrew derives from Ephraim as from Ephrathah. Over time one would expect some confusion over the terms. The significance of these texts is that they would seem to point to a movement of the clan from north to south to the area around Bethlehem.

The evidence for Ephrathah as a clan name is thus rather complicated and confusing. There are clues that point to an origin of the clan both north in Ephraim and in the extreme south. The evidence for an association with Bethlehem, however, is relatively late. What can be said with certainty? The late eighth-century prophet Micah is the first to connect Ephrathah with Bethlehem as a tribal designation. The text of Ruth, however, is post-exilic although it may preserve traditions going back to Micah's time. Likewise, the inserted single reference to Jesse as an Ephrathite in 1 Samuel 17:12 appears later than the other Deuteronomic traditions.

In contrast, the Genesis 35 reference to Ephrath does appear to be early. Yet, unlike the many references above, the Genesis term points to a specific place, likely a town or a village. There is no evidence in the Hebrew Bible that the town Bethlehem ever went by that name. However, one is faced with the fact that Bethlehem is missing from the list of towns in Judah in Joshua 15.[7] In the Septuagint, however, one finds an additional verse between Joshua 15:59 and 60. This insertion includes the city Ephrathah along with a parenthetical "that is, Bethlehem."[8] The insertion includes eleven town names altogether, including several near Bethlehem such as Tekoa, Aitan, and Bethir. On the other hand, Gallim is listed, a town in Benjamin near Anathoth.[9] The dating for this entire chapter, however, is problematical. Its organization in various districts suggests the kind of orga-

---

[6] Luker, vol. 2, 557.

[7] From the 1 Chronicles 2 list of names, also missing is Tekoa. Kiriath-jearim shows up as a gloss identifying Kiriath-baal in Joshua 15:60.

[8] *Ephratha [hautē estin Baithleem]*, basically the same as Septuagint Genesis 35:20; 48:7.

[9] In verse 62, one finds Kiriath-baal, that is, Kiriath-jearim, a city connected with Ephrathah, but north of Jerusalem.

nization that took place under Solomon (1 Kgs 4) or perhaps even as late as Josiah. Nevertheless, it seems to reflect the time of the monarchy (when the name Bethlehem was well known) rather than the period of conquest.

There have been many attempts to link the name Ephrath to a place in the north. W. F. Albright[10] identified Ephrath with the town of Ophrah about four miles northeast of Bethel. This town has had a number of names over the years. In modern times it is known as Taiyibeh. Under the Greeks it was known as Aphairema (1 Macc 11:34), and as a site visited by Jesus it was called Ephraim (John 11:54), a name already used at the time of David (2 Sam 13:23). Ophrah (Ephraim, Aphairema) was located in the territory of Benjamin (Josh 18:23; 1 Sam 13:17) and known in Hebrew also by Ephron (Josh 18:15; 2 Chr 13:19). With all these different spellings it is easy to see how the names could be confused, but also the similarity with Ephrath.[11] Orphah was located in the tribal territory of Benjamin within a short distance of Bethel, yet near the northern boundary with Ephraim.

Another interpretation by Matitiahu Tsevat[12] identifies Ephrath with Kiriath-jearim on the southern boundary of Benjamin, modern-day Deir al-ʿAzar about eight miles west of Jerusalem (Josh 15:60; 18:14). The connection with Ephrathah is made in the 1 Chronicles genealogy where Kiriath-jearim was designated as one of the descendants of Ephrathah, Caleb's wife (1 Chr 2:50). It is likely confirmed in Psalm 132:6 where the poetic parallelism brings together Ephrathah and "the fields of Jaar":

> We heard of it in Ephrathah;
> we found it in the fields of Jaar.

Most scholars understand this final expression in reference to Kiriath-jearim where the ark of the covenant was kept before David brought it to Jerusalem (1 Sam 7:1-2). So Kiriath-jearim does fit within the territory of the

---

[10] W. F. Albright, "Ophrah and Ephraim," *AASOR* (1922: 4) 124–37. Followed also by von Rad, 335; see Luker and Henry Thompson, "Ephraim," *Anchor Bible Dictionary*, vol. 2, 586.

[11] In fact, Codex Vaticanus of LXX Joshua 18:23 reads Ephrathah (Ephratha). Codex Alexandrinus of LXX Jos 18.23 reads *Aphra*. The LXX also translates as Ephrathah another town named Ophrah, the home of Gideon, farther north near Megiddo (Judg 6:11, 24; 8:27, 32; 9:5).

[12] Matitiahu Tsevat, "Interpretation of 1 Sam. 10:2," *Hebrew Union College Annual*, XXXIII (1962) 107–18. Also Tsevat, "Rachel's Tomb," *IDB Supplement* (Nashville: Abingdon, 1976) 724–25.

Ephrathah clan and is consistent with the narrative of Genesis 35. It may be more difficult to fit this location into the itinerary of Saul in 1 Samuel 10. However, Tsevat notes the term used by the seventh-century pilgrim Theodosius for Kiriath-jearim is Silona, which he links to the 1 Samuel 10:2 name Zelzah.

A third proposal, made by Lombardi,[13] links Ephrath of Genesis 35 with modern Farah, two miles east of er-Ram and five miles north of Jerusalem. The nearby ain-Farah is a major water source for modern Jerusalem. Farah is most certainly ancient Parah, listed among the towns of Benjamin in Joshua 18:23. It is easy to see how pronunciation of Farah/Parah could be related to Ephrath, especially when a preceding word ends in a vowel. The Vaticanus LXX manuscript, in fact, reads *Aphar*.[14] Many modern scholars see a connection of Parah with the vision in which the prophet buries a loincloth in the crevice of the rocks of Perat (Jer 13:4, 6, 7). Most translations, including NRSV, read "the Euphrates," which is symbolically meaningful in pointing ahead to the exile, but impractical. Parah was only a short distance from the prophet's home of Anathoth and the rocky terrain around ain-Farah fit perfectly the description of Jeremiah 13 in contrast to the flat and silted Euphrates River valley. Thus the NEB reads Parah, as does Holladay's translation in the *Hermeneia* commentary series.[15] This proposal goes back to early Western explorers of the Holy Land who were also aware that Septuagint Manuscript A Jeremiah 13:4 reads *eis pharan*.[16] Just as significant are the early proposals that the text of Jeremiah be read as Ephrathah—Samuel Bochart (1646), Venema (1765), and Hitzig (1841).[17] Interestingly, the Dead Sea Scrolls provide a reading that emphasizes the *t* sound Pharatah (4QJer). However, the absence of the initial *alef* remains a problem.

These three proposals demonstrate that scholars have long sought a northern alternative to Bethlehem for Ephrath of Genesis 35, and thus the site of Rachel's tomb. All three sites have their merits. Both Ophrah and Kiriath-jearim are attractive because of early connections with the name

---

[13] G. Lombardi, "H. Farah – W. Farah presso Anatot e la questione della Tomba di Rahel (Gen 35,16-20; 1 Sam 10,2-5; Ger 31,15)," *Liber Annuus*, XX (1970) 299–352.

[14] Ms A LXX Josh 18:23 reads *phara*.

[15] Holladay, 393. See also Fretheim, 203–4.

[16] Karl Marti, "Mittheilungen von Baurath C. Schick in Jerusalem," ZDPV 3 (1880) 11; W. F. Birch, "Hiding Places in Canaan. I. Jeremiah's Girdle and Farah," PEFQS (1880) 235–36.

[17] Cited in Holladay, 396.

Ephrathah and because they do fit into the broad parameters of the descriptions of Genesis 35 and 1 Samuel 10. Parah fits the closest geographically to those ancient texts and has linguistic affinities to the name Ephrathah, but the name connection is looser than the others. One can conclude then that the name Ephrath/Ephrathah does fit Bethlehem for the period of the late monarchy. Yet the name also fits three sites in the north. The connection of the name Bethlehem with the story of Rachel's death is thus late, likely from a setting disconnected from the physical presence of Bethlehem.

Bibliography

The Biblical Rachel

Alter, Robert. *The Art of Biblical Narrative*. New York: Basic Books, 1981.

Brueggemann, Walter. *The Land: Place as Gift, Promise, and Challenges in Biblical Faith*. 2nd ed. Minneapolis: Fortress, 2002.

Burrows, E. "Cuneiform and Old Testament: Three Notes." *Journal of Theological Studies (JTS)* 28 (1927): 185.

Callaway, Mary. *Sing O Barren One: A Study in Comparative Midrash*. Atlanta: Scholars Press, 1986.

Carroll, Robert P. *Jeremiah: Old Testament Library*. Philadelphia: Westminster, 1986.

Dresner, Samuel H. *Rachel*. Minneapolis: Fortress, 1994.

Fretheim, Terence E. *Jeremiah: Smyth & Helwys Bible Commentary*. Macon, GA: Smyth & Helwys, 2002.

Holladay, William L. *Jeremiah: Hermeneia Commentary Series*. Minneapolis: Fortress, 1989.

Jacob, B. *Genesis*. New York: KTAV, 1974.

Jeansonne, Sharon Pace. *The Women of Genesis: From Sarah to Potiphar's Wife*. Minneapolis: Fortress, 1990.

Niedner, Frederick A. "Rachel's Lament." *Word & World* 22 (Fall 2002): 406–14.

Noth, Martin. *A History of Pentateuchal Traditions*. Chico, CA: Scholars Press, 1981.

Ringe, Sharon H. *The Women's Bible Commentary*. Louisville: Westminster John Knox Press, 1992.

Skinner, John. *Genesis: The International Critical Commentary*. Edinburgh: T&T Clark, 1956.

Speiser, E. A. *Genesis: The Anchor Bible*. Garden City, NY: Doubleday, 1964.

Trible, Phyllis. *God and the Rhetoric of Sexuality*. Philadelphia: Fortress, 1978.

Westermann, Claus. *Genesis 12–36: A Commentary*. Trans. John J. Scullion. Minneapolis: Augsburg, 1985.

———. *Genesis 37–50: A Commentary*. Trans. John J. Scullion. Minneapolis: Augsburg, 1986.

Vogt, Ernst. "Benjamin geboren 'eine Meile' von Ephrata." *Biblica* 56 (1975): 30–36.

Von Rad, Gerhard. *Genesis: A Commentary*. Trans. John Marks. Philadelphia: Westminster, 1961.

Rachel in Jewish Literature

Attridge, Harold W. *The Interpretation of Biblical History in the Antiquitates Judaicae of Flavius Josephus*. Missoula, MT: SBL, 1976.

Bailey, James L. "Josephus' Portrayal of the Matriarchs." In Louis H. Feldman and Gohei Hata, eds. *Josephus, Judaism, and Christianity*. Detroit: Wayne State University Press, 1987. 154–79.

Charlesworth, James. *The Old Testament Pseudepigrapha. Anchor Bible*. Vol. 2. Garden City, NY: Doubleday, 1985.

Colson, F. H., and G. H. Whitaker. *Philo. The Loeb Classical Library*. 5 vols. Cambridge, MA: Harvard University Press, 1968.

Franxman, Thomas W. *Genesis and the "Jewish Antiquities" of Flavius Josephus*. Rome: Biblica et Orientalia, 1979.

Ginzberg, Louis. *The Legends of the Jews*. Vol. 2. Trans. Henrietta Szold. Philadelphia: The Jewish Publication Society of America, 1910.

Kasher, M. M. "Torah Shlemah." *Encyclopedia of Biblical Interpretation*. New York: KTAV, 1979.

Neusner, James, ed. and trans. *Genesis Rabbah. Scripture and Midrash in Judaism*. Vol. 2. Frankfurt: Peter Lang, 1995.

———. *Lamentations Rabbah and Leviticus Rabbah. Scripture and Midrash in Judaism*. Vol. 3. Frankfurt: Peter Lang, 1995.

Scholem, Gershom. *On the Kabbalah and Its Symbolism*. New York: KTAV, 1965.

Simon, Maurice, ed. and trans. *The Zohar*. 5 vols. Brooklyn: Soncino Press, 1984.

Thackeray, H. St. J., and Ralph Marcus. *Josephus, Flavius: Jewish Antiquities* 1.285–344 *(Josephus*, Vol. 4). *The Loeb Classical Library*. Cambridge, MA: Harvard University Press, 1977.

Zatelli, Ida. "Rachel's Lament in the Targum and Other Ancient Jewish Interpretations." *Revista Biblica* 39 (1991): 477–90.

Rachel in Christian Literature

Alighieri, Dante. *The Divine Comedy, Purgatorio*. Trans. Dorothy Sayers. New York: Penguin Classics, 1962.

Aquinas, St. Thomas. "Active and Contemplative Life," *Summa Theologiae*. Vol. 46. Trans. Jordan Aumann. New York: McGraw-Hill, 1964.

Brown, Raymond E. *The Birth of the Messiah*. Garden City, NY: Doubleday, 1977.

Giannarelli, E. "Rachele e il pianto della madre nella tradizione cristiana antica." *Annali de storia dell'esegise* 3 (1986): 215–26.

Hibbard, H. *Michelangelo*. New York, 1978.

Jeffrey, David Lyle. *A Dictionary of Biblical Tradition in English Literature*. Grand Rapids, MI: Wm. B. Eerdmans, 1992.

Luther, Martin. "Lectures on Genesis: Chapters 26–30." In Jaroslav Pelikan, ed., *Luther's Works*. Vol. 5. American Edition. St. Louis: Concordia, 1968.

———. "Lectures on Genesis: Chapters 31–37." In Jaroslav Pelikan, ed., *Luther's Works*. Vol. 6. American Edition. St. Louis: Concordia, 1970.

Melville, Herman. *Moby Dick*. New York: Quality Paperback, 1996.

Menken, Martinus J. J. "The Quotation from Jeremiah 31 (38).15 in Matthew 2.18: A Study of Matthew's Scriptural Text." In Steve Moyise, ed., *Old Testament in the New Testament*. Sheffield: Sheffield Academic Press, 2000. 106–25.

Migne, Jacques-Paul, ed. "Gregory of Nyssa: *Moralia and Homil. In Ezech*," *Patrologia Latina*. Vols. 75–76. Paris, 1844–1864.

Richard of St. Victor. *The Twelve Patriarchs: Benjamin*. Trans. Grover A. Zinn. New York: Paulist Press, 1979.

Roberts, Alexander, and James Donaldson. "Justin: Dialogue with Trypho," *The Anti-Nicene Fathers*. Vol. 1. Grand Rapids, MI: Wm. B. Eerdmans, 1981.

Schaff, Philip, ed. "Augustine: *Contra Faustum*." Trans. Richard Stothert. In *A Select Library of the Nicene and Post-Nicene Fathers of the Christian Church*. Vol. 4. New York: Charles Scribner's Sons, 1909.

Zatelli, L. "Lea e Rachele," In *Atti del seminario*. "*Giacobbe, o l'avventure del figlio ruinore*." *Biblia*. Florence (1990): 51–74.

Rachel in Muslim Literature

ʿAlī, ʿAbdullah Yūsuf. *The Meaning of the Holy Qurʾān*. Beltsville, MD: Amana Publications, 1989.

Brinner, William M. *The History of al-Tabari: Volume II: Prophets and Patriarchs*. New York: State University of New York Press, 1987.

———. *Abū Ishāq Ahmad b. Muhammad b. Ibrāhīm al-Thaʾlabī al-Nīsābūrī al-Shāfiʾī: Lives of the Prophets*. Leiden: E. J. Brill, 2002.

Haleem, Muhammad Abdel. "The Story of Joseph in the Qurʾan and the Bible." In *Understanding the Qurʾan: Themes and Style*. New York: St. Martin's Press, 1999. 138–57.

Kaltner, John. *Inquiring of Joseph: Getting to Know a Biblical Character through the Qurʾan*. Collegeville, MN: Liturgical Press, 2003.

Stowasser, Barbara Freyer. *Women in the Qurʾan, Traditions, and Interpretation*. Oxford: Oxford University Press, 1994.

Thackston Jr., Wheeler M. *Muhammad b. ʿAbdallāh al-Kisāʾī: Tales of the Prophet*. Chicago: Great Books of the Islamic World Inc, 1997.

Rachel's Tomb in the Biblical Record

Albright, W. F. "Ophrah and Ephraim." *AASOR* (1922: 4): 124–37.

Birch, W. F. "Hiding Places in Canaan. I. Jeremiah's Girdle and Farah." *PEFQS* (1880): 235–36.

Campbell, Anthony F., and Mark O'Brien. *Sources of the Pentateuch: Texts, Introductions, Annotations*. Minneapolis: Fortress, 1998.

Cartledge, Tony W. *1 & 2 Samuel: Smyth & Helwys Commentary*. Macon, GA: Smyth & Helwys, 2001.

Finkelstein, Israel, and Yizhak Magen. *Archaeological Survey of the Hill Country of Benjamin*. Jerusalem: Israel Antiquities Authority Publications, 1993.

Charles Clermont Ganneau. *Archaeological Researches in Palestine in the Years 1873–74*. London: Palestine Exploration Fund, 1899.

Kallai, Zecharia. "Rachel's Tomb: A Historiographical Review." In *Vielseitigkeit des Altes Testaments*. Frankfurt: Peter Lang, 1999. 215–23.

Lombardi, G. "H. Farah—W. Farah presso Anatot e la questione della Tomba di Rahel (Gen 35,16-20; 1 Sam 10,2-5; Ger 31,15)." *Liber Annuus* (20.1970): 299–352.

Luker, Lamonette. "Ephrathah." In David Noel Freedman, ed. *Anchor Bible Dictionary*. Vol. 2. Garden City, NY: Doubleday, 1992.

———. "Rachel's Tomb." In David Noel Freedman, ed. *Anchor Bible Dictionary*. Vol. 5. Garden City, NY: Doubleday, 1992.

Macalister, R. A. S. "The Topography of Rachel's Tomb." *Palestine Exploration Fund Quarterly* (1912): 74–82.

Marti, Karl. "Mittheilungen von Baurath C. Schick in Jerusalem." *ZDPV* 3 (1880): 11.

Tsevat, Matitiahu. "Interpretation of 1 Sam. 10:2." *Hebrew Union College Annual*, *XXXIII* (1962): 107–18.

———. "Rachel's Tomb." *IDB Supplement*. Nashville: Abingdon, 1976.

Vincent, H. "Cronique." *RB* (1901): 287–89.

Pilgrim Accounts and Eyewitness Reports

Primary Sources

Adler, Elkan Nathan. *Jewish Travelers in the Middle Ages: 19 Firsthand Accounts*. New York: Dover Publications, Inc., 1987.

Adler, William, and Paul Tuffin. *The Chronology of George Synkellos: A Byzantine Chronicle of Universal History from the Creation*. Oxford: University Press, 2002.

al-Mukaddasi, Muhammed. *Description of Syria, including Palestine*. In *The Library of the Palestine Pilgrims' Text Society*. Vol. 3. London: Palestine Exploration Fund, 1886.

Baedeker, Karl. *Jerusalem and Its Surroundings: Handbook for Travelers*. London: Dulau and Co., 1876.

Baldi, P. Donatus. *Enchiridion Locorum Sanctorum*. Jerusalem: Tupis PP Franciscanorum, 1955.

Barnai, Jacob. *The Jews in Palestine in the Eighteenth Century: Under the Patronage of the Istanbul Committee of Officials for Palestine*. Trans. Naomi Goldblum. Tuscaloosa, AL: University of Alabama Press, 1992.

Bartlett, W. H. *Walks about the City and Environs of Jerusalem*. Jerusalem: Canaan Publishing House, 1974.

Bellorini, T., E. Hoade, and B. Bagatti. *Fra Bernardino Amico, Plans of the Sacred Edifices of the Holy Land*. Jerusalem, 1953.

Conder, Capt. C. R. and Capt. H. H. *The Survey of Western Palestine: Memoirs of the Topography, Orography, Hydrography and Archaeology*. Vol. 3. London: Palestine Exploration Fund, 1872.

Damer, Mrs. G. L. Dawson. *Diary of a Tour in Greece, Turkey, Egypt, and the Holy Land*. Vol. 2. London: Henry Colburn, Publisher, 1841.

Ellis, Henry, ed. *Pylgrymage of Sir Richard Guyleford to the Holy Land, A.D. 1506*. London: Camden Society, 1851.

Eusebius. *Das Onomastikon der biblischen Ortsnamen*. Erich Klostermann, ed. Hildesheim: Georg Olms Verlagsbuchhandlung, 1966.

Finn, Elizabeth Anne. *Reminiscences of Mrs. Finn*. London: Marshall, Morgon and Scott, 1929.

Finn, James. *Stirring Times, or Records from Jerusalem Consular Chronicles of 1853–1856*. 2 vols. London: C. Kegan Paul, 1878.

Garitte, Gérad. *The Calendrier palestino-georgien du Sinaiticus, 34*. Brussels: Society of Bollandistes, 1958.

Garver, Rev. Daniel. "Visit to Hebron and Bethlehem." *Ohio Repository* (Canton, OH), July 7, 1859. http://www.shalomjerusalem.com/jerusalem/jerusalem27 _1858-59.html.

Gorenberg, Gershom. "The Tomb Cult: Outside the Fence." *The Jerusalem Report* (September 23, 2002): 31.

Greenslade, S. L. *Early Latin Theology: Selections from Tertullian, Cyprian, Ambrose, and Jerome*. Library of Christian Classics. Vol. 5. Philadelphia: The Westminster Press, 1956.

Jerome. "Letter 46." In Philip Schaff, ed. *A Select Library of the Nicene and Post-Nicene Fathers of the Christian Church*. Vol. 6. New York: Charles Scribner's Sons, 1909.

———. "Letter 58." *Patrologia Latina*. Vol. 29, ed. Jacques-Paul Migne. Paris, 1844–1864.

Johnson, B. W. *Young Folks in Bible Lands*. St. Louis: Christian Publishing Co., 1892.

Khosraw, Naser-e. *Book of Travels*. Trans. W. M. Thackston, Jr. Albany: State University of New York Press, 1986.

Lanneau, Rev. John F. "Letter from Jerusalem: The Earthquake in Syria." *Adams Sentinel* (Gettysburg, PA), June 12, 1837.

Loftie, W. J., ed. *Ye Oldest Diearie of Englysshe Travell: Being Hitherto Unpublished Narrative of the Pilgrimage of Sir Richard Torkyington to Jerusalem in 1517*. London: Leadenhalle, 1857.

Loewe, L., ed. *Diaries of Sir Moses and Lady Montefiore in Two Volumes*. Vol. 1. Chicago: Belford-Clarke Co., 1890.

Margoliouth, Rev. Moses. *A Pilgrimage to the Land of My Fathers*. London: Richard Bentley, 1850.

Maundeville, Sir John. "Bethlehem." In Thomas Wright, ed. *Early Travels in Palestine*. London: Bohn, 1848.

Montefiore, Judith. *Private Journal of a Visit to Egypt and Palestine: 1827*. London: 1836.

Newett, M. Margaret. *Canon Pietro Casola's Pilgrimage to Jerusalem in the Year 1494*. Manchester: Manchester University Press, 1907.

Pfeiffer, Madame Ida. *Visit to the Holy Land, Egypt, and Italy*. Trans. H. W. Dulcke. 1842. http://www.gutenberg.org/files/12561/12561.txt.

Porter, Josias Leslie. *A Handbook for Travellers in Syria and Palestine*. Part 1. London: John Murray, 1858.

———. *Jerusalem, Bethany, and Bethlehem*. London: Nelson, 1886.

Robinson, Edward. *Biblical Researches in Palestine, Mount Sinai and Arabia Petraea.* Vol 1. Boston: 1841.

Schwarz, Rabbi Joseph. *A Descriptive Geography and Brief Historical Sketch of Palestine.* Trans. Isaac Leeser. Philadelphia: A. Hart, 1850.

Signer, Michael A. *The Itinerary of Benjamin of Tudela: Travels in the Middle Ages.* Malibu, CA: Joseph Simon Pangloss Press, 1983.

Spencer, Jesse Amos. *The East: Sketches of Travel in Egypt and the Holy Land.* New York: George P. Putnam, 1850.

Stephens, John Lloyd. *Incidents of Travel in Egypt, Arabia Petraea and the Holy Land.* Reprint Edition. Mineola, NY: Dover Publications, 1996.

Turner, William. *Journal of a Tour in the Levant.* Vol. 2. London: J. Murray, 1820.

Twain, Mark. *The Innocents Abroad.* New York: Oxford University Press, 1996.

Van de Velde, C. W. M. *Narrative of a Journey through Syria and Palestine in 1851 and 1852.* Vol. 2. London: William Blackwood and Sons, 1854.

Wilkinson, John. *Egeria's Travels to the Holy Land.* Jerusalem: Ariel, 1981.

———. *Jerusalem Pilgrims Before the Crusades.* Warminster, England: Aris & Phillips Ltd., 2002.

Wilkinson, John, with Joyce Hill and W. F. Ryan. *Jerusalem Pilgrimage, 1099–1185.* London: The Hakluyt Society, 1988.

Secondary Sources

Aharoni, Y. "Ramat Rachel." In *Encyclopedia of Archaeological Excavations in the Holy Land.* Vol. 4, ed. Michael Avi-Yonah. Englewood Cliffs, NJ: Prentice Hall, 1976.

Avigad, N. "Jerusalem." In Michael Avi-Yonah, ed. *Encyclopedia of Archaeological Excavations in the Holy Land.* Vol. 2. Englewood Cliffs, NJ: Prentice Hall, 1976.

Barnes, T. D. "The Composition of Eusebius's Onomasticon." *JTS.* New series 26 (1975): 412–15.

Blumberg, Arnold. *A View from Jerusalem, 1849–1858: The Consular Diary of James and Elizabeth Anne Finn.* Rutherford: Farleigh Dickinson University Press, 1980.

Chareyron, Nicole. *Pilgrims to Jerusalem in the Middle Ages.* New York: Columbia University Press, 2005.

Collard, George. *Moses, the Victorian Jew.* Oxford: The Kensall Press, 1990.

Davidson, Linda Kay, and David M. Gitlitz. *Pilgrimage: From the Ganges to Graceland.* Santa Barbara, CA: ABC-Clio, 2002.

Elad, Amikam. *Medieval Jerusalem and Islamic Worship: Holy Places, Ceremonies, Pilgrimage.* Leiden: Brill, 1995.

Gil, Moshe. *A History of Palestine, 634–1099.* Trans. Ethel Broido. Cambridge: Cambridge University Press, 1992.

Goodman, Paul. *Moses Montefiore.* Philadelphia: The Jewish Publication Society of America, 1925.

Green, Abigail, "Rethinking Sir Moses Montefiore: Religion, Nationhood, and International Philanthropy in the Nineteenth Century." *The American Historical Review* 110:3 (June 2005). http://www.historycooperative.org/journals/ahr/110.3/green.html.

Hunt, E. D. *Holy Land Pilgrimage in the Late Roman Empire,* A.D. *312–460.* Oxford: Clarendon Press, 1982.

Janin, Hunt. *Four Paths to Jerusalem: Jewish, Christian, Muslim, and Secular Pilgrimages, 1000* B.C.E. *to 2001* C.E. Jefferson, NC: McFarland & Co., 2002.

Kollek, Teddy, and Moshe Pearlman. *Pilgrims to the Holy Land: The Story of Pilgrimage through the Ages.* New York: Harper & Row, 1970.

Landes, David S. "Palestine before the Zionists." *Commentary* (February 1976): 52.

Le Strange, Guy. *Palestine under the Moslems: A Description of Syria and the Holy Land from* A.D. *650 to 1500.* London: Alexander P. Watt, 1890.

Peters, Joan. *From Time Immemorial—The Origins of the Arab-Jewish Conflict over Palestine.* New York: Harper & Row, 1984.

Raheb, Mitri, and Fred Strickert. *Bethlehem 2000: Past and Present.* Heidelberg: Palmyra, 1998.

Scholem, Gershom. *Sabbatai Sevi: The Mystical Messiah.* New York: Littman, 1997.

Sered, Susan Starr. "Rachel's Tomb and the Milk Grotto of the Virgin Mary: Two Women's Shrines in Bethlehem." *Journal of Feminist Studies in Religion* 2.2 (Fall 1986): 7–22.

———. "Rachel's Tomb: Societal Liminality and the Revitalization of a Shrine." *Religion* 19 (1989): 27–40.

Shoemaker, Stephen J. "The (Re?)Discovery of the Kathisma Church and the Cult of the Virgin in Late Antique Palestine." *Maria* 2 (2001): 21–72.

Webster, Sir Charles. *The Foreign Policy of Palmerston 1830–1841, Britain, the Liberal Movement and the Eastern Question.* Vol. 2. New York: Humanities Press, 1969.

Modern Political Developments

Assad, Samar. "Palestinian boy fights for life." *AP News Service,* November 12, 1997.

Barnett, Denis. "Palestinian boy, policeman die in day of anti-summit rage." *Agence France Press,* October 17, 2000.

Bennet, James. "New Wall Sharpens Arab-Israel Divisions." *New York Times*, February 18, 2003.

Benzimann, Uzi. *Jerusalem, A City without a Wall.*

Cust, L. G. A. *The Status Quo in the Holy Places.* Jerusalem: Ariel Publishing House, 1980.

Dudkevitch, Margot. "Parents of child killed by IDF: 'Organs can go to Jew or Arab.'" *Jerusalem Post*, November 16, 1997.

———. "Activists try to reach Rachel's Tomb despite IDF ban." *Jerusalem Post*, November 10, 2000.

Dumper, Michael. *The Politics of Sacred Space: The Old City of Jerusalem in the Middle East Conflict.* London: Lynne Rienner Publishers, 2002.

Geller, Doron. "Sense of Mission." *Jerusalem Post*, November 12, 1997.

"Grabbing Rachel's Tomb." *Haaretz*, September 12, 2002.

Greenberg, Joel. "Strife Claims Small Victim as Rachel's Tomb is Reopened." *New York Times*, November 12, 1997.

Hauser, Christine. "In Bethlehem, faithful pray in the shadow of the gun." *Reuters News Service*, October 28, 2000.

Jansen, Michael. "If the Palestinian-Israeli Conflict is to be Resolved." *Jordan Times*, March 23, 2005.

Kraft, Dina. "Thousands worship at fortified tomb." *AP News Service*, November 11, 1997.

Lapidot, R., and M. Hirsch. *The Arab-Israeli Conflict and Its Resolution: Selected Documents.* Dordrecht, Netherlands: Kluwer Academic Publishers, 1992.

Mitnick, Joshua. "Christmas behind Israel's Walls." *Christian Science Monitor*, December 22, 2005.

"MKS Pray at Besieged Tomb." *Haaretz*, November 10, 2000.

Rodan, Steve, and Margot Dudkevitch. "Rachel's Tomb reopens after renovations." *Jerusalem Post*, November 12, 1997.

Sennott, Charles. *The Body and the Blood: The Holy Land at the Turn of a New Millennium.* New York: Public Affairs, 2001.

Shagai, Nadav. "Rachel's Tomb: Beyond or within?" *Haaretz*, 2002.

———. "Two Jewish families move into house near Rachel's Tomb." *Haaretz*, October 25, 2004.

Tarabay, Jamie. "For ninth-grade boys, clashes are a game of cat and mouse." *Associated Press*, October 18, 2000.

"To Rachel's Tomb in a Bulletproof Bus." *Haaretz*, November 23, 2000.

Index of Names, Places, and Subjects

Biblical Index